HISTORY OF INDIA

HISTORY OF INDIA

Edited by
A. V. WILLIAMS JACKSON, Ph. D., LL.D.

VOLUME V

The Mohammedan Period as Described by its Own Historians

BY
Sir Henry Miers Elliot, K.C.B.

GYAN

Published by

Gyan Publishing House
5, Ansari Road
Daryaganj, New Delhi-110002
Phone: 011-47034999, 9811692060
E-mail: books@gyanbooks.com

Distribution Network
gyanbooks.com
India, USA, Canada, UK, Australia, France

ISBN : 978-81-212-6772-4 (Set)
978-81-212-6768-7 (PB)
First Published, 1906

2nd Impression 2022

Printed at: Gyan Press, Delhi.

HISTORY OF INDIA (VOL. V)
Author: Sir Henry Miers Elliot

The Lake of Udaipur

Udaipur, the capital of the ancient state of Mewar, is the centre of what has been called the "Lake District of India." The lake itself, on which the city is located, is one of the most picturesque sheets of water in the world. The dazzling marble of royal palaces, imaged in its mirror-like face, stands out in contrast to the dark hills in the background.

History of India

Edited by

A. V. WILLIAMS JACKSON, Ph. D., LL. D.
Professor of Indo-Iranian Languages in Columbia University

VOLUME V

The Mohammedan Period as Described by its Own Historians

Selected from the Works of the late

SIR HENRY MIERS ELLIOT, K. C. B.
East India Company's Bengal Civil Service

INTRODUCTION BY THE EDITOR

This volume, consisting of selections from Sir Henry M. Elliot's great work on the history of Mohammedan India as told by its own historians, may be regarded as a new contribution, in a way, because it presents the subject from that standpoint in a far more concise form than was possible in the original series of translations from Oriental chroniclers, and it keeps in view at the same time the two volumes of Professor Lane-Poole immediately preceding it in the present series. Tributes to the value of Elliot's monumental work are many, but one of the best estimates of its worth was given by Lane-Poole himself, from whom the following paragraph is, in part, a quotation.

"To realize Mediæval India there is no better way than to dive into the eight volumes of the priceless *History of India as told by its own Historians*, which Sir H. M. Elliot conceived and began, and which Professor Dowson edited and completed with infinite labour and learning. It is a revelation of Indian life as seen through the eyes of the Persian court annalists. As a source it is invaluable, and no modern historian of India can afford to neglect it. It is, however, a mine to be worked, not a consecutive history, and its wide leaps in chronology, its repetitions, recurrences, and omissions, render it no easy guide for general readers."

On this latter point I desire to lay emphasis and also to add that in order to bring so extensive a mass of material within the compass of a single volume I have been obliged to exercise the utmost circumspection and to confine the selections simply to those which would represent the main outlines of the most important reigns, spread over nearly a thousand years, keeping in view at the same time the aim of supplementing the two preceding books in the series without undue crossing or unnecessary repetition. In discharging this somewhat difficult task I have received material aid, which I desire to acknowledge, from my friend and pupil, Dr. Louis H. Gray. I hope that those who may use the book will find that fair justice has been done to the merits of the various Mohammedan historians included in it. We owe much to their records as a means of understanding the Moslem conquest of Hindustan better than would otherwise be possible, and we also find them helpful in preventing us from being led away too far in other directions, if former prejudice might incline us to be biassed or to see only the side of the conquered.

In dealing with the text of the excerpts, considerable latitude has been used—an example which was set by Sir Henry Elliot himself, as well as by Professor Dowson and the various translators who lent their aid in converting the original Oriental accounts into English. Condensation was essential, excisions were often necessary, while certain changes in phraseology seemed frequently advisable; but never has the tone or spirit of the original been departed from, as will be clear to any one who will take the trouble to consult Elliot's complete work, which must always remain the standard and the ultimate source for the special student and historian to use.

In arranging the selections I have tried to make the story a more or less continuous one and have endeavoured to make the connections clear by introductory and transfer paragraphs, indicating also by 'single quotes' the point where the account of the native annalist begins and ends. The story as told by these Oriental writers has a quality of its own; and that will best be appreciated when the events described are read in connection with the two preceding volumes, to which this volume forms a supplement and sequel. The photogravures, half-tones, and cuts which serve as illustrations have been selected with the same attention as throughout the rest of the series. With these words I leave the Eastern chroniclers to narrate their own events after their own manner.

A. V. Williams Jackson.

CONTENTS

LIST OF ILLUSTRATIONS

ARABESQUE FROM A MOHAMMEDAN TOMB.

CHAPTER I

ARAB CONQUEST OF SIND

AS the history of Mohammedan rule in India begins with the conquest of Sind by the Moslems, it seems fitting to present an account of the Arab invasion as told by one of their own historians. Such a narrative we have, for example, from the pen of al-Baladhuri of Baghdad, a Mussulman chronicler who wrote contemporaneously with many of the events he described, and died in the year 892 A. D., hardly a hundred years after the Mohammedans had gained their first foothold in Hindustan. His narrative, which is here slightly abridged, should be compared with the main current of events described in the first chapter of the third volume of this series for a clearer understanding of some of the incidents whose importance was not fully realized in his time. But it is best to allow al-Baladhuri to tell his own story.

'Ali ibn Mohammad ibn Abdallah ibn Abu Saif has related that the Caliph Omar ibn al-Khattab appointed

Osman ibn Abu-l-Asi of the tribe of Sakif to Bahrain and Oman in the year 15 A. H. (636 A. D.). Osman sent his brother Hakam to Bahrain, while he himself went to Oman and despatched an army to Tana. When the army returned, he wrote to the Caliph Omar to inform him of it. Omar wrote in reply: "O brother of Sakif, thou has placed the worm in the wood, but I swear that if our men had been killed, I would have slain an equal number from thy tribe." Hakam despatched a force to Barauz (Broach); he also sent to the bay of Daibul his brother Mughira, who met and defeated the enemy.

When Osman ibn Akkan became caliph, he appointed Abdallah ibn Amar ibn Kuraiz to the government of Irak, and wrote to him an order to send some one to the confines of Hind in order to acquire knowledge and bring back information. He accordingly deputed Hakim ibn Jaballa al-Abdi. When this man returned, he was sent to the caliph, who questioned him about the state of those regions. He replied that he knew them because he had examined them. The caliph then told him to describe them. He said: "Water is scarce, the fruits are poor, and the robbers are bold; if few troops are sent there, they will be slain; if many, they will starve." Osman asked him whether he spoke literally or metaphorically. He said that he spoke according to his knowledge. The caliph abstained from sending any expedition there.

At the end of the year 38 or the beginning of the

year 39 A. H. (659 A. D.), in the caliphate of Ali ibn Abu-Salib, Haras ibn Marra-al-Abdi went with the sanction of the caliph to the same frontier as a volunteer. He was victorious, got plunder, made cap-

OSMAN. ABU BAKR.

ALI. OMAR.

SEALS OF EARLY CALIPHS.

tives, and distributed a thousand heads in one day. He and all but a few of those who were with him were slain in the land of Kikan in the year 42 A. H. (662 A. D.). Kikan is in Sind near the frontiers of Khorasan.

In the year 44 A. H. (664 A. D.), and in the days of the Caliph Mu‘awiya, Muhallab ibn Abu-Safra made war upon the same frontier, and advanced as far as Banna (Bannu) and Alahwar (Lahore), which lie between Multan and Kabul. The enemy opposed him and killed him and his followers. In the reign of Mu'awiya, the Amir Abdallah ibn Amir or, according to some, Mu'awiya himself, sent Abdallah ibn Suar-al-Abdi to the frontier of Hind. He fought in Kikan and captured booty. He then came to Mu'awiya and presented him with some Kikan horses. He staid near the caliph some time, and then returned to Kikan, whereupon the Turks mobilized their forces and slew him.

In the reign of this same Mu'awiya, Ziyad ibn Abu-Sufian appointed Sinan, a good and godly man, commander. He proceeded to the frontier, and having subdued Mekran and its cities by force, he staid there and established his power in the country.

Ziyad then appointed Rashid ibn Omar-al-Judaidi, of the tribe of Azd, to the frontier. He proceeded to Mekran and was victorious in warring against Kikan, but was slain fighting against the Meds. Sinan ibn Salama then succeeded to the command and was confirmed therein by Ziyad. He remained there two years.

Abbad ibn Ziyad then made war on the frontier of Hind by way of Seistan. He went to Sanaruz, whence he proceeded by way of Khaz to Rudbar in Seistan on the banks of the Hilmand. He then descended to Kish, and crossing the desert came to Kandahar. He fought against the inhabitants, routed them, put them to flight, and subdued the country; but many Mussulmans also perished.

Ziyad next appointed al-Manzar ibn al-Jarud-al-Abdi to the frontiers of India. He was known by the name of Abu-l-Ash'as. He attacked and conquered Nukan and Kikan. The Mussulmans obtained great plunder, and their forces spread over all the country. He captured Kusdar, which Sinan had already taken, but which had again revolted, and took prisoners there. Abu-l-Ash'as died in Kusdar, and after that the governor, Ubaid-Allah ibn Ziyad, appointed Ibn Harri al-Bahali. God, by his hands, subdued these countries, for he waged cruel war in them and conquered and plundered them.

The people of Nukan are now Mohammedans. Amran ibn Musa ibn Yahya, son of Khalid the Barmacide, built a city there in the caliphate of Mu'tasim bi-Allah which he called al-Baiza (the white). When al-Hajjaj ibn Yusuf was governor of Irak, Sa'id ibn Aslam was appointed to Mekran and its frontiers. He was opposed and slain there by Mu'awiya and Mohammad, sons of al-Haras al-Alafi. Hajjaj then appointed Mujja' ibn Si'r at-Tamimi to the frontier. He made war upon, plundered, and defeated the tribes about Kandabil, and this conquest was subsequently completed by Mohammad ibn Kasim. Mujja' died in Mekran after being there a year.

After the death of Mujja', Hajjaj appointed as his successor Mohammad ibn Harun ibn Zara' al-Namari. Under the government of Mohammad, the king of the

Isle of Rubies (Ceylon, so called from the beauty of its women), sent as a present to Hajjaj certain Mohammedan girls who had been born in his country, the

A TYPE OF CEYLON BEAUTY.

orphan daughters of merchants who had died there. The king hoped by this measure to ingratiate himself with Hajjaj; but the ship in which he had embarked these girls was attacked and taken by some barks belonging to the Meds of Daibul. When this news reached Hajjaj, he sent an ambassador to Dahir to demand their release, but Dahir replied: "They are pirates who have captured these women, and over them I have no authority." Hajjaj then sent Ubaid-Allah ibn Nabhan against Daibul. Ubaid-Allah being killed, Hajjaj wrote to Budail ibn Tahfa, of the tribe of Bajali, who was at Oman, directing him to proceed to Daibul. When he arrived there, his horse took fright and threw him, and the enemy surrounded him and killed him, although some say that he was killed by the Jats of Budha.

Hajjaj afterwards appointed Mohammad ibn Kasim to govern the Sindian frontier. Mohammad was in Fars when the order arrived, and had previously received instruction to go to Rai (in Persia, south of the Caspian Sea). Abu-l-Aswad Jahm ibn Zahr-al-Ju'fi was at the head of the advance-guard, and was ordered to return to Mohammad, whom he joined on the borders of Sind. Hajjaj ordered six thousand Syrian warriors to attend Mohammad, and others besides. He was provided with all he could require, without omitting even thread and needles. He had leave to remain at Shiraz until all the troops who were to accompany him had assembled and all the preparations had been duly made. Hajjaj had some dressed cotton saturated with strong vinegar, and then dried it in the shade, and said: "When you arrive in Sind, if you find the vinegar scarce, soak the cotton in water, and with the water you can cook your food and season your dishes as you wish." Some authors say that when Mohammad arrived on the frontiers, he wrote to complain of the scarcity of vinegar, and this was the reason which induced Hajjaj to send cotton soaked in vinegar.

Mohammad ibn Kasim then went to Mekran and remained there some time. He then went to Kannazbur and took it, and then to Armail, which he also took. After this he left Armail, accompanied by Jahm, and arrived at Daibul on Friday, where ships brought him a supply of men, arms, and engines of war. He dug an entrenchment, which he defended with spearmen, and unfurled his banners; each body of warriors was arrayed under its own banner, and he fixed the *manjanīk*, a catapult or ballista, which was called "the bride" and required five hundred men to work it. There was at Daibul a lofty temple surmounted by a long pole, and on the pole was fixed a red flag, which, when the breeze blew, was unfurled over the city. The temple is a high steeple, below which the idol or idols are deposited, as in this instance. The Indians give the general name of *budd* (temple) to anything connected with their worship or which forms the object of their veneration, so that an idol itself is called *budd*.

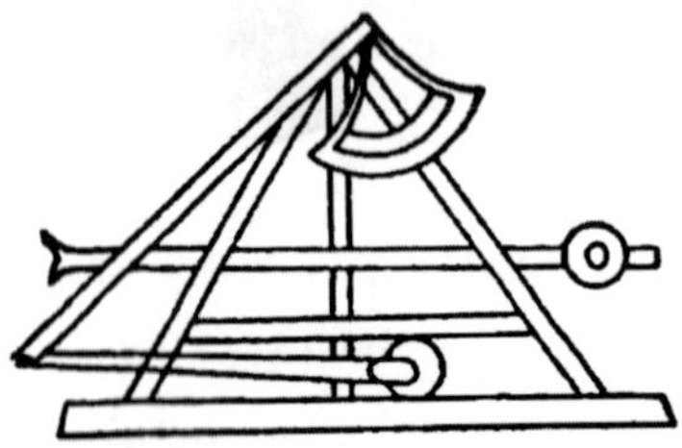

THE MANJANIK, A CATAPULT OR BALLISTA.
From Egerton's Indian Armour.

In the correspondence which ensued, Mohammad informed Hajjaj of what he had done, and solicited advice respecting the future. Letters were written every three days. One day a reply was received to this effect: "Fix the manjanik, and shorten its foot, and place it on the east; you will then call the manjanik-master, and tell him to aim at the flagstaff, of which you have given a description in your letter." So he brought down the flagstaff, and it was broken; at which the infidels were sore afflicted. The idolaters advanced to the combat, but were put to flight; ladders were then brought and the Mussulmans scaled the wall. The first who gained the summit was a man of Kufa, of the tribe of Murad. The town was thus taken by assault, and the slaughter lasted three days. The governor of the town, who had been appointed by Dahir, fled, and the priests of the temple were massacred. Mohammad marked out a place for the Mussulmans to dwell in, built a mosque, and left four thousand Moslems to garrison the city.

Ambissa ibn Ishak az-Zabbi, the governor of Sind, in the caliphate of Mu'tasim bi-Allah, knocked down the upper part of the minaret of the temple and converted it into a prison. At the same time he began to repair the ruined town with the stones of the minaret; but before he had completed his labours, he was deprived of his office and was succeeded by Harun ibn Abi Khalid-al-Maruruzi, after which he was slain there.

Mohammad ibn Kasim then went to Nirun, the inhabitants of which had already sent two Samanis, or priests, of their town to Hajjaj to treat for peace. They furnished Mohammad with supplies, and permitting him to enter the town, they were allowed to capitulate. Mohammad conquered all the towns successively which he met on his route, until he had crossed a river which runs on this side of the Mihran (Indus). He then saw approaching him Sarbidas, the Samani, who came to sue for peace in the name of the inhabitants. Mohammad imposed tribute upon them, and then went towards S a h b a n, and took it. He then went to the banks of the Mihran, and remained there. When this news reached Dahir, he prepared for battle. Mohammad ibn Kasim had sent Mohammad ibn Mus'ab to Sadusan, with men mounted on horses and asses, and at their approach the inhabitants begged for quarter and peace, the terms of which were negotiated by the Samani. Mohammad granted them peace, but he imposed tribute on the place and took pledges from them, and then returned to his master. He brought with him four thousand Jats, and left an officer in command at Sadusan.

JAT PEASANTS AND LANDLORDS.

Mohammad now sought means for crossing the Mihran, and effected the passage in a place which adjoined the dominions of Rasil, chief of Kassa, in Hind, upon a bridge which he had caused to be constructed. Dahir had neglected every precaution, not believing that the Mussulmans would dare to advance so far. Mohammad and his Mussulmans encountered Dahir mounted on his elephant, and surrounded by many of these animals, and with his Thakurs near his person. A dreadful conflict ensued, such as had never been heard of. Dahir dismounted and fought valiantly, but he was killed toward evening, whereupon the idolaters fled and the Mussulmans glutted themselves with slaughter.

Mohammad ibn Kasim then went to old Brahmanabad, two parasangs from Mansura, which did not then exist, its site being a forest. The remnant of the army of Dahir rallied at Brahmanabad and offered resistance, so that Mohammad was obliged to resort to force, and eight, or as some say, twenty-six, thousand men were put to the sword.

Mohammad then marched toward Alrur (Alor) and Baghrur. The people of Sawandari came out to meet him and sued for peace, which was granted them on condition that they should entertain the Mohammedans and furnish guides. At this time they profess the Mohammedan creed. After that he went to Basmad, where the inhabitants obtained peace on the same terms as those accorded to the Sawandarians. At last he reached Alrur, one of the cities of Sind, which is situated on a hill. Mohammad besieged it for several months and compelled it to surrender, promising to spare the lives of the inhabitants and not to touch the temples. "The temples," he said, "shall be unto us like as the churches of the Christians, the synagogues of the Jews, and the fire-temples of the Magians."

A TOMB AT MULTAN.

He imposed tribute upon the inhabitants, however, and built a mosque in the city.

Mohammad then advanced to Alsakah, a town on this side of the Biyah, which was captured by him, and is now in ruins. He then crossed the Biyah and went toward Multan, where, in the action which ensued, Zaid ibn Omar, of the tribe of Tai, covered himself with glory. The infidels retreated in disorder into the town and Mohammad commenced the siege, but the provisions being exhausted, the Mussulmans were reduced to eat asses. Then came a man who sued for quarter and pointed out to them an aqueduct, by which the inhabitants were supplied with drinking-water from the river of Basmad. It flowed within the city into a reservoir like a well, which they call *talāh* or *talāo.* Mohammad destroyed the water-course, whereupon the inhabitants, oppressed with thirst, surrendered at discretion. He massacred the men capable of bearing arms, but the children were taken captive, as well as the ministers of the temple, to the number of six thousand. The Mussulmans found much gold in a chamber ten cubits long by eight broad, and there was an aperture above, through which the gold was poured into the chamber, whence they call Multan "the Frontier of the House of Gold." The temple of Multan received rich presents and offerings, and the people of Sind resorted to it as a place of pilgrimage. They circumambulated it and shaved their heads and beards. They believed that the image in the temple was that of the prophet Job, the peace of God be upon him!

Upon the death of Hajjaj in 95 A.H. (714 A.D.), Mohammad left Multan and returned to Alrur and Baghrur, which had previously been captured. He made donations to his men, and sent an army toward al-Bailaman, the inhabitants of which place surrendered without any resistance. He made peace with the inhabitants of Surast, who are Meds, seafarers, and pirates. He went against the town of Kiraj. Duhar advanced to oppose him, but the enemy was put to flight and Duhar fled, although some say he was killed. The inhabitants surrendered, and Mohammad slew all those capable of bearing arms and reduced the rest to slavery.

Meanwhile, Walid ibn Abd-al-Malik died and was

AN INDIAN BARBER.

succeeded by his brother Sulaiman, who appointed Salih ibn Abd-ar-Rahman to collect the tribute of Irak. Yazid ibn Abu-Kabsha as-Saksaki was made governor of Sind, and Mohammad ibn Kasim was sent back a prisoner with Mu'awiya ibn Muhallab. The people of Hind wept for Mohammad, and preserved his likeness at Kiraj. He was imprisoned by Salih at Wasit. Salih put him to torture, together with other persons of the family of Abu-Ukail, until they expired, but of him Hamza ibn Baiz Hanafi says:

> "Verily, courage, and generosity, and liberality,
> Belonged to Mohammad, son of Kasim, son of Mohammad;
> He led armies at the age of seventeen years;
> He seemed destined for command from the day of his birth."

Yazid ibn Abu-Kabsha died eighteen days after his arrival in Sind. Sulaiman then appointed Habib ibn al-Muhallab to carry on the war in Sind, and he departed for that purpose. Meanwhile the princes of Hind had returned to their states, and Jaishiya ibn Dahir had come back to Brahmanabad. Habib proceeded to the banks of the Mihran, where the people of Alrur made their submission; but he warred against a certain tribe and reduced them.

When the Caliph Sulaiman ibn Abd-al-Malik died, he was succeeded by Omar ibn Abd-al-Aziz in 717 A. D. He wrote to the princes of Hind, inviting them to become Mussulmans and submit to his authority, whereupon they would be treated like all other Mussulmans. These princes had already heard of his promises, character, and creed, so Jaishiya and other princes turned Mussulmans and took Arab names. Amru ibn Muslim al-Bahali was lieutenant of Omar on this frontier. He invaded several places in Hind and subdued them.

In the days of Yazid ibn Abd-al-Malik, who reigned from 720 to 724 A. D., the sons of al-Muhallab fled to Sind, and Hilal ibn Ahwaz at-Tamimi was sent after them. He fell in with them and killed Mudrak ibn Muhallab at Kandabil. He also slew Mufazzal, Abd-al-Malik, Ziyad, Marun, and Mu'awiya, sons of Muhallab, and last of all he killed Mu'awiya ibn Yazid.

Junaid ibn Abd-ar-Rahman al-Marri was appointed to the frontier of Sind, under the authority of Omar ibn Hubaira al-Fazari, and was confirmed in the government by the Caliph Hasham ibn Abd-al-Malik, who ascended the throne in 724. When Khalid ibn Abdallah al-Kasri was sent to Irak as governor, Hasham wrote to Junaid, directing him to keep up a correspondence with Khalid. Junaid went to Daibul, and from thence to the banks of the Mihran, but Jaishiya ibn Dahir forbade him to cross, and sent to him, saying, "I have become a Mussulman, and an excellent man confirmed me in my estates, but I have no faith in thee." Junaid, however, gave him pledges and took pledges from him, together with the tribute due from his territories. They thus exchanged guarantees, but Jaishiya acted like an infidel and took up arms, although some say that he did not begin the attack, but that Junaid dealt unjustly with him. Jaishiya assembled his troops, fitted out ships, and prepared for war. Junaid proceeded against him in ships and they fought in the lake of ash-Sharki. Jaishiya's ship was destroyed, and he himself was taken prisoner and slain.

Thereupon, Sasah ibn Dahir fled and proceeded toward Irak to complain of the treachery of Junaid, but the latter did not cease to conciliate him until they had shaken hands, and then he slew him. Junaid then made war against Kiraj, where the people had rebelled. He made use of battering-rams, and battered the walls of the town with them until they were breached, and then he stormed the place, slaying, plundering, and making captives. He then sent his officers to Marmad, Mandal, Dahnaj, and Barus (Broach). He sent a force against Uzain (Ujjain) and he also sent Habid ibn Marra with an army against the country of Maliba (Malabar). They made incursions against Uzain, and attacked Baharimad and burnt its suburbs. Junaid conquered al-Bailaman and Jurz (Gujarat), and he received at his abode, in addition to what his visitors presented to him, forty millions, while he himself carried off a similar sum.

The successor of Junaid was Tamim ibn Zaid al-Utbi. He was feeble and imbecile, and died near Daibul in a water called the "Buffalo-water," so named because buffalos took refuge there from the bears which infested the banks of the Mihran. Tamim was one of the most generous of Arabs and soon spent the eighteen million Tartar dirhams which he found in the treasury of Sind. In his days, the Mussulmans retired from several parts of India and left some of their positions, nor have they up to the present time advanced so far as in days gone by.

Hakim ibn Awana al-Kalbi succeeded Tamim. The people of India had returned to idolatry, excepting those of Kassa, and the Mussulmans had no place of security in which they could take refuge, so he built a town on the other side of the lake facing India, and called it al-Mahfuzah, "the secure," and this he made a place of refuge and security for them, and their chief town. He asked the elders of the tribe of Kalb, who were of Syrian descent, what name he should give the town. Some said Dimashk (Damascus), others, Hims (Emessa), and others Tadmur (Palmyra), whereupon Hakim chose the latter name for his city, to which he gave the epithet of al-Mahfuzah, and dwelt there.

Amr ibn Mohammad ibn Kasim was with Hakim, and the latter advised with him, trusted him with many important matters, and sent him out of al-Mahfuzah on a warlike expedition. He was victorious in his commission, and was made an amir. He founded a city on this side of the lake, which he called Mansura, in which the governors now dwell. Hakim recovered from the enemy those places which they had subjugated, and gave satisfaction to the people in his country, so that Khalid said: "It is very surprising—I gave the charge of the country to the most generous of Arabs, that is, to Tamim, and they were disgusted; I gave it to the most niggardly of men, and they were satisfied." Hakim was killed there.

The governors who succeeded him continued to kill the enemy, taking whatever they could acquire and subduing the people who rebelled. When the dynasty of the Abbasids was established, Abu Muslim appointed Abd-ar-Rahman ibn Abu Muslim Mughallis-al-Abdi to the frontier of Sind. Abd-ar-Rahman went by way of Tokharistan, and proceeded against Mansur ibn Jamhur al-Kalbi, who was in Sind, but he was met by Mansur and slain, and his forces were put to flight. When Muslim heard this, he appointed Musa ibn Kab at-Tamimi and sent him to Sind. When he arrived, the river Mihran lay between him and Mansur ibn Jamhur. Still he

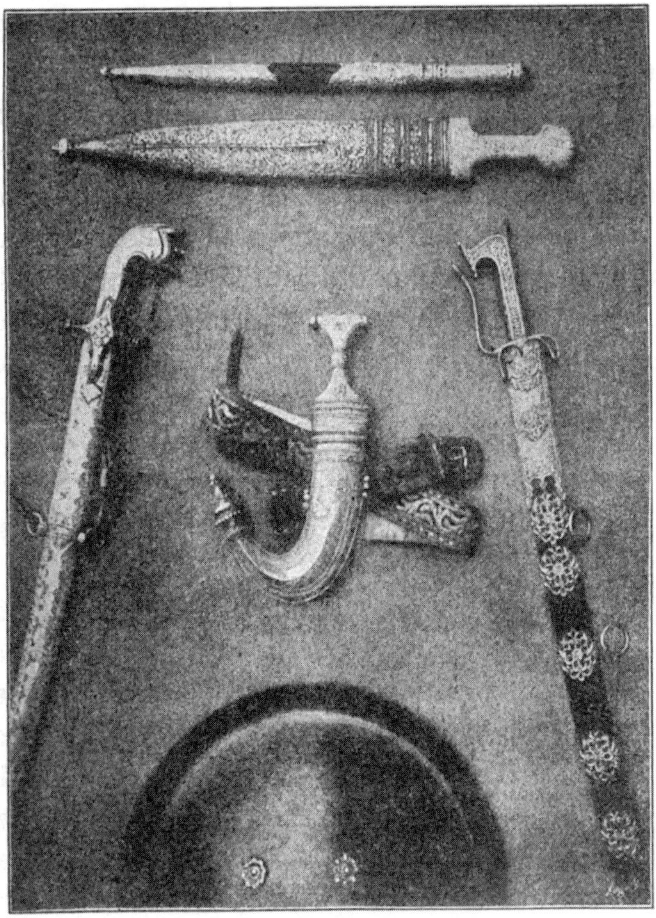

ARAB ARMOUR.

came up with Mansur, put him and his forces to flight, and slew his brother Manzur. Mansur fled in wretched plight to the sands, where he died of thirst. Musa ruled in Sind, repaired the city of Mansura, and enlarged its mosque. He was victorious in his campaigns.

The Caliph al-Mansur sent Hasham ibn Amr at-Taghlabi to Sind, and he reduced those places which still held out. He sent Amr ibn Jamal in boats to Narand. He also sent a force to the territories of Hind, subdued Kashmir, and took many prisoners and slaves. Multan was reduced, and he overpowered a body of Arabs who were in Kandabil, and drove them out. He then went to Kandahar in boats, and conquered it. He destroyed the temple there, and built a mosque in its place. There was abundance in the country under his rule, and the people blessed him; he extended the frontier and enforced his decrees.

Omar ibn Hafs ibn Osman Hazarmard was then appointed governor of Sind, and after him came Daud ibn Yazid ibn Hatim. There was with him Abu-l-Samma, who had been a slave of the tribe of Kanda, and who later became governor. The affairs of the frontier went on prosperously until Bashar ibn Daud was appointed under the caliphate of Mamun, who began to reign in 813 A. D. He rebelled and set up in opposition. Ghassan ibn Abbad, who was a native of the neighbourhood of Kufa, was sent against him. Bashar proceeded to meet Ghassan under a safe-conduct, and they both proceeded to Baghdad, the Mohammedan capital. Ghassan deputed Musa ibn Yahya ibn Khalid to the charge of the frontier. Musa killed Bala, King of ash-Sharki, although the latter had given him five hundred thousand dirhams to preserve his life. Bala was faithful to Ghassan and wrote to him in the presence of his army through the princes who were with him, but his request was rejected. Musa died in 221 A. H. (836 A. D.), leaving a high reputation, and appointed his son Amran as his successor. The Caliph Mu'tasim bi-Allah wrote to him confirming him in the government of the frontier. He marched to Kikan against the Jats, whom he defeated and subjugated. He built a city there, which he called al-Baiza (the white), and posted a military force there.

He proceeded thence to Multan and then to Kandabil, which stands upon a hill. Mohammad ibn Khalil was reigning there, but Amran slew him, conquered the town, and carried its inhabitants to Kusdar. He then made war upon the Meds, and killed three thousand of them. There he constructed a *band*, or dike, called Sakr-al-Med, "Band of the Meds." He encamped on the river at Alrur, and summoned the Jats, who came to his presence, whereupon he sealed their hands, took from them the *jizya* (the poll-tax levied on all who are not Mussulmans), and ordered that every man of them should bring a dog with him when he came to wait upon him, so that the price of a dog rose to fifty dirhams. He again attacked the Meds, having with him the chief men of the Jats. He dug a canal from the sea to their tank, so that their water became salt, and he sent out several marauding expeditions against them.

Dissensions then arose between the Nizarians and Yamanians, and Amran joined with the latter. Omar ibn Abu-l-Aziz al-Habbari consequently went to him and killed him unawares.

Mansur ibn Hatim related to me that Fazl ibn Mahan, formerly a slave of the sons of Sama, got into Sindan and subdued it. He then sent an elephant to the Caliph Mamun, wrote to him, and offered up prayers for him in the Jami' Masjid, which he built there. When he died, he was succeeded by Mohammad ibn Fazl ibn Mahan. He proceeded with sixty vessels against the Meds of Hind. He killed a great number of them, captured Kallari, and then returned toward Sindan. But his brother, named Mahan, had made himself master of Sindan, and wrote to the Caliph Mu'tasim bi-Allah, and sent him as a present the largest and longest teak-tree that had ever been seen. But the Indians were under the control of his brother whom they liked, so they slew Mahan and crucified him. The Indians afterwards made themselves masters of Sindan, but they spared the mosque, and the Mohammedans used to meet in it on Fridays and pray for the caliph.

Abu Bakr, who had been a slave of the Karizis, related to me that the country called al-Usaifan, lying between Kashmir and Multan and Kabul, was governed by a wise king. The people of this country worshipped an idol for which they had built a temple. The son of the king fell sick and the king desired the priests of the temple to pray to the idol for his son's recovery. They retired for a short time, and then returned and said: "We have prayed and our supplications have been accepted." But no long time passed before the youth died, whereupon the king attacked the temple, destroyed and broke in pieces the idol, and slew its priests. He afterwards invited to his court a party of Mohammedan traders, who made known to him the unity of God, so that he believed in the unity and became a Mussulman. This happened in the caliphate of Mu'tasim bi-Allah.'

This last section concludes al-Baladhuri's account of the conquest of Sind, but by way of supplement and to bring the history of this particular province down to the time of Mahmud of Ghazni, it seems appropriate to add here, in abridged form, the excellent sketch by Sir Henry M. Elliot himself, tracing the main current of events down to the extinction of the Arab dominion in Sind. His account occupies the remainder of this chapter.

'During the nine reigns which occupied the period between the reigns of al-Mu'tasim (833 - 841 A. D.) and al-Muktadar (908 - 932 A. D.), the power of the caliphs had been gradually on the decline. The Turkish guard had become more and more outrageous and arbitrary; independent dynasties, such as the Tahirids and Safarids, after having shorn the kingdom of some of its fairest provinces, had themselves died out; eunuchs, and even women, had sat upon the judgment seat and dispensed patronage, while corruption and venality openly prevailed; and now, at a later period, notwithstanding the fact that literature flourished and the personal dignity of the caliph was maintained in the highest splendour, nevertheless, not only had the Samanids conquered the whole of Mawara-an-nahr and Khorasan, not only had the Dailamites penetrated to the borders of Irak, not only had all northern Africa, except Egypt, been lost to the caliphate for ever, but, as if to crown the measure of its misfortunes, the Karmathian heretics, after plundering Kufa, Basra, and Samarra, had possessed themselves of Mecca during the very time of pilgrimage, had massacred the pilgrims, and had even carried off the sacred black stone itself, the principal and universal object of Mohammedan veneration.

Under such circumstances, the most distant provinces necessarily partook of the decline from which the heart of the empire was suffering; and Sind, neglected by the imperial government, came to be divided among several petty princes, who, though they transmitted no revenue and rendered no political allegiance to the caliph, were, like other more powerful chiefs who had assumed independence, glad to fortify their position by acknowledging his spiritual supremacy and by flattering him with the occasional presentation of some rarity from the kingdoms which they had usurped.

The virtual renunciation of political control in Sind may be dated from the year 257 A. H. (870 A. D.), when the Caliph Mu'tamad, to divert the Safarids from their hostile designs against Irak, conferred upon Ya'kub ibn Lais the government of Sind, as well as of Balkh and Tokharistan, in addition to that of Seistan and Kirman, with which he had already been invested.

AN OLD PAVILION AT THATTA IN SIND.

The two principal kingdoms which were established in Sind a few years after this event were those of Multan and Mansura, both of which attained a high degree of power and prosperity. It is probable that the independence of those states commenced immediately after the death of Ya'kub ibn Lais in 265 A. H. (879 A. D.), for his successors were comparatively powerless, and the Samanis, at the commencement of their rule, had little leisure to attend to so remote a province as Sind.

Mas'udi, who visited the valley of the Indus in the year 303 - 304 A. H. (915 - 916 A. D.) and completed his "Meadows of Gold" in 332 A. H. (943 - 944 A. D.), furnishes a brilliant account of the state of Islam in that country. The Amir of Multan was an Arab of the noble tribe of Kuraish, named Abu-l-Dalhat al-Munabba ibn Assad as-Sami, and the kingdom of Multan is represented to have been hereditary in his family for a long time, "nearly from the beginning of Islam" (meaning, probably, from its introduction into Sind). Kanauj, Mas'udi asserts, was then a province of Multan, "the greatest of the countries which form a frontier against unbelieving nations." Abu-l-Dalhat himself was descended from Sama ibn Lawi ibn Ghalib, who had established himself on the shores of Oman before the birth of Mohammed. The amir had an army in his pay, and there were reckoned to be 120,000 hamlets around the capital, while his dominion extended to the frontier of Khorasan.

Mansura was governed by another Kuraishi, whose name was Abu-l-Mundar Omar ibn Abdallah. He was descended from Habbar ibn Aswad, who was celebrated for his opposition to Mohammed, and who, on the return of the prophet to Mecca in triumph, was among the few that were excepted from the terms of the amnesty which was proclaimed at that time. He subsequently became a convert, and toward the year 111 A. H. (729 A. D.) one of his descendants came to the valley of the Indus to seek his fortune. Some time after, his family, taking advantage of the anarchy which prevailed in the country, made themselves masters of the lower Indus, and established themselves at Mansura, a principality which extended from the sea to Alor, where that of Multan commenced. It was said to contain three hundred thousand villages, which is, of course, an exaggeration, but the whole country was well cultivated and covered with trees and fields. Nevertheless, the inhabitants were continually obliged to protect themselves against the aggressions of the Meds and other savage tribes of the desert.

A few years after Mas'udi, the valley of the Indus was visited by the Arab geographer and traveller Istakhri, and by Ibn Haukal, who has included nearly the whole of Istakhri's relation in his own and has entered into some further details. With respect to the condition of the country at the time of his visit, Ibn Haukal, who wrote his work after the year 366 A. H. (976 A. D.), when he was for a second time in India, observes that Multan was not so large as Mansura and was defended by a citadel, and that the territory was fertile, although it was inferior to that of Mansura, and not cultivated with the same care. The amir lived outside the town and never entered it, except for the purpose of going to the mosque on Fridays, mounted on an elephant.

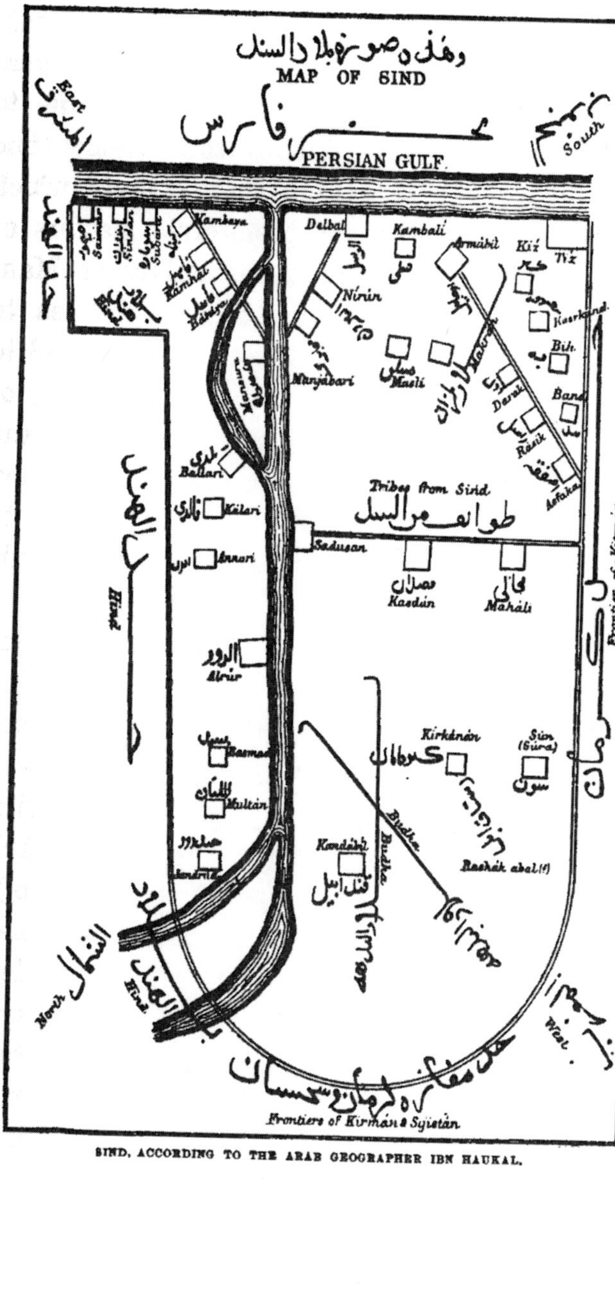

SIND, ACCORDING TO THE ARAB GEOGRAPHER IBN HAUKAL.

There appears to have been no native coinage, but the money in circulation was chiefly Kandahar and Tartar dirhams. The dress of the Sindians was like that of the people of Irak, but the amirs habited themselves like the native princes. Some persons wore their hair long, and their dresses loose, with waistbands, on account of the heat, and there was no difference between the garb of the faithful and of idolaters.

The Amirs of Multan and Mansura were independent of one another, but both deferred to the spiritual authority of the Caliph of Baghdad. The former was still a descendant of Sama ibn Lawi, in the days of Ibn Haukal, and the latter a descendant of the Habbari family.

Alor, the ancient Hindu capital, surrounded by a double wall, was nearly as large as Multan, and was a dependency of Mansura. Its territory was fertile and rich, and it was the seat of considerable commerce. Rahuk (or Dahuk), on the borders of Mekran and to the west of the Hala range, was also included in Mansura. There were other principalities to the west, besides the two in the valley of the Indus, such as Turan, Kusdar, Mekran, and Mushki.

With respect to those other parts of India to which the Mussulmans resorted, such as the maritime towns in the jurisdiction of the Balhara, between Cambay and Saimur, Ibn Haukal observes that they were covered with towns and villages. The inhabitants were idolaters, but the Mohammedans were treated with great consideration by the native princes. They were governed by men of their own faith, and had the privilege of living under their own laws, nor could any one give testimony against them, unless he professed the Mohammedan faith. They had also erected their mosques in these infidel cities and were allowed to summon their

A RUINED MOHAMMEDAN MOSQUE AT HAIDARABAD IN SIND.

congregations by the usual mode of proclaiming the times of prayer.

The revenues, which the Arab princes of Sind derived from their several provinces, are pronounced to have been very small, barely more than sufficient to provide food and clothing and the means of maintaining their position with credit and decency; and, as a necessary consequence, only a few years elapsed before they were driven from their kingdoms, and compelled to yield their power to more enterprising and energetic assailants.

The Karmathians of India are nowhere mentioned by Ibn Haukal, but it could not have been long after his visit that these heretics, who probably contained within their ranks many converted natives and foreigners as well as Arabs, began to spread in the valley of the Indus. It must have been about the year 375 A. H. (985 A. D.) that, finding their power expiring in the original seat of their conquests, they sought new settlements in a distant land and tried their success in Sind. There the weakness of the petty local governments favoured their progress and led to their early occupation both of Mansura and Multan, from which latter place history records their expulsion by the overwhelming power of Mahmud of Ghazni, whose victories brought Sind under his triumphant sway, resulting ultimately in the extinction of the Arab dominion in that province after a duration of three centuries.'

GOLD COIN OF MAHMUD, STRUCK AT NAISHAPUR IN KHORASAN, A. H. 402 (A. D. 1011 - 1012).

CHAPTER II

THE HOLY WARS OF ISLAM WAGED AGAINST HINDUSTAN BY SABUKTAGIN AND MAHMUD OF GHAZNI

975 - 1030 A. D.

THE Mohammedan conquest of India, as has been shown in the third volume of this series, was effected in reality not by the Arabs but by the Moslem Turks from Central Asia, who had settled in Afghanistan and made the mountain fortress of Ghazni their stronghold in the latter part of the tenth century. Sabuktagin, a slave by birth but a sovereign by achievement, ruled as lord of the Afghan tribes around his little kingdom of Ghazni (976 - 997 A. D.) and brought province after province under his imperial sway until he was prepared to invade northwestern India. His sword had a double sanctification in this endeavour, since it was to be drawn to fight the battle for the faith under the crescent and green banner of Islam against the infidels and idolaters of Hindustan, and a rich reward of booty was also in prospect for the puissant commander. He advanced from Afghanistan into the fertile districts of the Panjab, triumphed over the Indian raja Jaipal, reduced him to temporary subjection and repeated the victorious inroad more than once. The way pointed out by Sabuktagin was followed by his son Mahmud of Ghazni, with true Mohammedan zeal and with still greater results, in a dozen or more successive invasions, and we have a good account of the various campaigns, written by an Arab historian Utbi, who was secretary to Sultan Mahmud up to the time of Mahmud's death in 1030 A.D. Sir Henry Elliot translated selections from this Arabic chronicle, entitled "Tarikh-i Yamini," and extracts from his version are here given to recount the history of these holy wars waged against Hindustan by two famous rulers of Afghanistan, as viewed through the eyes of a Mohammedan annalist.

'Sabuktagin, the ruler of Ghazni, in Afghanistan, made frequent expeditions into Hindustan in the prosecution of holy wars, and he conquered forts there upon lofty hills, in order to seize the treasures they contained, and expelled their garrisons. He took all the property in their treasuries, and captured cities in Hind, which had up to that time been tenanted only by infidels, and not trodden by the camels and horses of Mussulmans.

When Jaipal, the king of Hind, ascertained the calamity which had befallen him, and learned how Sabuktagin was taking different parts of the territory into his own possession and injuring all who opposed him in his projects of ambition, the deepest grief seized him and made him restless, and his lands became narrow under his feet, though their expanse was broad. Then he arose with his relations, and the generals of his army, and his vassals, and hastened with his huge elephants to wreak his revenge upon Sabuktagin, by treading the field of Islam under his feet, and doing dishonour to that which should be treated with respect. In this disposition he marched on until he passed Lamghan and approached the territory of Sabuktagin, trusting to his own resources and power, for Satan had laid an egg in Jaipal's brain and hatched it; so that he waxed proud, entertaining absurd thoughts, and anticipating an immediate accomplishment of his wishes, impracticable as they were.

When the amir heard of Jaipal's approach toward his territory, and of his great power, he girt up his loins to fight, and collecting his vassals and the Mohammedan forces whose duty it was to oppose infidels, he advanced from Ghazni against Jaipal, who was encamped between that place and Lamghan, with soldiers as black as night and as impetuous as a torrent. Yamin-ad-daulah Mahmud accompanied Amir Sabuktagin, his father, like a lion of the forest or a destructive eagle, and they attempted no difficult undertaking which they did not easily accomplish.

The armies fought several days successively against each other, and cups filled to the brim with blood, drawn from wounds inflicted by sword and spear, circulated among them till they were drunken. In consequence of the great fear which fell upon Jaipal, who confessed he had seen death before the appointed time, he sent a deputation to the amir, promising to pay down a sum of money if he might have peace, and offering to obey any order he might receive respecting his elephants and his country. The Amir Sabuktagin consented on account of the mercy he felt toward those who were his vassals, or for some other reason which seemed expedient to him. The Sultan Yamin-ad-daulah Mahmud, however, addressed the messengers in a harsh voice, and refused to abstain from battle until he should obtain a complete victory suited to his zeal for the honour of Islam and of Mussulmans, and one which he was confident God would grant to his arms. They returned, therefore, and Jaipal, being in great alarm, again sent most humble supplications that the battle might cease.

A SPECIES OF INDIAN DAGGER.

When the amir received this conciliatory message and knew what Jaipal would do in his despair, he thought that religion and the views of the faithful would best be consulted by peace and the acquisition of tribute. The Amir Mahmud accordingly agreed with Sabuktagin as to the propriety of withdrawing the hand of vengeance, on condition of the immediate receipt of a million dirhams of royal stamp and fifty elephants, in addition to some cities and forts in the midst of his country. Jaipal was to deliver these forts to the officers nominated by the amir, and was to send hostages from among his relatives and friends to remain with the amir until the terms of surrender were fulfilled. The amir sent two deputies with Jaipal to see that he did not swerve from his engagements, and they were accompanied by confidential officers who were to take charge of the places which were ceded.

When Jaipal had marched to a great distance and thought that the demand upon him had relaxed, his evil disposition prompted him to break his engagements, and his folly made him beget enmity, insomuch that he imprisoned those who accompanied him on the part of the amir, in reprisal for those of his relations whom the amir had taken as hostages.

When this intelligence reached the amir, he considered it false, as being opposed to the usual habits of Jaipal; but after repeated accounts to the same effect had been brought, the veil which obscured the truth was withdrawn, and he knew that God had set his seal upon Jaipal's heart, so that he might obtain the reward of his evil deeds. The Sultan, therefore, sharpened the sword of intention in order to make an incursion upon his kingdom, and to cleanse it from impurity and from his rejection of Islam. He accordingly departed with his valiant servants and allies, relying upon the one God, and trusting in the fulfilment of the promise of victory; and he went on till he arrived with his troops in the country of Hind, where he killed every one who came out to oppose him on the part of Jaipal.

The amir marched toward Lamghan, which is a city

celebrated for its great strength and abounding in wealth. He conquered it, and after setting fire to the places in its vicinity which were inhabited by infidels, he demolished the idol-temples and established Islam in them. He also captured other cities and killed the polluted wretches, destroying the idolatrous and gratifying the Mussulmans. After wounding and killing

HINDU IDOLS.

beyond all measure, his own hands and those of his friends became cold in counting the value of the plundered property. On the completion of his conquest, he returned and promulgated accounts of the victories obtained for Islam, and every one, great and small, concurred in rejoicing over this result and thanking God.

When Jaipal saw what had befallen him on account of the infraction of his engagements, he became greatly agitated, and knew not whether to retire or advance. He at last determined to fight once more and satisfy his revenge. Thereupon he collected troops to the number of more than one hundred thousand, and when Amir Sabuktagin heard of this, he again advanced to fight him, and ascended a lofty hill, from which he could see the whole army of the infidels, which resembled scattered ants and locusts. He urged the Mussulmans against the infidels, and they willingly obeyed his orders. He made detachments of five hundred attack the enemy with their maces in hand, and relieve each other when one party became tired, so that fresh men and horses were constantly engaged, till the accursed enemy complained of the heat which arose from that iron oven. These detached parties then made one united charge to exterminate their numerous opponents. Officers and men mingled in close conflict, and all weapons were useless except the sword. The dust which arose prevented the eyes from seeing; swords could not be distinguished from spears, men from elephants, or heroes from cowards. It was only when the dust was allayed that it was found that the infidels had fled, leaving behind them their property, utensils, arms, provisions, elephants, and horses. The jungles were filled with the carcasses of the infidels, some wounded by the sword, and others fallen dead through fright.

The Hindus were like frightened curs, and the raja was glad to offer the best things in his most distant provinces to the conqueror, on condition that the hair on the crowns of their heads should not be shaved off. The country in that neighbourhood thus became clear and open before Amir Sabuktagin, and he seized all the wealth which was found in it. He levied tribute and obtained immense booty, besides two hundred elephants of war. He increased his army, and since the Afghans and Khaljis had submitted to him, he admitted thousands of them into the ranks of his army whenever he wished, and thereafter expended their lives in his service.'

Having given this account of Sabuktagin's invasion

AFGHAN TYPES.
(Copyright by Underwood & Underwood, N. Y.)

of Hindustan, the Arab chronicle proceeds to describe the continuation of the holy wars against the idol-worshipping Hindus carried on by Sabuktagin's famous son, Mahmud of Ghazni, under the sanction of the Caliph of Baghdad.

'Kadir bi-Allah, the Caliph of Baghdad, sent a robe of honour, such as had never before been heard of, for the use of Sultan Saif-ad-daulah, and he addressed Mahmud in his imperial rescript as "Yamin-ad-daulah, Commander of the Faith, and friend of the Commander of the Faithful," a title which had never yet been bestowed upon any prince, either far or near, notwithstanding their intense desire to receive such an honour. The Sultan sat on his throne and vested himself with his new robe, professing his allegiance to the successor of the prophet of God. The amirs of Khorasan stood before him in order, with respectful demeanour, and did not take their seats till so directed. He then bestowed upon the nobles, his slaves, his confidential servants, and his chief friends valuable robes and choice presents, beyond all calculation, and vowed that every year he would undertake a holy war against Hind.

Sultan Mahmud at first designed to go to Seistan, but subsequently preferred to engage in a holy war against Hind. He accordingly distributed arms before convening a council on the subject, that he might secure a blessing on his designs of exalting the standard of religion, of widening the plain of right, of illumining the words of truth, and of strengthening the power of justice. He departed toward the country of Hind in full reliance on the aid of God, who guided him by his light and power, bestowed dignity upon him, and gave him victory in all his expeditions. When he reached Peshawar, he pitched his tent outside the city. There he received intelligence of the bold resolve of Jaipal, the king of Hind and the enemy of God, to offer opposition, and of his rapid advance to meet his fate on the field of battle. He then took a muster of his horses and of all his warriors and their vassals, after which he selected from among his troops fifteen thousand cavalry and strictly prohibited those who were rejected and not fit or disposed for war, from joining those who had been chosen, and who were like dragons of the desert and lions of the forest. With them he advanced against the wicked and accursed enemy, whose hearts were firm as hills, and were as twigs of patience on the boughs of affection. The villainous infidel came forward, proud in his strength of head and arm, with twelve thousand horsemen, thirty thousand foot-soldiers, and three hundred elephants, at whose ponderous weight the lighter earth groaned, little reflecting that, under the dispensation of God, a small army can overturn a host, as the ignorant man would have learnt, if he could have read the word of God, which says: "Oftentimes a small army overcomes a large one by the order of God."

That infidel remained where he was, avoiding action for a long time, and craftily awaiting the arrival of reinforcements; but Sultan Mahmud would not allow him to postpone the conflict, and the Mussulmans commenced the action, assailing the enemy with sword, arrow, and spear—plundering, seizing, and destroying; at all which the Hindus, being greatly alarmed, began to kindle the flame of fight. Jaipal now set his cavalry in and beat his drums. The elephants moved on from their posts, and line advanced against line, shooting their arrows at one another, while swords flashed like lightning amid the blackness of clouds, and fountains of blood flowed like the fall of setting stars. The Mussulmans defeated their obstinate opponents, and quickly put them to a complete rout. Noon had not arrived when they had wreaked their vengeance on the enemies of God, killing fifteen thousand of them, spreading them like a carpet over the ground, and making them food for beasts and birds of prey. Fifteen elephants fell on the field of battle, as their legs, being pierced with arrows, became as motionless as if they had been in a quagmire, and their trunks were cut with the swords of the valiant heroes.

AN INDIAN NECKLACE.

The enemies of God, Jaipal, his children and grandchildren, his nephews, the chief men of his tribe, and his relatives, were taken prisoners, and being strongly bound with ropes, were carried before the Sultan. Some had their arms forcibly tied behind their backs, some were seized by the cheek, some were driven by blows on the neck. From Jaipal's throat was taken a necklace composed of large pearls and shining gems and rubies set in gold, the value of which was two hundred thousand dinars; and twice that value was obtained from the necks of those of his relatives who were taken prisoners or slain. God also bestowed upon his friends such an amount of booty as was beyond all bounds and all calculation, including five hundred thousand slaves, beautiful men and women. The Sultan returned with his followers to his camp, thankful to God, the lord of the universe, who had given them victory over a province of the country of Hind broader and longer and more fertile than Khorasan. This splendid and celebrated action took place on Thursday, the eighth of Muharram, 392 A. H. (November 27, 1001 A. D.).

After the victory, Sultan Mahmud directed that the polluted infidel Jaipal should be paraded about, so that his sons and chieftains might see him in that condition of shame, bonds, and disgrace, and that the fear of Islam might fly abroad through the country of the misbelievers. He then entered into conditions of peace with him, after demanding fifty elephants, and took from him his son and grandson as hostages till he should fulfil the terms imposed upon him.

The infidel returned to his own country and remained there, and wrote to his son Andpal, whose territory, on which he prided himself, was on the other side of the Indus, explaining the dreadful calamity which had befallen him, and beseeching him with many entreaties to send the elephants which were to be given to the Sultan according to agreement. Upon this, Andpal sent the elephants to Jaipal, and they were delivered over to the Sultan. The Sultan, therefore, ordered the release of the hostages, and his myrmidons gave them a sound thump, telling them to return to their own country.

Andpal reflected that his father, Jaipal, had put on

the sheaf of old age and had fallen under the influence of Lyra and other unlucky constellations, and that it was time he should contemplate his death and devote himself to religious exercises. There is a custom among these people that if any one is taken prisoner by an enemy, as in this case Jaipal was by the Mussulmans, it is not lawful for him to continue to reign. When, therefore, Jaipal saw that he was captive in the prison of old age and degradation, he thought death by cremation preferable to shame and dishonour. So he commenced with shaving off his hair, and then threw himself upon the fire till he was burnt.

When Sultan Mahmud had accomplished every wish and reduced all his enemies, he resolved, in his happiness, on another holy war. Marching toward Waihind, he encamped there in state, until he had established himself in that country and had relieved himself from the toils of the campaign. News reached him that the Hindus had taken refuge in the passes of the neighbouring hills, where they had concealed themselves in the forests and jungles, consulting among themselves how to attack the Mussulmans. He therefore despatched an army against them, to conquer their country and disperse them. The army fell upon them, and committed such slaughter that their swords were covered with blood. Those who escaped death fled away like mountain goats, having seen the swords flashing as bright as stars at noonday and dealing black and red death around them. Thus did the infidels meet with the punishment and loss due to their deserts. The standards of the Sultan then returned happy and victorious to Ghazni, the face of Islam was made resplendent by his exertions, the teeth of the true faith displayed themselves in their laughter, the breasts of religion expanded, and the back of idolatry was broken.

When Sultan Mahmud had settled the affairs of

THE RIVER INDUS AT ATTOK.

Seistan, and when the action of his beating pulse had subsided and the clouds had dispersed, he determined to invade Bhatia. He accordingly collected armies with trustworthy guides and valiant standard-bearers, and crossing the Indus in the neighbourhood of Multan, he marched toward the city of Bhatia, whose walls the wings of the eagle could not surmount, and which was surrounded as by the ocean with a ditch of exceeding depth and breadth. The city was as wealthy as imagination can conceive in property, armies, and weapons of war. There were elephants as headstrong as Satan. The ruler at that time was Biji Rai, and the pride which he felt in the state of his preparations induced him to leave the walls of his fort and come forth to oppose the Mussulmans, that he might frighten them with his warriors and elephants and great prowess.

The Sultan fought against him for three days and nights, and the lightnings of his swords and the meteors of his spears fell on the enemy. On the fourth morning a most furious onslaught was made with swords and arrows which lasted till noon, when Mahmud ordered a general charge to be made upon the infidels. The Mussulmans, advancing against the masters of lies and idolatry with cries of "God is exceeding great!" broke their ranks, and rubbed their noses upon the ground of disgrace. The Sultan himself, like a stallion, dealt hard blows around him on the right hand and on the left, and cut in twain those who were clothed in mail, making the thirsty infidels drink the cup of death. In this single charge he took several elephants, which Biji Rai regarded as the chief support of his centre. At last God granted victory to the standards of Islam, and the infidels retreated behind the walls of their city for protection. The Mussulmans obtained possession of the gates of the city, and employed themselves in filling up the ditch and destroying the scarp and counterscarp, widening the narrow roads and opening the closed entrances.

When Biji Rai saw the desperate plight to which he was reduced, he escaped by stealth and on foot into the forest with a few attendants and sought refuge on the top of some hills. Mahmud despatched a select body of his troops in pursuit of them, and when Biji Rai saw that there was no chance of escape, he drew his dagger, struck it into his breast, and went to the fire which God has lighted for infidels and those who deny a resurrection, for those who say no prayers, hold no fasts, and tell no beads.

The army of the Sultan kept moving on and committing slaughter and pillage. One hundred and twenty elephants fell to the share of the Sultan, besides the usual share of property and arms. He also obtained an accession of territory without any solicitation. He remained at Bhatia till he had cleansed it from pollution, and appointed a person there to teach those who had embraced Islam and to lead them in the right way. He then returned to Ghazni in triumph and glory, and his fortune was in the ascendent; but since his return was during the rains, when the rivers were full and foaming, and as the mountains were lofty, and he had to fight with enemies, he lost the greater part of his baggage in the rivers, and many of his valiant warriors were dispersed. God, nevertheless, preserved his person, for God is the friend of the virtuous.

Intelligence reached Mahmud of the acts committed by Abi-al-futuh, the ruler of Multan, and also of the impurity of his religion, the seditious designs of his heart, the evidence of his evil doings, and his endeavours to make proselytes of the inhabitants of his country. The Sultan, zealous for the Mohammedan religion, thought it a shame to allow him to retain his government while he practised such wickedness and disobedience, and he besought the assistance of a gracious God in bringing him to repentance, and in attacking him with that end in view.

He then issued orders to assemble an army from

EXTERIOR OF SULTAN MAHMUD'S TOMB AT GHAZNI.

among the Mussulmans for the purpose of joining him in this holy expedition, and departed with them toward Multan in the spring, when the rivers were swollen with the rain, and when the Indus and other rivers prevented the passage of the cavalry, and offered difficulties to his companions. The Sultan desired Andpal, the chief of Hind, to allow him to march through his territory, but Andpal would not consent, and offered opposition, which resulted in his discomfiture. The Sultan, consequently, thought it expedient to attack Rai Andpal first, notwithstanding his power, to bow down his broad neck, to cut down the trees of his jungles, to destroy every thing he possessed, and thus to obtain the fruit of two paradises by this double conquest.

He accordingly stretched out upon him the hand of slaughter, imprisonment, pillage, depopulation, and fire, and hunted him from ambush to ambush, into which he was followed by his subjects. The spears were wearied with penetrating the rings of the coats of mail, the swords became blunt by the blows on the sides, and the Sultan pursued the raja over hill and dale, until his followers either became a feast to the rapacious wild beasts of the passes and plains or fled in distraction to the neighbourhood of Kashmir.

When Abi-al-futuh, the ruler of Multan, heard what had happened to the chief of Hind, notwithstanding all his power and the lofty walls of his fort, and despite his shining sword, and when he began to measure their relative strength and considered how Andpal, a much greater potentate than himself, had been subdued, he looked upon himself, as compared with Sultan Mahmud, as a ravine in comparison with the top of a mountain. He therefore determined to load all his property on elephants, and carry it off to Sarandip, and he left Multan empty for the Sultan to deal with as he chose. Mahmud accordingly invested Multan, took it by assault, treated the people with severity, and levied from them twenty thousand thousand dirhams with which to respite their sins. The reports of Sultan Mahmud's conquests then spread over distant countries, and over the salt sea, even as far as Egypt. Sind and her sister Hind trembled at his power and vengeance; and his fame exceeded that of Alexander the Great, and heresy, rebellion, and enmity were suppressed.

When Sultan Mahmud heard that Ilak Khan had crossed the Jihun with fifty thousand men or more, he hastened from Tokharistan to Balkh, where he remained to anticipate Ilak Khan, who wished to obtain supplies from that province. The Sultan advanced ready for action with an army composed of Turks, Hindus, Khaljis, Afghans, and Ghaznavids, and after routing Ilak Khan disastrously, he resolved to go to Hind to make a sudden attack upon Nawasa Shah, one of the rulers of Hind, who had been established as governor over some of the territories in the country conquered by the Sultan. Satan had got the better of Nawasa Shah, however, for he had thrown off the mantle of Islam and held converse with the chiefs of idolatry, designing to cast the firm rope of religion from his neck. The Sultan, therefore, went in that direction more swiftly than the wind and made the sword reek with the blood of his enemies. He turned Nawasa Shah out of his government, took possession of all the treasures which he had accumulated, resumed his sceptre, and then cut down the harvest of idolatry with the sickle of his sword and spear, after which he returned without difficulty to Ghazni.

Contrary to the disposition of man, which induces him to prefer a soft couch to a hard one and the splendour of the cheeks of pomegranate-bosomed girls to well-tempered sword-blades, Sultan Mahmud was so incensed at the standard which Satan had raised in

AN AFGHAN BOY.

Hind, that he determined to wage another holy war against that land. On the last day of Rabi'-al-akhir of the same year, he prayed to God for the fulfilment of his wishes. When he reached the river of Waihind, he was met by Brahmanpal, the son of Andpal, at the head of a valiant army, with white swords, blue spears, yellow coats of mail, and ash-coloured elephants. Battle opened its crooked teeth, attacks like flaming meteors were frequent, arrows fell like rain from bows, and the grinding-stone of slaughter revolved, crushing the bold and the powerful. The battle lasted from morning till evening, and the infidels had well-nigh gained the victory, when God brought aid by sending the slaves of the household to attack the enemy in the rear and to put them to flight. The victors obtained thirty large elephants and slew the vanquished wherever they were found in jungles, passes, plains, and hills.

The Sultan himself joined in the pursuit and went after them as far as the fort called Bhimnagar, which is very strong, being situated on the promontory of a lofty hill and in the midst of impassable waters.

He brought his army under the fort and surrounded it, and prepared to attack the garrison vigorously, boldly, and wisely. When the defenders saw the hills covered with the armies of plunderers and perceived the arrows ascending toward them like flaming sparks of fire, great fear came upon them and they opened the gates, entreating mercy, and fell on the earth like sparrows before a hawk or rain before lightning. The Sultan entered the fort with Abu Nasr Ahmad ibn Mohammad Farghuni, the ruler of Juzjan, and all his private attendants, and appointed his two chief chamberlains, Altuntash and Asightigin, to take care of the treasures of gold and silver and all the valuable property, while he himself assumed charge of the jewels. The treasures were laden on the backs of as many camels as they could procure, and the officers carried away the rest. The stamped coin amounted to seventy thousand thousand royal dirhams, and the gold and silver ingots were 700,400 *mans* in weight, besides wearing-apparel and fine cloths of Sus, respecting which old men said they never remembered to have seen any so fine, soft, and embroidered. Among the booty was a house of white silver, like to the houses of the rich, which was thirty yards in length and fifteen in breadth. It could be taken to pieces and put together again. There was also a canopy, made of fine Byzantine linen, forty yards long and twenty broad, supported on two golden and two silver poles, which had been cast in moulds.

Sultan Mahmud thereupon appointed one of his most confidential servants to take charge of the fort and the property in it. After this he returned to Ghazni in triumph; and on his arrival there, he ordered the court-yard of his palace to be covered with a carpet, on which he displayed jewels and unbored pearls and rubies, shining like sparks or like wine congealed with ice, and emeralds like fresh sprigs of myrtle, and diamonds like pomegranates in size and weight. Thereupon, ambassadors from foreign countries, including the envoy from Taghan Khan, King of Turkistan, assembled to see such wealth as they had never even read of in books of the ancients and whose like had never been accumulated by kings of Persia or of Greece.

The Sultan again resolved on an expedition to Hind, and marching toward Narain, he moved over ground, hard and soft, until he came to the middle of Hind, where he reduced chiefs who up to that time had obeyed

INTERIOR OF SULTAN MAHMUD'S TOMB AT GHAZNI.

no master, overthrew their idols, put the vagabonds of that country to the sword, and with delay and circumspection proceeded to accomplish his design. He fought a battle with the chiefs of the infidels, in which God granted him much booty in property, horses, and elephants, and the Mussulmans committed slaughter in every hill and valley. The Sultan returned to Ghazni with all the plunder he had obtained.

When the ruler of Hind witnessed the calamities

which had inflicted ruin on his country and his subjects in consequence of his contests with Mahmud, and saw their effects far and near, he became satisfied that he could not war against him. He accordingly sent some of his relatives and chiefs to the Sultan, imploring him not to invade India again and offering him money to abstain from that purpose. The envoys were told to yield a tribute of fifty elephants, each equal to two ordinary ones in size and strength, laden with the products and rarities of the country. The King of Hind promised to send this tribute every year, accompanied by two thousand men for service at the court of the Sultan.

Mahmud accepted his proposal, since Islam was promoted by the humility of his submission and by the payment of tribute, and sent an envoy to see that these conditions were carried into effect. The ruler of Hind fulfilled them strictly and despatched one of his vassals with the elephants to see that they were duly presented to the Sultan. Thus peace was established and tribute was paid, and caravans travelled in full security between Khorasan and Hind.

When the Sultan had purified Hind from idolatry and had raised mosques therein, he determined to invade the capital of the land, that he might punish those who kept idols and refused to acknowledge the unity of God. After collecting his warriors and distributing money among them, he set forth with a large army in the year 404 A. H. (1013 A. D.), choosing the close of autumn for his expedition on account of the purity of the southern breezes at that season. When he arrived near the frontier of Hind, snow fell such as had never been seen before, insomuch that the passes of the hills were closed, and the mountains and valleys became of one level. The roads were concealed, and the right could not be distinguished from the left, or what was behind from that which was before, and they were unable to return until God should give command. In the meantime the Sultan employed himself in collecting supplies, and summoned his generals from the different provinces. Having thus accumulated the means of warfare and having been joined by his soldiers, who had come from different directions, and who were equal in number to the drops of an autumnal rain, he left these winter quarters in the spring, and, had the earth been endowed with feeling, it would have groaned beneath the weight of the iron, the warriors, the horses, and the beasts of burden. The guides marched on in front over hill and dale before the sun arose and even before the light of the stars was extinguished. He urged on his horses for two months, among broad and deep rivers and among jungles in which even wild cattle might lose their way.

When the Sultan drew near the end of his destination, he set his cavalry in array and formed them into different bodies, appointing his brother, Amir Nasr, to command the right wing, consisting of valiant heroes; Arslan-al-Jazib to the left wing, consisting of powerful young men; and Abu Abdallah Mohammad ibn Ibrahim-at-Tai to the vanguard, consisting of fiery Arab

A SKETCH OF THE KHAIBAR PASS.
From Roskoschny's Afghanistan.

cavaliers. To the centre he appointed 'Altuntash the chamberlain, together with his personal slaves and attendants, as firm as mountains.

Nidar Bhim, the enemy of God and the chief of Hind, alarmed at this sudden invasion, summoned his vassals and generals and took refuge within a pass, which was narrow, precipitous, and inaccessible. They intrenched themselves behind stones and closed the entrance to the pass by their elephants, which looked like so many hills because of their lofty stature. Here he remained in great security, being persuaded that the place was impervious to attack, but he did not know that God is the protector of the faithful and the annihilator of infidels!

When Mahmud learned that Nidar Bhim intended to prolong the war, he advanced against him with his Dailamite warriors and Afghan spearmen, who penetrated the pass like gimlets into wood, ascending the hills like mountain goats and descending them like torrents of water. The action lasted for several days without intermission, till at last some of the Hindus were drawn out into the plain to fight, where they were attacked and killed by the cavalry, just as the knight on the chess-board demolishes pawns.

When his vassals had joined Nidar Bhim with reinforcements, he consented to leave his intrenchments and come into the plain, having the hills behind him, and the elephants drawn up on each wing. The battle raged furiously, and when the elephants of the Hindus advanced to destroy their opponents, they were assailed by showers of arrows upon their trunks and eyes. When Abu Abdallah had bravely advanced into the midst of the infidels, he was wounded in his head and body; but Sultan Mahmud, seeing the extreme danger to which his general was exposed, despatched some of his own guards to his assistance, and they rescued him from the conflict. They then brought him to the Sultan, who ordered him to be placed on an elephant to relieve him from the pain of his wounds, and thus he was exalted like a king above all the leaders of the army.

The conflict continued as before until God blew the gale of victory on his friends, and the enemy were slain on the tops of the hills, and in the valleys, ravines, and beds of torrents. A large number of elephants, which the enemy had regarded as strongholds to protect them, fell into the hands of the victors, as well as much other booty. Thus God granted the Sultan the victory of Nardin and added to the adornment of the mantle of Islam, which had not hitherto extended to that place. On his return, the Sultan marched in the rear of his immense booty, and slaves were so plentiful that they became very cheap; and men of respectability in their native land were degraded by becoming slaves of common shopkeepers. But this is the goodness of God, who bestows honours on his own religion and degrades infidelity.

Sultan Mahmud learned that in the country of Thanesar there were large elephants of the Ceylon breed, celebrated for military purposes. On this account the chief of Thanesar was obstinate in his infidelity and denial of God. The Sultan marched against him, therefore, with his valiant warriors, for the purpose of planting the standards of Islam and extirpating idolatry. He marched through a desert which had never yet been crossed, save by birds and wild beasts, for the foot of man and the shoe of horse had not traversed it. There was no water in it, much less any other kind of food. The Sultan was the first to whom God had granted a passage over this desert, in order that he might attain the fulfilment of his wishes.

Beneath Thanesar flowed a pure stream; the bottom was covered with large stones, and the banks were precipitous and sharp as the points of arrows. The Sultan reached this river at a place where it takes its course through a hill-pass, behind which the infidels posted themselves, in the rear of their elephants. The Sultan adopted the stratagem of sending some of his troops to cross the river by two different fords and attack the enemy on both sides; and when they were all engaged in close conflict, he ordered another body of men to go up the bank of the stream, which was flowing through the pass with fearful impetuosity, and to attack the enemy among the ravines, where they were posted in the greatest number. The battle raged fiercely, but about evening, after a vigorous attack on the part of the Mussulmans, the enemy fled, leaving their elephants, which were all driven into the camp of the Sultan, except one, which ran off and could not be found. The largest were reserved for the Sultan.

The blood of the infidels flowed so copiously that the stream was discoloured, notwithstanding its purity, and people were unable to drink it. Had not night come on and concealed the traces of their flight, many more of the enemy would have been slain. The victory was gained by God's grace, who has established Islam for ever as the best of religions, notwithstanding that idolaters revolt against it. The Sultan returned with plunder which it is impossible to enumerate. Praise be to God, the protector of the world, for the honour He bestows upon Islam and Mussulmans!

INDIAN ARMOUR.

As no part of Hind remained unconquered except Kashmir, the Sultan Mahmud resolved on an expedition to that country. It happened that twenty thousand men from Mawara-an-nahr and its neighbourhood, who were with the Sultan, were anxious to be employed in a holy war, and the Sultan accordingly determined to march with them toward Kanauj, which no other king but the all-powerful Gushtasp had been able to take, as has been related in certain histories of the Magians.

Between Ghazni and Kanauj the journey occupies three months, even for camels and horses. The Sultan therefore bade farewell to sleep and ease, and praying to God for success, he departed with his valiant warriors. He safely crossed the Sihun (Indus), Jihlam, Chandraha, Ubra (Ravi), Bah (Biyah), and Sataldur (Sutlaj). All these rivers are deep beyond description; even elephants' bodies are concealed in them, so it may easily be imagined what is the case with horses. The currents of these streams carry along large stones, so that camels and horses are in danger of being swept down the stream. In every country traversed by the Sultan, ambassadors were sent to him proffering submission, insomuch that Sabli ibn Shahi ibn Bamhi, who held the passes leading into Kashmir, also came forward, offering his allegiance and his services as a guide. He led the way, crossing forest after forest. At midnight the drum sounded for the march, and the Mussulmans mounted their horses, ready to bear the inconvenience of the journey; and they marched on until the sun began to decline from the meridian. On the twentieth of Rajab, 409 A. H. (December 2, 1018 A. D.), they crossed the river Jumna.

The Sultan took all the lofty hill forts which he passed on the road, and at length arrived at the fort of Baran in the country of Hardat. When Hardat heard of this invasion by the warriors of God, who advanced like the waves of the sea, he became greatly agitated, his steps trembled, and he feared for his life, which was forfeit under the law of God. He accordingly reflected that his safety would best be secured by conforming to the religion of Islam, since the sword of God was drawn from the scabbard and the whip of punishment was uplifted. He came forth, therefore, with ten thousand men, all of whom proclaimed their anxiety for conversion and their rejection of idols. God confirmed the promises He had made, and rendered assistance to the Sultan Mahmud.

After some delay the Sultan marched against a fort held by Kulchand, who had assumed superiority over other rulers and was inflated with pride, and who employed his whole life in infidelity and was confident in the strength of his dominions. Whoever fought with him sustained defeat and flight, and he possessed much power, great wealth, many brave soldiers, large elephants, and strong forts, which were secure from attack and capture. When he saw that the Sultan advanced against him in the endeavour to engage in a holy war, he drew up his army and elephants within a deep forest ready for action.

Sultan Mahmud sent an advance-guard to attack Kulchand, and this vanguard, penetrating through the forest like a comb through a head of hair, enabled the Sultan to discover the road which led to the fort. The Mussulmans exclaimed, "God is exceeding great," and those of the enemy, who were anxious for death, stood their ground. Swords and spears were used in close conflict, but when the infidels found all their efforts were in vain, they deserted the fort and tried to cross the foaming river which flowed on the other side of their stronghold, thinking that beyond it they would be in security; but nearly fifty thousand of them were slain, taken, or drowned in the attempt, and went to the fire of hell. Kulchand himself, drawing his dagger, slew his wife, and then drove it into his own body. By this victory the Sultan obtained 185 powerful elephants, besides other booty.

AN INDIAN DAGGER.

The Sultan then departed from the environs of the city, in which was a temple of the Hindus. The name of this place was Maharat-al-Hind (Mathura). The wall of the city was constructed of hard stone, and two gates, erected upon strong and lofty foundations to protect them against the floods of the river and the rains, opened on the stream which flowed beneath the town. On both sides of the city there were a thousand houses to which idol-temples were attached, all strengthened from top to bottom by rivets of iron, and all made of masonry work; and opposite them were other buildings, supported on broad wooden pillars to give them strength.

In the middle of the city there was a temple larger and firmer than the rest, which can neither be described nor painted. The Sultan wrote thus concerning it:

"If any one should wish to construct a building equal to this, he would not be able to do it without expending a hundred thousand thousand red dinars, and it would occupy two hundred years, even though the most experienced and able workmen were employed." Among the idols there were five made of red gold, each five yards high, fixed in the air without support. In the eyes of one of these idols there were two rubies of such value that if any one were to sell such as are like them, he would obtain fifty thousand dinars. On another there was a sapphire purer than water and more sparkling than crystal; the weight was 450 miskals (nearly six pounds Troy). The feet of another idol weighed 4,400 miskals (nearly fifty-six pounds Troy), and the entire quantity of gold yielded by the bodies of these idols was 98,300 miskals (almost 1,246 pounds Troy). The idols of silver amounted to two hundred, but they could not be weighed without breaking them to pieces and putting them into scales. The Sultan gave orders that all the temples should be burnt with naphtha and fire, and levelled to the ground.

After this, the Sultan went on with the intention of proceeding to Kanauj. He left the greater part of his army behind and took only a small body of troops with him against Rai Jaipal, who also had but a few men with him and was preparing to fly for safety to some of his dependent vassals.

The Sultan levelled to the ground every fort which Jaipal had in this country and the inhabitants either accepted Islam or took arms against Mahmud. He collected so much booty, prisoners, and wealth that the fingers of those who counted them would have been tired.

On the eighth of Sha'ban he arrived at Kanauj, which was deserted by Jaipal on hearing of his approach, for he fled across the Ganges, which the Hindus regard as of exceeding sanctity, and as having its source in the paradise of heaven. When they burn their dead, they throw the ashes into this river, as they believe that its waters purify them from sin. Devotees even come to it from a distance and drown themselves in its stream in the hope of obtaining eternal salvation, but in the end it will only carry them to hell, so that it will neither kill them nor make them alive.

The Sultan advanced to the fortifications of Kanauj, which consisted of seven distinct forts, washed by the Ganges which flowed under them like the ocean. In Kanauj there were nearly ten thousand temples, which the idolaters asserted had been founded by their ancestors two or three hundred thousand years ago. They worshipped and offered their vows and supplications to them in consequence of their great antiquity. Many of the inhabitants of the place fled and were scattered abroad like so many wretched widows and orphans from the fear which oppressed them in consequence of witnessing the fate of their deaf and dumb idols. Many of them thus effected their escape and those who did not fly were put to death. The Sultan took all seven forts in one day and gave his soldiers leave to plunder them and take prisoners.

A BURNING-GHAT ON THE BANK OF THE GANGES AT BENARES.

He then went to Munj, known as the fort of Brahmans, the inhabitants of which were independent as headstrong camels. They prepared to offer opposition like evil demons and obstinate Satans, and when they found they could not withstand the Mussulmans and that their blood would be shed, they took to flight, throwing themselves down from the apertures and the broad and lofty battlements, but most of them were killed in this attempt.

After this, Mahmud advanced against the fort of Asi, which was ruled by Chandal Bhor, one of the chief men and generals of the Hindus. Around his fort there were broad and deep ditches, as well as an impenetrable and dense jungle, full of snakes which no enchanters could tame and so dark that even the rays of the full moon could not be discerned in it.

When Chandal heard of the advance of the Sultan, he lost heart from excess of fear, and as he saw death with his mouth open toward him, he had no resource but flight. The Sultan therefore ordered that his five forts should be demolished to their very foundations, the inhabitants buried in the ruins, and the soldiers of the garrison plundered, slain, and imprisoned.

Hearing of the flight of Chandal, the Sultan was sorely afflicted and turned his horse's head toward Chand Rai, one of the greatest men in Hind, who resided in the fort of Sharwa.

Between him and Puru Jaipal there had been constant battles, in which many men and warriors had fallen in the field, so that at last they made peace to prevent further bloodshed and invasion of their respective borders. Puru Jaipal sought his old enemy's daughter that he might give her in marriage to his son Bhimpal, thus cementing the peace between them for ever. He sent his son to obtain his bride from Chand Rai, but the latter imprisoned the son and demanded retribution for the losses which had been inflicted by the father. Jaipal was thus compelled to refrain from proceeding against Chand Rai's fort and country, being unable to release his son; but constant skirmishes occurred between them until the arrival of Sultan Mahmud in those parts, who, through the kindness of God, had wish after wish gratified in a succession of conquests.

To save his life, Puru Jaipal entered into an alliance with Bhoj Chand, who was arrogant because of the strength of his forts and their difficulty of access, and there he considered himself secure against pursuit in his inaccessible retreat. Chand Rai, on the contrary, took up arms, trusting in the strength of his fort; but had he remained in it, he would undoubtedly have had it destroyed, and had he trusted to his army, it would have been of no avail. Under these circumstances, Bhimpal wrote him a letter to this effect: "Sultan Mahmud is not like the rulers of Hind and is not the leader of black men. It is obviously advisable to seek safety from such a person, for armies flee away before the very name of him and his father. I regard his bridle as much stronger than yours, for he never contents himself with one blow of the sword nor does his army satisfy itself with one hill out of a whole range. If, therefore, you design to contend with him, you will suffer; but do as you like—you know best. If you wish for your own safety, you will remain in concealment."

Chand Rai considered that Bhimpal had given him sound advice and that danger was to be incurred by acting contrary to his suggestions. He therefore departed secretly with his property, elephants, and treasure to the hill country, which was exceedingly lofty, hiding himself in jungles which the sun could not pene-

The Kanch Mahal at Amber

The ruined city of Amber, adjoining Jaipur, was once the capital of its district, but has been practically deserted for two centuries and has fallen into decay and desolation. Yet its crumbling and tenantless palaces still retain signs of departed glory and exhibit some of the most exquisite specimens of Indian art in inlaid work, mosaic panels, and the mirror and spangle decorative design for which Jaipur is renowned.

trate and concealing even the direction of his flight, so that no man could know whither he was gone or whether he had sped by night or day. The object of Bhimpal in recommending the flight of Chand Rai was that the king should not fall into the net of the Sultan and thus be made a Mussulman, as had happened to Bhimpal's uncle and relations, when they demanded quarter in their distress.

Sultan Mahmud invested and captured the fort, notwithstanding its strength and height. Here he got plenty of supplies and booty, but he did not obtain the real object of his desire, which was to seize Chand Rai, and which he now determined to effect by proceeding in pursuit of him. Accordingly, after marching fifteen parasangs, or leagues, through the jungle, which was so thorny that the faces of his men were scarred and bleeding, and through stony tracts which battered and injured the horses' shoes, he at last came up to his enemy shortly before midnight on the twenty-fifth of Sha'ban, 409 A. H. (January 6, 1019 A. D.).

The Sultan summoned the most religiously disposed of his followers and ordered them to attack the enemy at once. Many infidels were consequently slain or taken prisoners in this sudden attack, but the Mussulmans paid no regard to the booty till they had sated themselves with the slaughter of the infidels and worshippers of the sun and fire. The soldiers of the Sultan searched the bodies of the slain for three whole days to obtain booty.

The plunder of gold and silver, and of rubies and

pearls, amounted to nearly three thousand thousand dirhams, and the number of prisoners may be imagined from the fact that each brought from two to ten dirhams. These were afterwards taken to Ghazni, and merchants came from distant cities to purchase them, so that the countries of Mawara-an-nahr, Irak, and Khorasan were filled with them, and the fair and the dark, the rich and the poor, were commingled in one common slavery.

After an expedition against the Afghans, Sultan Mahmud again turned toward Hind with his bold warriors, whose greatest pleasure was to be in the saddle, which they regarded as their throne; while they deemed hot winds refreshing breezes and the drinking of dirty water seemed pure wine, so prepared were they to undergo every kind of privation and annoyance. When Mahmud arrived in that country, he granted quarter to all those who submitted, but slew those who opposed him. He obtained a large amount of booty before he reached a river known by the name of Rahib. It was very deep, and its bottom was muddy like tar used for anointing scabby animals. The feet of the horses and camels sank deeply into it, so that the men took off their coats of mail and stripped themselves naked before crossing it.

Puru Jaipal was encamped on the other side of the river, as a measure of security in consequence of this sudden attack, with his warriors dusky as night and with his elephants all caparisoned. He showed a determination to resist the passage of the Sultan, but at night he was making preparations to escape down the river. When the Sultan learnt this, he ordered inflated skins

CROSSING THE RIVER SUTLAJ ON SKINS.
(Copyright by Underwood & Underwood, New York.)

to be prepared, and directed some of his men to swim over on them. Jaipal, seeing eight men swimming over to that distant bank, ordered a detachment of his army, accompanied by five elephants, to oppose their landing, but the eight men plied their arrows so vigorously that the detachment was not able to effect its purpose. When the Sultan witnessed the full success of these men, he ordered all his soldiers who could swim to pass over at once, and promised them a life of repose after that day of trouble. His own personal guards first crossed this difficult stream, and they were followed by the whole army. Some swam over on skins, and others were nearly drowned, but eventually all landed safely.

When they all had reached the opposite bank, the Sultan ordered his men to mount their horses and charge in such a manner as to put the enemy to flight. Some of the infidels asked for mercy after being wounded, some were taken prisoners, some were killed, and the rest took to flight, while 270 gigantic elephants fell into the hands of the Mussulmans.'

CHAPTER III

RISE OF THE HOUSE OF GHOR

WHEN the power of the house of Ghazni declined, the ascendency passed to another Afghan line, the house of Ghor. Two brothers, Sultan Ghiyas-ad-din and Sultan Mu'izz-ad-din (the latter afterwards known as Mohammad Ghori), made the history of this short dynasty famous, as has been narrated in the third chapter of the third volume. The former of these able chieftains came to the throne in 558 A. H. (1163 A. D.), and with the aid of his brother Mu'izz-ad-din, who succeeded him as Sultan Mohammad Ghori (599 - 603 A. H., or 1202 - 1206 A. D.), extended the domain of Afghan authority by a series of ravaging campaigns in Hindustan rivalling those which Mahmud of Ghazni had previously carried on. We have an account of the main current of these events recorded by the pen of a native chronicler of Ghor, named Minhaj-as-Siraj, who wrote a general history from the earliest times down to the year 658 A. H. (1259 A. D.), and a brief selection from his annals is here given in a slightly abridged form.

'When Ghiyas-ad-din succeeded to the throne of

Ghor after the death of Saif-ad-din and the intelligence thereof came to Bamian, Fakhr-ad-din addressed his nephew Mu'izz-ad-din (later the Sultan Mohammad Ghori), saying: "Your brother is an active prince, what do you mean to do? You must bestir yourself." Mu'izz-ad-din bowed respectfully to his uncle, left the court, and started at once for Firoz-koh. When he arrived there, he waited upon his brother and paid his respects. One year he served his brother, but having taken some offence, he went to Seistan to Malik Shams-ad-din Sijistani and staid there one winter. His brother sent messengers to bring him back, and when he arrived, he assigned to him the countries of Kasr-kajuran and Istiya. When he had established his authority over the whole of Garmsir, he entrusted to his brother the city of Takinabad, which was the largest town in Garmsir. This Takinabad is the place which was the cause of the quarrel with the house of Mahmud Sabuktagin, and it passed into the hands of the kings of Ghor.

When Sultan Mu'izz-ad-din became master of Takinabad, the armies and leaders of the Ghuzz fled before the forces of Khita toward Ghazni, where they remained for twelve years, having wrested the country from the hands of Khusru Shah and Khusru Malik. Sultan Mu'izz-ad-din kept continually assailing them from Takinabad and troubling the country. At length, in the year 569 A. H. (1173 A. D.), Sultan Ghiyas-ad-din conquered Ghazni and returned to Ghor, after placing his brother Mu'izz-ad-din upon the throne.

THE BALA HISSAR AT PESHAWAR.

This prince secured the territories of Ghazni, and conquered Gurdez two years afterwards, in 570 A. H. (1174 A. D.). In the third year he led his forces to Multan and delivered that place from the hands of the Karmathians. In the same year, 571 A. H. (1175 A. D.), the people of Sankaran revolted and made great confusion, so that he marched against them and put most of them to the sword.

In the year after this victory, he conducted his army by way of Uchh and Multan toward Nahrwala. The Raja of Nahrwala, Bhim-deo, was a minor, but he had a large army and many elephants. In the day of battle the Mohammedans were defeated and the Sultan was compelled to retreat. This happened in the year 574 A. H. (1178 A. D.).

In 575 A. H. (1179 A. D.), Ghiyas-ad-din attacked and conquered Peshawar, and two years afterwards he advanced to Lahore. The power of the Ghaznavids was now drawing to a close, and their glory was departed, so Khusru Malik sent his son as a hostage and also an elephant as a present to the Sultan. This was in the year 577 A. H. (1181 A. D.). Next year the Sultan marched to Daibul, subdued all that country even to the sea, and returned with great booty. In 580 A. H. (1184 A. D.), he went to Lahore, ravaged all the territories of that kingdom, and returned after building the fort of Sialkot, in which he placed Husain Kharmil as governor. When the Sultan was gone, Khusru Malik assembled the forces of Hindustan, and having also obtained a body of Gakkars, he laid siege to Sialkot, but, after some time, was obliged to withdraw. The Sultan returned to Lahore in 581 A. H. (1185 A. D.).

The house of Mahmud had now come to its end; the sun of its glory was set; and the registrar of fate had written the mandate of its destruction. Khusru Malik could offer no resistance; he came forth peacefully to meet the Sultan and was made prisoner. Lahore fell completely into the power of the Ghori prince and he secured all its dominions in Hindustan.

Ali Karmakh, chief of Multan, was appointed commander at Lahore, and the father of the author of this book, Maulana A'jubat-az-Zaman Afsah-al-Ajam Siraj-ad-din Minhaj, was appointed judge of the army of Hindustan and received the honour of investiture from Mu'izz-ad-din. He held his court at the headquarters of the army, and twelve camels were assigned for moving his Bench of Justice from place to place.

The Sultan returned to Ghazni, carrying Khusru Malik with him, and on arriving there, he sent him on to Firoz-koh, to the court of the great king Ghiyas-ad-din. This monarch sent him as a prisoner to the fort of Bahrawan and confined his son Bahram Shah in the fort of Saifrud. When the war with Khwarizm Shah broke out in the year 587 A. H. (1191 A. D.), Khusru Malik and his son were put to death.

The victorious Sultan then prepared another army, with which he attacked and conquered the fort of Sirhind. This fort he placed under the command of Zia-ad-din ibn Mohammad Abd-as-Salam Tolaki. At his request, Majd-ad-din Tolaki selected twelve hundred men of the tribe of Tolaki and placed them all under his command in the fort, so as to enable him to hold it until the Sultan's return from Ghazni.

Raja Kolah Pithaura marched against the fort, whereupon the Sultan returned and faced him at Narain. All the rajas of Hindustan were with Kolah. The battle was formed, and the Sultan, seizing a lance, made a rush upon the elephant which carried Govind Rai of Delhi. The latter advanced to meet him in front of the battle, and then the Sultan drove his lance into the raja's mouth and knocked two of his teeth down his throat. The raja, on the other hand, returned the blow, and inflicted a severe wound on the arm of his adversary. The Sultan reined back his horse and turned aside, but the pain of the wound was so insufferable that he could not support himself on horseback. The Mussulman army gave way and could not be controlled. The Sultan was just falling, when a brave young Khalji recognized him, jumped upon the horse behind him, and clasping him round the bosom, spurred on the horse and bore him from the midst of the fight.

When the Mussulmans lost sight of the Sultan, panic fell upon them; they fled, and halted not until they were safe from the pursuit of the victors. A party of nobles and youths of Ghor had seen and recognized their leader with that lion-hearted Khalji, and when he came up, they drew together, and forming a kind of litter with broken lances, they bore him to the halting-place. The hearts of the troops were consoled by his appearance, and the Mohammedan faith gathered new strength in his life. The Sultan collected his scattered forces and retreated to the territories of Islam, leaving Tolak in the fort of Sirhind. Raja Pithaura advanced and invested the fort, which he besieged for thirteen months.

A KHALJI CHIEFTAIN AND HIS WIFE.

Next year the Sultan assembled another army and advanced to Hindustan to avenge his defeat. A trustworthy person named Mu'in-ad-din, one of the principal men in the hills of Tolak, informed me that he was in this army, and that its force amounted to 120,000 horsemen bearing armour. Before the Sultan could arrive, the fort of Sirhind had capitulated, and the enemy were encamped in the vicinity of Narain. The Sultan drew up his battle-array, leaving his main body in the rear with the banners, canopies, and elephants, to the number of several divisions. His plan of attack being formed, he advanced quietly. The light unarmoured horsemen were made into four divisions of ten thousand each, and were directed to advance and harass the enemy with their arrows on all sides, on the right and on the left, in the front and in the rear. When the enemy collected his forces to attack, they were to support each other and to charge at full speed. By these tactics the infidels were worsted; the Almighty gave us the victory over them, and they fled.

Pithaura alighted from his elephant, mounted a horse, and galloped off, but was captured near Sarsuti and killed. Govind Rai of Delhi was slain in the battle, and the Sultan recognized his head by the two teeth which he had broken. Ajmir, the capital, and all the Siwalik hills, Hansi, Sarsuti, and other districts were the results of this victory, which was gained in the year 588 A. H. (1192 A. D.).

On his return homeward, the Sultan placed Kutb-ad-din in command of the fort of Kahram, and in the same year this chief, advancing to Mirat, conquered that town and took possession of Delhi. In the following year he captured the fort of Kol. In the year 590 A. H. (1193 A. D.), the Sultan came back from Ghazni by way of Benares and Kanauj, defeated Rai Jai Chand in the neighbourhood of Chandawal, and captured over three hundred elephants in the battle.

Sultan Sa'id Ghiyas-ad-din died at Herat in 599 A. H. (1201 A. D.), while his brother Sultan Mu'izz-ad-din, or Mohammad Ghori, was between Tus and Sarakhs in Khorasan, but the latter returned and secured his elevation to the throne.

Two years later a rebellion broke out among the Gakkars and the tribes of the hills of Jud, and in the winter Sultan Mohammad went to Hindustan to put down the revolt. He defeated the rebels and made their blood to flow in streams, but as he was returning home to Ghazni he fell into the hands of these infidels and was put to death in the year 602 A. H. (1206 A. D.). The period of his reign was thirty-two years.'

The detailed history of Mohammad Ghori's reign has been given in the third chapter of the third volume of the series, a reference to which will be sufficient.

ARABESQUE SCROLL FROM THE MINARET OF KUTB-AD-DIN AYBEK.

CHAPTER IV

KUTB-AD-DIN AYBEK AND ALTAMISH—TWO OF THE SLAVE KINGS

1206-1236 A.D.

AT the beginning of the thirteenth century a line of slaves, born from the blood of Turks, rose to be kings of Northern India and formed a powerful dynasty that governed Hindustan for more than eighty years (1206-1290 A. D.). The strain of royal democracy in their veins seemed to possess the qualities that make for greatness, and three of the ten "Slave Kings"—Kutb-ad-din Aybek, Altamish, and Balban—were men of remarkable power, while the administrative strength of all of them was enhanced by the special advantage of not ruling India at a distance, from Ghazni and Ghor in Afghanistan, but sitting directly on the throne of Delhi itself.

Kutb-ad-din Aybek, the first of these dynasts, was a slave of Mohammad of Ghor, but was raised by his imperial master to the rank of viceroy because of his merit, and became the nominal founder of the Slave

Sultans, although his rule as an independent sovereign at Delhi (1206 - 1210 A. D.) was too short to enable him to consolidate an empire. There is a concise account of his short career written by Minhaj-as-Siraj, who was quoted in the preceding chapter, and it is reproduced in the following paragraphs.

'Sultan Kutb-ad-din was a brave and liberal king, and the Almighty bestowed on him such courage and generosity that in his time there was no king like unto him from the east to the west. When the Almighty God wishes to exhibit to His people an example of greatness and majesty He endows one of His slaves with the qualities of courage and generosity, and then friends and enemies are influenced by His bounteous generosity and warlike prowess. So this king was generous and brave, and all the regions of Hindustan were filled with friends and cleared of foes. His bounty was continuous and his slaughter was unceasing.

When Kutb-ad-din was first brought from Turkistan, his lot fell in the city of Naishapur, where he was bought by the chief judge, Kadi Fakhr-ad-din Abd-al-Aziz of Kufa, one of the descendants of the great Imam Abu Hanifa of Kufa and governor of Naishapur and its dependencies. Kutb-ad-din grew up in the service and society of his master's sons, and with them he learned to read the Koran and also acquired the arts of riding and archery. In a short time he became remarkable for his manly qualities. When he had nearly arrived at the age of manhood, merchants brought him to Ghazni, and Sultan Ghazi Mu'izz-ad-din Mohammad Sam (Mohammad Ghori) purchased him from them. He was possessed of every quality and virtue, but he was not comely in appearance. His little finger was broken from his hand, and he was therefore called Aybek, "maimed in the hand."

A HINDU MUSICIAN.

Sultan Mu'izz-ad-din (Mohammad Ghori) used occasionally to indulge in music and conviviality, and one night he had a party; and in the course of the banquet he graciously bestowed gifts of money and of uncoined gold and silver upon his servants. Kutb-ad-din received his share among the rest, but whatever he got, whether gold or silver, coined or uncoined, he gave it all, when he went out of the assembly, to the Turkish soldiers, guards, farashes, and other servants. He kept nothing, either small or great, for himself. Next day when this was reported to the king, Kutb was looked upon with great favour and condescension, and was appointed to some important duties about the court. He thus became a great officer, and his rank grew higher every day, until by the king's favour he was appointed Master of the Horse.

While he held this station, the kings of Ghor, Ghazni, and Bamian went toward Khorasan, and Kutb-ad-din showed great activity in repelling the attacks of Sultan Shah. He held the command of the foragers, and one day, while in quest of supplies, he was unexpectedly attacked by the cavalry of the enemy. Kutb-ad-din showed great bravery in the fight which ensued, but his party was small, so he was overpowered, made a prisoner, and carried to Sultan Shah. This prince ordered him to be placed in confinement, but when the battle was fought and Sultan Shah was defeated, the victors released Kutb-ad-din and brought him in his iron fetters, riding on a camel, to his master Sultan Mu'izz-ad-din. The Sultan received him kindly and, on his arrival at his capital, Ghazni, conferred on him the districts of Kahram. From thence he went to Mirat, of which he took possession in 587 A. H. (1191 A. D.). In the same year he marched from Mirat and captured Delhi.

In 590 A. H. (1194 A. D.) he and Izz-ad-din Husain Kharmil, both being generals of the army, accompanied the Sultan and defeated Rai Jai Chand of Benares in the neighbourhood of Chandawal. In the year 591 A. H. (1195 A. D.) Thankar was conquered, and two years later Kutb-ad-din went toward Nahrwala, defeated Raja Bhim-deo, and took revenge on behalf of the Sultan. He also reduced other countries of Hindustan as far as the outskirts of the dominions of China on the east.

When Sultan Mohammad of Ghor died, Sultan

Ghiyas-ad-din Mahmud Mohammad Sam, his nephew, gave Kutb-ad-din the royal canopy and the title of Sultan. In 602 A. H. (1205 A. D.) the new monarch marched from Delhi to attack Lahore, and on Tuesday, the eighteenth of the month of Zu-l-ka'da, 602 A.H. (June 26, 1206), he ascended the throne in that city. After some time a dispute arose between him and Sultan Taj-ad-din Yildiz respecting Lahore, and it ended in a battle, in which the victory was gained by Sultan Kutb-ad-din. Taj-ad-din fled, and Sultan Kutb-ad-din then proceeded toward Ghazni, which he captured, and he sat upon the throne of that city for forty days, at the end of which time he returned to Delhi.

MINAR OF KUTB-AD-DIN AT DELHI.

Death now claimed his own, and in the year 607 A. H. (1210 A. D.) the Sultan fell from his horse in the field while he was playing polo (*chaugān*), and the horse came down upon him, so that the pommel of the saddle entered his chest and killed him. The period of his government, from his first conquest of Delhi up to this time, was twenty years, and the time of his reign, during which he wore the crown and had the Khutba read and caused coin to be struck in his name, was something more than four years.'

Some confusion followed upon the death of Kutb-ad-din Aybek, since his son Aram proved unworthy to succeed him. The throne then passed to his son-in-law, Shams-ad-din Altamish, who was likewise originally a slave but had raised himself by his ability and had married Kutb-ad-din's third daughter. In the words of Minhaj, our Arab chronicler, the monarch had regarded him "as well suited for empire and had called him his son;" in fact "it was destined from all eternity by the Most High and Holy God that the country of Hindustan should be placed under the protection of this great king, the light of the world and of religion." The remainder of the chapter is abridged from the chronicler's own account of Altamish, or Sultan Shams-ad-din, as he prefers to call him.

'It is related by credible persons that Sultan Shams-ad-din Altamish was chosen in early childhood by the destiny of Providence from the tribes of Albari in Turkistan for the sovereignty of Islam and of the dominions of Hindustan. His father, whose name was Yalam Khan, had numerous dependents, relatives, and followers in his employ. The future monarch was remarkable from his childhood for beauty, intelligence, and grace, which excited such jealousy in the hearts of his brothers that, like Joseph's brethren, they enticed him away from his father and mother on the pretence of going to see a drove of horses; but when they brought him there, they sold him to a horse-dealer. Some say that his sellers were his cousins. The horse-dealers took him to Bokhara and sold him to one of the relatives of the chief judge of that city. For some time he remained with that great and noble family, whose chiefs nourished and educated him like a son.

A PIOUS MENDICANT.

A credible person has related that he heard in the gracious words of the king himself that on a certain occasion one of the members of the family gave him a piece of money and ordered him to go to the bazaar and buy some grapes. He went to the bazaar, and on the way lost the coin. Being of tender age, he began to cry for fear; and while he was weeping and crying, a dervish came to him, took his hand, purchased some grapes, and gave them to him, saying: "When you obtain wealth and dominion, take care that you show respect to dervishes and holy men, and uphold their rights." He gave his promise to the dervish, and whatever fortune and power he obtained he always ascribed to the favour shown him by that kindly man.

Altamish was purchased from his noble and distinguished owner by a merchant whose name was Haji

Bokhari, and he sold him to another merchant named Jamal-ad-din Chast Kaba, who brought him to Ghazni. No slave equal to him in beauty, virtue, intelligence, and nobility had ever been brought to that city. Mention was made of him before his Majesty Sultan Mu'izz-ad-din Mohammad Sam of Ghor, who commanded a price to be named for him. A thousand dinars in refined gold was fixed as his value, but Jamal-ad-din Chast Kaba declined to sell him for that price, and the Sultan accordingly gave orders that nobody should purchase him. After this, Jamal-ad-din Chast Kaba staid for a year in Ghazni, and then went to Bokhara, carrying the future Sultan with him. After staying there three years, he brought him back to Ghazni; but no one ventured to purchase him, for fear of the king's orders.

The youth had been there a year, when Kutb-ad-din returned to Ghazni with Malik Nasir-ad-din Husain after the invasion of Nahrwala and the conquest of Gujarat. Kutb heard an account of Shams-ad-din Altamish and asked Sultan Mu'izz-ad-din for permission to purchase him. The Sultan replied that orders had been issued that he should not be purchased in Ghazni, but said that he might take him to Delhi and buy him there. Kutb-ad-din entrusted the management of the affair to Nizam-ad-din Mohammad and ordered him to take Jamal-ad-din Chast Kaba with him to Hindustan, that he might purchase Shams-ad-din Altamish there. According to these directions, Nizam-ad-din took them to Delhi, where Kutb-ad-din pur-

The Kutb Minar at Delhi.
From a Photograph.

chased him. Altamish was made chief of the guards, and Kutb-ad-din called him his son and kept him near his person. His rank and honour increased every day, and such marks of intelligence were evident in all his acts that he was elevated to the rank of chief huntsman. When Gwalior was taken, he became amir of that place, and after that he obtained the district and town of Baran and its dependencies. Some time after this, when proofs of his energy, bravery, and heroism had been fully displayed and had been witnessed by Kutb-ad-din, the country of Badaun was entrusted to him. When Sultan Mu'izz-ad-din Mohammad Sam returned from Khwarizm, after being defeated in the battle of Andkhod by the armies of Khita, the Gakkar tribes broke out in rebellion, and the Sultan marched against them from Ghazni. Kutb-ad-din, according to his orders, brought up an army from Hindustan, and Shams-ad-din Altamish accompanied him with the forces of Badaun.

In the midst of the battle the Sultan observed his feats of daring and courage, and inquired who he was. When his Majesty was enlightened upon this point, he called him into his presence and honoured him with especial notice. Kutb-ad-din was commanded to treat Altamish well, as he was destined for great works. His Majesty then ordered the deed of his freedom to be written out, and graciously granted him his liberty.

When Sultan Kutb-ad-din expired at Lahore in 607 A. H. (1210 A. D.), the commander-in-chief, Ali Isma'il, who had charge of Delhi, joined with some other nobles and principal men, and sent letters to Badaun, inviting Shams-ad-din Altamish to succeed the late ruler. When he arrived, he mounted the throne of Delhi and established his authority. The Turks and the Mu'izzi chiefs assembled at Delhi from all quarters, but the Turks and Mu'izzi chiefs of that city did not

VIEW OF LAHORE FROM THE PALACE IN THE FORT.

join them. They resolved to try the effect of resistance, so they went out from Delhi, collected in the environs, and raised the standard of revolt. Sultan Shams-ad-din Altamish marched out of the city with a body of horse and his own personal followers, defeated the rebels in the plains of the Jumna, and put most of their horsemen to the sword. Sultan Taj-ad-din later made a treaty with him from Lahore and Ghazni, and sent him some insignia of royalty. Repeated disputes arose between Sultan Shams-ad-din Altamish and Malik Nasir-ad-din Kubacha about Lahore, Tabarhindh, and Kahram, and in the year 614 A. H. (1217 A. D.) the Sultan defeated Kubacha. Hostilities also broke out at different times between him and the chiefs of various parts of Hindustan and the Turks, but as he was assisted by divine favour, every one who resisted him or rebelled was subdued. Heaven still continued to favour him, and all the territories belonging to Delhi, Badaun, Oudh, Benares, and the Siwalik Hills came under his sway.

Sultan Taj-ad-din Yildiz came to Lahore, fleeing before the army of Khwarizm. A dispute arose between him and Sultan Shams-ad-din Altamish regarding the limits of their possessions, and a battle was fought between them at Narain in 612 A. H. (1215 A. D.), in which Altamish won the victory, and Taj-ad-din Yildiz was taken prisoner. He was taken, according to orders, to Delhi and then sent to Badaun, where he was put to death and buried. After this another battle was fought in the year 614 A. H. (1217 A. D.) with Malik Nasir-ad-din Kubacha, and he was again defeated.

Great events now occurred in Khorasan through the appearance of the Moghul Chingiz Khan. In 615 A. H. (1218 A. D.) Jalal-ad-din, King of Khwarizm, came toward Hindustan, fleeing from the army of the infidels, and some fighting followed on the frontiers of Lahore. Shams-ad-din Altamish led his forces out of

Delhi toward Lahore, and Khwarizm Shah fled before the army of Hindustan and went toward Sind and Siwistan.

After this, in 622 A. H. (1225 A. D.), Sultan Shams-ad-din carried his arms toward Lakhnauti, and Ghiyas-ad-din Auz Khalji placed the yoke of servitude on the neck of submission, and presented thirty elephants and eight millions of the current coin. He also ordered sermons to be read and coinage to be struck in the name of Shams-ad-din.

In 623 A. H. (1226 A. D.) Sultan Shams-ad-din marched to conquer the fortress of Rantambhor, which is celebrated in all parts of Hindustan for its great strength and security, and it is related in the Hindu histories that it had been invaded by more than seventy kings, but that no one had been able to take it. In the space of a few months in the year 623 A. H. (1226 A. D.), through the favour of God, the fortress fell into the hands of Shams-ad-din. One year after this, in 624 A. H. (1227 A. D.), he attacked the fort of Mandur in the Siwalik Hills, where God again bestowed victory on him, and where much plunder fell into the hands of his followers.

After the lapse of another year, in 625 A. H. (1228 A. D.), an army was sent from Delhi toward the cities of Uchh and Multan. On the first of Rabi'-al-awwal, 625 A. H. (Feb. 9, 1228 A. D.), Sultan Sa'id Shams-ad-din Altamish reached the foot of the fort of Uchh. Malik Nasir-ad-din Kubacha had pitched his camp at the gate of the fort of Amravat, and all his followers and baggage were in ships and boats moored in front of the camp.

On Friday, after the time of prayer, some swift runners came from the direction of Multan and reported that Malik Nasir-ad-din Aitamur had been detached from Lahore and had come to the fort of Multan; and also that Sultan Shams-ad-din Altamish himself was marching onward to Uchh by way of Tabarhindh. Malik Nasir-ad-din Kubacha immediately fled with all his army in boats to Bhakkar and ordered his minister, Ain-al-Mulk Husain Ashghari, to remove all the treasure from the fortress of Uchh and transfer it to Bhakkar.

A HOUSE AT MULTAN.

Sultan Shams-ad-din then sent two of his principal generals in advance with an army to the walls of Uchh. Four days later, the Sultan himself arrived at Uchh with all his elephants and baggage, and pitched his tents there. He sent his minister, Nizam-ad-din Mohammad Junaidi, with other nobles, in pursuit of Malik Nasir-ad-din to the fort of Bhakkar. Fighting continued for a month under the walls of Uchh, and on Tuesday, the twenty-ninth of Jumada-l-awwal, 625 A. H. (May 5, 1228 A. D.), the place capitulated. In the same month Malik Nasir-ad-din Kubacha drowned himself at the fort of Bhakkar in the waters of the Indus, a few days after sending his son, Malik Ala-ad-din Bahram Shah, to wait upon Sultan Shams-ad-din. A few days later, the treasures were seized, and the remaining forces of Malik Nasir-ad-din entered the service of the conqueror. All the country down to the seashore was subdued, and Malik Sinan-ad-din Habsh, chief of Daibuḷ and Sind, came and did homage to the Sultan. When the noble mind of the king was satisfied with the conquest of the country, he returned to Delhi.

In 627 A. H. (1230 A. D.) Balka Malik Khalji rebelled in the territories of Lakhnauti, and Sultan Shams-ad-din Altamish led thither the armies of Hindustan, and having captured the rebel, he gave the throne of Lakhnauti to Malik Ala-ad-din Jani, and returned to his capital in the month of Rajab of the same year.

In 629 A. H. (1232 A. D.) the Sultan marched forth to conquer Gwalior, and when his royal tents were pitched beneath the walls of the fort, Milak Deo the accursed began the hostilities. For eleven months the camp remained under the fort, until on Tuesday, the twenty-sixth of Safar, 630 A. H. (Dec. 12, 1232 A. D.), the citadel was taken.

The accursed Milak Deo escaped from the fort in the night-time and fled. About seven hundred persons were ordered to receive punishment at the door of the royal tent, and after this, promotions were made in the ranks of the nobles and great officers. On the second of Rabi'-al-awwal in the same year, his Majesty started on his return from the fort, and after reaching the capital he sent the army of Islam toward Malwa, and took the fort and city of Bhilsa in 632 A. H. (1234 A. D.). There was a temple there which was three hundred years in building and was about one hundred and

THE ROAD NEAR A RUINED TEMPLE AT UJJAIN.

five cubits high. He demolished it. From thence he proceeded to Ujjain, where there was a temple of Maha-kal, which he destroyed, as well as the image of Vikramajit, who was King of Ujjain and reigned 1316 years before his time. The Hindu era dates from his reign. Some other images cast in copper were carried to Delhi with the stone image of Maha-kal.

In 633 A. H. (1236 A. D.) Sultan Shams-ad-din Altamish led the armies of Hindustan toward Banyan, but in this journey his Majesty fell sick and was obliged by his severe illness to return home. Wednesday morning, the first of Sha'ban, was fixed by the astrologers for his entrance into Delhi, the seat of his government, and he entered the city in a howdah on the back of an elephant. His illness increased, and nineteen days later, on the twentieth of Sha'ban, 633 A. H. (end of April, 1236 A. D.), he departed from this perishable world to everlasting life. The length of his reign was twenty-six years.'

PAINTED DECORATION ON THE CEILING OF ITMAD-AD-DAULAH'S TOMB.

CHAPTER V

RAZIYA, THE MOHAMMEDAN EMPRESS OF INDIA

1236-1240 A.D.

UPON the death of Altamish in 1236, his good-for-nothing son, Firoz, succeeded to the throne, but died after a brief and dissipated reign of seven months. India then experienced a novel sensation in having a woman upon the throne of Delhi. By a curious coincidence, noted by Lane-Poole, " the only three women who were ever elected to the throne in the Mohammedan East, reigned in the thirteenth century. Shajar-ad-durr, the high-spirited slave-wife of Saladin's grand-nephew, the woman who defeated the crusade of Louis IX and afterwards spared the saintly hero's life, was queen of the Mamluks in Egypt in 1250. Abish, the last of the princely line of Salghar, patrons of Sa'di, ruled the great province of Fars for nearly a quarter of a century during the troubled period of Mongol supremacy. Raziya, daughter of Altamish, less fortunate, sat on the throne of Delhi for only three years and a half (1236 - 1240)."

The story of Raziya's short-lived reign has already been sketched in this History, but we have also a good description of it from the Oriental chronicler Minhaj-as-Siraj, and this, with one unimportant omission, is used here. It will be noted that Minhaj always speaks of the queen as "Sultan," since this title, or that of Padshah, "king," was given to her, as well as to a few queens regent, despite the Mohammedan aversion to female rulers.[1] The account by Minhaj follows.

'Sultan Raziya was a great monarch. She was wise, just, and generous, a benefactor to her kingdom, a dispenser of justice, the protector of her subjects, and the leader of her armies. She was endowed with all the qualities befitting a king, but she was not born a man, and for that reason, in the estimation of men, all these virtues were worthless. In the days of her father, Sultan Shams-ad-din Altamish, she had exercised authority with great dignity. Her mother was the chief wife of his Majesty, and Raziya herself resided in the chief palace in the Kushk-firozi. The Sultan discerned in her countenance the signs of power and bravery, and although she was a girl and lived in retirement, yet when he returned from the conquest of Gwalior, he directed his secretary, Taj-al-Malik Mahmud, who was the director of the government, to

[1] The title Sultan is retained in the translation, especially as Sultana would not be an appropriate rendering, since *sultāna*, in its original meaning, signifies "a scold."

put her name in writing as heiress of the kingdom and successor to the throne. Before this firman was executed, the servants of the State, who were in close intimacy with his Majesty, represented that there would be little wisdom in making a woman heir to a Mohammedan throne, especially as the king had grown-up sons who were worthy of the dignity. They besought him, therefore, to set their minds at ease, for the course that he proposed seemed very inexpedient. The king replied: "My sons are devoted to the pleasures of youth, and no one of them is qualified to be king. They are unfit to rule the country, and after my death you will find that there is no one more competent to guide the State than my daughter." It was afterwards agreed by common consent that the king had judged aright.

When Sultan Raziya succeeded to the throne, all things reverted to their old order. The vizir of the State, Nizam-al-mulk Junaidi, however, refused to give allegiance, and he, together with Malik Jani, Malik Kochi, Malik Kabir Khan, and Malik Izz-ad-din Mohammad Salari, who assembled from different parts of the country at the gates of Delhi, made war for a long time against the Sultan Raziya. After awhile, Malik Nasir-ad-din Tabashi Mu'izzi, who was governor of Oudh, hurried his forces to Delhi to the assistance of Sultan Raziya; but when he had crossed the Ganges, the generals who were fighting against the city met him unexpectedly and took him prisoner, after which he fell sick and died.

Since the stay of the insurgents at the gates of Delhi was protracted, Sultan Raziya went out from the city and ordered her tents to be pitched at a certain place on the banks of the Jumna. Several engagements took place between the insurgent chiefs and the Turkish nobles who were on the side of the Sultan, but at last peace was effected with great adroitness. Malik Izz-ad-din Mohammad Salari and Malik Izz-ad-din Kabir Khan Ayyaz secretly joined the Sultan, and came at night to her Majesty's tents, with the understanding that Malik Jani, Malik Kochi, and Nizam-al-Mulk Junaidi were to be summoned and closely imprisoned, so that the rebellion might subside. When these chiefs were informed of this matter, they fled from their camp, and some horsemen of the Sultan pursued them. Malik Kochi and his brother Fakhr-ad-din were captured, and were afterwards killed in prison. Malik Jani was slain in the neighbourhood of Babul and Nakwan, and Nizam-al-Mulk Junaidi went into the mountains of Bardar, where he died.

When the affairs of Raziya were thus settled, she conferred the office of vizir on an upright officer who had been the deputy of Nizam-al-Mulk, and he likewise received the title of Nizam-al-Mulk. The command of the army was given to Malik Saif-ad-din Aybek Bahtu, with the title of Katlagh Khan. To Kabir Khan was assigned the province of Lahore. The country now enjoyed peace, and the power of the State became manifest. Throughout its territories, from Lakhnauti to Daibul, all the princes and nobles made their submission.

Shortly afterward, Malik Aybek Bahtu died, whereupon Malik Kutb-ad-din Hasan Ghori was appointed to his office and was ordered to march against the fort of Rantambhor. The Hindus had laid siege to this fortress after the death of Shams-ad-din, and had beleaguered it for some time, but when Kutb-ad-din arrived, he drew the Mussulman forces out of the fort and destroyed it, after which he returned to Delhi.

A MOHAMMEDAN WOMAN.

About this time Malik Ikhtiyar-ad-din Itigin was appointed lord chamberlain, and Amir Jamal-ad-din Yakut, the Abyssinian superintendent of the stables, was made a personal attendant of her Majesty, an act which created jealousy among the Turkish nobles. The Sultan Raziya now threw off the dress and veil of women. She put on a coat and cap, and showed herself among the people, so all men saw her openly as she rode on her elephant. She now ordered an army to march to Gwalior, and sent with it rich gifts. As there was no possibility of resistance, Minhaj-as-Siraj, the well-wisher of the victorious government, and the author of this book, together with Majd-al-Umara Zia-ad-din Junaidi, chief justice of Gwalior, and other principal officers, came out of the fort of Gwalior on the first of Sha'ban, 635 A. H. (Feb., 1238 A. D.), and proceeded to the Court of Delhi. In the month of Sha'ban of the same year, Sultan Raziya appointed the writer of these lines to the Nasiriya college and to the office of Judge of Gwalior. In 637 A. H. (1239 A. D.), Malik Izz-ad-din Kabir Khan, governor of Lahore, broke out in revolt. The Sultan led her army from Delhi in that direction and pursued him. After a time he made peace and did homage. The province of Multan, which had been held by Malik Karakash, was given to Malik Izz-ad-din Kabir Khan.

On Thursday, the nineteenth of Ramazan, 637 A. H. (April, 1240 A. D.), the Sultan Raziya returned to the capital. Malik Altuniya, who was governor of Tabarhindh, revolted, and some of the high officials on the frontier supported him. On Wednesday, the ninth of the same month and year, she marched with a numerous army toward Tabarhindh to put down these rebels. When she arrived there, she was attacked by the Turks, who put the Abyssinian Amir Jamal-ad-din Yakut to death. They then seized the Sultan Raziya and sent her a prisoner to the fort of Tabarhindh.

When Sultan Raziya was taken to Tabarhindh as a captive, Malik Altuniya espoused her cause and led her army toward Delhi to regain possession of the kingdom, whereupon Malik Izz-ad-din Mohammad Salari and Malik Karakash left the capital and went to join them. Meanwhile, Mu'izz-ad-din had ascended the throne, Ikhtiyar-ad-din Itigin, the lord chamberlain, had been slain, and Badr-ad-din Sankar Rumi had been appointed his successor. In the month of Rabi'-al-awwal, 638 A. H. (Sept., 1240 A. D.), the Sultan marched from

Delhi to repel his opponents, and Sultan Raziya and Malik Altuniya were defeated. When they reached Kaithal in their flight, their remaining forces abandoned them, and they both fell into the hands of the Hindus and were killed. The date of this defeat was the twenty-fourth of Rabi'-al-awwal, 638 A. H. (Oct. 13, 1240 A. D.), and the Sultan Raziya was killed on the day following, after a reign of three years and six days.'

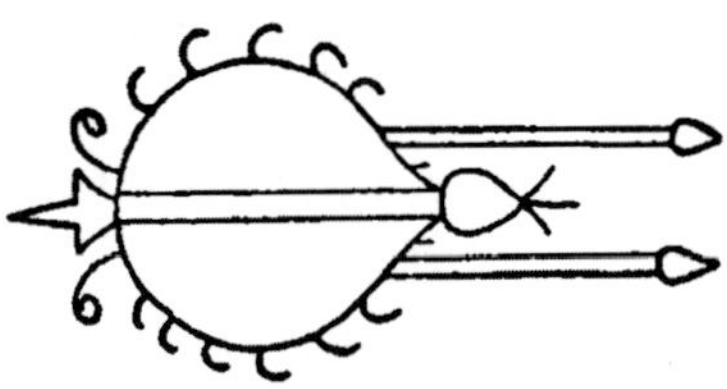

A PROJECTILE USED IN INDIAN WARFARE.

CHAPTER VI

THE EARLIER CAREER OF ULUGH KHAN, AFTERWARDS 'EMPEROR BALBAN

THE death of Queen Raziya was followed by six years of weak government by one of her brothers and a nephew, and then her younger brother Nasir-ad-din, the third son of the Slave King Altamish, took the throne and reigned for twenty years (1246-1266 A. D.). But during all this time the true power behind the throne was Ulugh Khan, who afterwards became Sultan Balban.

This remarkable man was originally a purchased slave from Turkistan, but he rose from that position and the menial services of water-carrier and huntsman to be prime minister and ultimately emperor. His devotion to his gentle master, Nasir-ad-din, was unswerving, whether as servant, general, or statesman, and on the death of Nasir he succeeded to the crown as Emperor Balban and reigned for twenty years himself, with the same qualities of noble greatness that marked all his previous life, which leave on our minds the impression that Balban was one of the strongest personalities among India's rulers.

The history of this notable man's earlier career is

told in the annals of Nasir-ad-din, which were written by Minhaj-as-Siraj, the Mohammedan historian who has already been quoted at length, and an excerpt from his work forms a suitable chapter to trace the upward steps by which Ulugh Khan rose to fame.

'The Sultan Ulugh Khan-i-Azam, otherwise called Ghiyas-ad-din Balban, belonged to the stock of the Khakans of Albari. His father was *khān* over ten thousand houses (*khānah*), and the family was well known in Albari, among the Turkish tribes of Turkistan. Now, inasmuch as the Almighty desired to grant a support to the power of Islam and strength to the Mohammedan faith, to extend His glorious shadow over it, and to preserve Hindustan within the range of His favour and protection, He removed Ulugh Khan in his youth from Turkistan, separating him from his race and kindred, and from his tribe and relations, and conveying him to the country of Hindustan, for the purpose of curbing the Moghuls. God conducted him to Baghdad, and from that city to Gujarat, where Khwaja Jamal-ad-din Basri, a man remarkable for piety and integrity, ability and worth, purchased him and brought him up carefully like a son. Intelligence and ability shone out clearly in his countenance, and his patron, Jamal, looked upon him with an eye of kindness and treated him with especial consideration.

In the year 630 A. H. (1232 A. D.), Jamal-ad-din took Ulugh Khan to Delhi, in the days when Sultan Shams-ad-din Altamish adorned the throne; and when the Sultan perceived that Ulugh was a youth of great promise, he bought him and made him his personal attendant, placing the hawk of fortune, so to say, upon his wrist. His power now became conspicuous; but when Sultan Rukn-ad-din ascended the throne, Ulugh accompanied the Turks from Delhi to Hindustan, and when they were brought back, he returned to Delhi in their army.

THE DIWAN-I-AAM AT DELHI.

He was imprisoned for some days and subjected to indignity. The design in this may have been (God knows!) that he should taste the sufferings of the miserable, so that when he attained to sovereign rank, he might have compassion on them and be thankful for his own exaltation.

When the Empress Raziya ascended the throne, Ulugh Khan continued to be one of the royal attendants till fortune favoured him and he became chief huntsman. Fate proclaimed that the earth was to be the prey of his fortune and the world the game of his sovereignty. He held this office and discharged its duties for some time, till the sun of the supremacy of Raziya set and that of Mu'izz-ad-din Bahram Shah shone forth. Fortune still befriended him. After remaining some time in his position of chief huntsman, performing his service and exhibiting marks of ability, he was made master of the horse. The steed of sovereignty and empire thus came under his bridle and control. When Badr-ad-din Sankar became lord chamberlain, he showed a paternal interest in Ulugh Khan and took such care of his advancement that he was raised to a higher position and received a grant of the lands of Riwari. He went to that place, and by his vigour and bravery punished the hill chiefs and brought the district under his sway.

When the power of the Mu'izzi dynasty was declining, the nobles conspired together and came to the gates of the city of Delhi. The princes and nobles all agreed as to the course to be pursued. Ulugh Khan, grantee of Riwari, displayed such energy and exhibited such remarkable resolution in securing the submission of the provinces, that no one of the princes and nobles, Turks or Arabs, was worth the hundredth part of him. All the confederates admitted that he surpassed them all in vigour, courage, and activity. When Delhi was conquered, he received a grant of Hansi. On taking possession of that territory, he applied himself to its improvement, and through his justice and generosity all the inhabitants were happy and contented. His success was so great that other nobles began to look upon him with jealousy and the thorn of envy commenced to rankle in their hearts. But it was the will of God that he should excel them all, so that the more the fire of their envy burnt, the stronger did the incense of his fortune rise from the censer of the times.

Trustworthy persons have recorded that in the year 641 A. H. (1243 A. D.) Ulugh Khan was appointed lord chamberlain. When the royal army marched from the capital, he inflicted a severe chastisement on the rebels of Jalali and Dewali, and also on the Mawas in the Doab district between the Ganges and Jumna. He fought much against the infidels and cleared the roads and neighbouring country from insurgents.

In the year 643 A. H. (1245 A. D.) the accursed Mangu Khan, who was one of the generals of the Moghuls and a prince of Turkistan, marched from the neighbourhood of Talikan and Kunduz into Sind. He laid siege to Uchh, one of the most renowned fortresses of Sind, which was commanded by a eunuch who belonged to the household of Taj-ad-din. When word regarding the invasion reached the court, Ulugh Khan made known his views to the Sultan and prepared an army to withstand the Moghuls. The princes and nobles were opposed to this expedition, but Ulugh Khan was very earnest about it.

When the royal army marched toward the seat of

warfare, Ulugh Khan appointed guides to lead the way, so that the marches might be made with the greatest celerity. In ordinary cases eight leagues would be one day's march, but under his arrangements twelve leagues, or even more, were accomplished. The army arrived on the banks of the Biyah, crossed the river, and reached Lahore on the banks of the Ravi. There Ulugh Khan showed great energy and bravery in pushing forward the expedition, and incited the Sultan and the nobles to be zealous in the repulse of the infidel Moghuls.

A SCENE AT LAHORE.

On Monday, the twenty-fifth of Sha'ban, 643 A. H. (Jan. 15, 1246 A. D.), word was brought to the royal camp that the Moghuls had raised the siege of Uchh. The reason of their retreat was that when Ulugh Khan had reached the Biyah, he had sent messengers bearing letters from the Sultan to the garrison of the fort, announcing the approach of the royal army and dilating upon the vast numbers of the soldiers and elephants and describing the great valour and spirit of the forces which followed the royal standards. He also sent an advance force to reconnoitre. When the messengers came near Uchh, some of the letters fell into the hands of the besiegers, and some reached the garrison of the fort. The drums were beaten in the fort to announce the joy of the besieged, and when the contents of the letters and the approach of the army of Islam became fully known to the foe, and when the horsemen of the vanguard were in the vicinity of Sind on the banks of the river Biyah, fear and dismay fell upon the hearts of the infidels, and the goodness of God lent its aid to the forces of Islam. Trusty men record that when Mangu Khan heard of the approach of the army of Islam under the royal standard, he was seized with panic and neither he nor his forces was able longer to make a stand. He divided his army into three bodies and fled.

After the achievement of this victory, Ulugh Khan advised that the royal army should march toward the river Sodra (Chinab), that it might impress the minds of the enemy with the great power, bravery, and magnitude of the army of Islam. The army accordingly proceeded to the banks of the Sodra, and from thence, on the twenty-seventh of Shawwal, 643 A. H. (Mar. 17, 1246 A. D.), it returned to Delhi, which it reached on Monday, the twelfth of Zu-l-hijja of the same year.

For some time past the mind of Sultan Ala-ad-din had been alienated from the nobles, he was seldom visible to the army, and besides this he had given himself up to depravity. The nobles all agreed to write secretly from Delhi to Nasir-ad-din, urging him to seize the throne. On Sunday, the twenty-third of Muharram, 644 A. H. (June 10, 1246 A. D.), he went to Delhi and sat upon the seat of empire. The Khutba of Islam was

Exterior of the Jami' Masjid at Delhi.

read and coin of the realm was struck in Nasir's auspicious name. When Ulugh Khan represented how the accursed foe had fled before the armies of Islam in the previous year and had gone to the upper districts, it seemed advisable that the royal army should proceed in that direction. This advice was approved and orders were given for the march.

The army set forth on Monday, the first of Rajab, 644 A. H. (Nov. 12, 1246 A. D.), and proceeded to the river Sodra. Here Ulugh Khan was detached with several nobles and generals to make an incursion into the hills of Jud. The Rana of these hills had acted as guide to the Moghuls, but the hour of revenge for this was at hand. Ulugh Khan accordingly attacked the hills of Jud and the countries on the Jihlam, and led his forces as far as the banks of the Indus. All the women and dependents of the infidels that were in those regions were obliged to flee, and a party of the Moghul army crossed over the Jihlam and saw the forces which were arrayed under the command of Ulugh Khan. The manifold lines of the army, the numbers of the horse, and the wealth of armour filled all beholders with wonder and dismay. The bravery and generalship which Ulugh Khan displayed in scaling mountains, breaking through defiles, capturing fortified places, and crossing jungles cannot be described in writing. The fame of this campaign extended to Turkistan. There was no husbandry or agriculture in this country, however, and fodder became unobtainable, so that he was compelled to retire; but he returned victorious and triumphant to the royal camp, bringing back all his officers and troops in safety.

On Thursday, the sixth of Zu-l-ka'da, 644 A. H. (March 16, 1247 A. D.), his Majesty returned to the capital, which he reached on Thursday, the second of Muharram, 645 A. H. The perseverance and resolution of Ulugh Khan had been the means of showing to the army of Turkistan and the Moghuls such bravery and generalship that in the course of this year no one came from the upper districts toward Sind. Ulugh Khan, therefore, represented to his Majesty, in the month of Sha'ban, that the time had come to make an expedition into Hindustan, by which spoil would fall into the hands of the soldiers of Islam and wealth would be gained to strengthen the hands of the State in resisting the Moghuls.

The royal armies accordingly marched to Hindustan, passing through the Doab region between the Ganges and the Jumna. After some fighting, the fort of Nandana was captured, and Ulugh Khan was sent with some other generals and a Mohammedan force to oppose Dalaki-wa-Malaki, a powerful prince in the vicinity of the Jumna, between Kalinjar and Karra, over whom the kings of Kalinjar and Malwa had no authority. When Ulugh Khan reached his abode, Dalaki-wa-Malaki provided so carefully for the safety of himself and his family that he kept quiet from dawn until the time of evening prayer, and when it grew dark he fled to some more secure place. At daybreak, the Mohammedan army entered his abode and then pursued him, but the accursed infidel had escaped into the lofty mountains, where he could not be reached except by stratagem and the use of ropes and ladders. Ulugh Khan incited his soldiers to make the attempt, and, under his able direction, they succeeded in taking the place. All Dalaki-wa-Malaki's wives, dependents, and children fell into the hands of the victors, together with many cattle, horses, and slaves, so that the spoil which was secured exceeded all computation. At the beginning of Shawwal, 645 A. H. (February, 1248 A. D.), the forces of Ulugh Khan returned to the royal camp with their booty, and after the festival of sacrifices, the whole army marched toward Delhi, which it reached on the fourth of Muharram, 646 A. H. (April, 1248 A. D.).

INDIAN VILLAGE WOMEN.

In Sha'ban, 646 A. H. (November, 1248 A. D.), the royal army marched through the upper country to the neighbourhood of the Biyah and then returned to the capital. Ulugh Khan, with several nobles under him, was sent with an ample force toward Rantambhor, the capital of Bahar Deo, who was the greatest of the rajas of Hindustan. He ravaged the whole of those territories and gained much booty.

On Monday, the third of Safar, 647 A. H. (May 18, 1249 A. D.), Ulugh Khan and his army arrived at Delhi. In the course of this year his Majesty was pleased to recognize the great ability and distinguished services of his general, whom he promoted from the rank of a general and the office of lord chamberlain to the dignity of a Khan, while on Tuesday, the third of Rajab, 647 A. H. (Oct. 12, 1249 A. D.), he named him lieutenant of the government, army, and royal fortune, with the title of Ulugh Khan. The truth of the adage that "the worth of titles is revealed by heaven" was proved in this case, for from that day forth the services of Ulugh Khan to the house of Nasir-ad-din became still more conspicuous.

On Tuesday, the twenty-fifth of Sha'ban, 649 A. H. (Nov. 12, 1251 A. D.), the royal army marched toward Malwa and Kalinjar. When Ulugh Khan arrived there with the army of Islam, he defeated Jahir of Ijari, a great king, who had a large army and many adherents, and destroyed both him and his kingdom. On Monday, the twenty-third of Rabi'-al-awwal, 650 A. H. (June 25, 1252 A. D.), the army returned to Delhi and remained there for six months. On the twelfth of Shawwal of the same year (Jan. 18, 1250 A. D.), it marched through the upper country to the Biyah, but when the army reached the banks of that river, Imad-ad-din Rihan conspired with other chiefs and excited envy and enmity against Ulugh Khan, since they found their own importance dimmed by his glory, and they resolved to do some hurt and injury to his august person, either in hunting, in passing through mountain defiles, or in crossing rivers. Ulugh Khan's good fortune preserved him, however, and his adversaries were unable to do him any harm. When they found that their plans were ineffectual, they agreed upon another course, and presenting themselves at the doors of the royal tent, urged upon his Majesty that Ulugh Khan ought to be sent to his estates at Hansi.

On Saturday, the new moon of Muharram, 651 A. H. (March, 1253 A. D.), Ulugh Khan accordingly proceeded to Hansi with his followers and family. When the Sultan reached Delhi, the thorn of envy, which still festered in the malicious heart of Rihan, impelled him to recommend his Majesty to send Ulugh Khan to Nagor and to give the country of Hansi to one of the royal princes. His Majesty accordingly went to Hansi, and the Khan was removed to Nagor. This happened in Jumada-l-akhir, 651 A. H. On his departure for Hansi, Imad-ad-din Rihan became viceroy, and the execution of the royal commands passed into his hands.

On returning to the capital, on the seventeenth of Shawwal, Malik Saif-ad-din Kishli Khan, brother of Ulugh Khan, was sent to his estate of Karra, and Izz-ad-din Balban, son-in-law of Katlagh Khan, was appointed lord chamberlain. All the officers who had been appointed at the instance of Ulugh Khan were removed, and the business and quietude of the State were disturbed through the machinations of Imad-ad-din.

At this period, Ulugh Khan, who was at Nagor, led a Mohammedan force in the direction of Rantambhor,

Hindi, and Chitor. Bahar Deo, Raja of Rantambhor, the most noble and illustrious of all the princes of Hindustan, assembled an army to inflict a blow on Ulugh

THE TOWER OF VICTORY AT CHITOR.

Khan; but it was the will of God that the name of the Khan should be celebrated for his victories, and although the raja's army was large and well equipped with arms and horses, it was put to flight and many of its valiant fighting-men were slain. The Mussulmans obtained great spoil and captured many horses and prisoners, after which they returned to Nagor, which had become a place of great importance in consequence of Ulugh Khan's presence.

At the opening of the year 651 A. H. (1253 A. D.) those who had suffered oppression and hardship through the disgrace of Ulugh Khan retired to their homes, and like fish out of water, and as sick men without slumber, from night till morn and from morn till night, they offered up their prayers to the Creator, imploring Him to let the dawn of Ulugh Khan's prosperity break forth in splendour and dispel by its brilliant light the darkness due to his rival Imad-ad-din Rihan. The Almighty graciously gave ear to the prayers of the wretched and harkened to the cries of the distressed, so that the victorious banners of Ulugh Khan were carried out from Nagor, and he went to Delhi, the capital.

The circumstances of his coming were as follows. The nobles and servants of the State were all Turks of pure origin and Arabs of good stock, but Imad-ad-din Rihan was a eunuch and belonged to one of the tribes of Hindustan. Notwithstanding all this, he exercised authority over the heads of all those chiefs until they became disgusted with the state of affairs and could no longer endure it. They suffered so much from the hands of the bullies who were retained by Imad-ad-din Rihan, that for six months they could not leave their houses nor even go to prayers on Fridays. The chiefs of Hindustan, Karra, Manikpur, Oudh, and the upper country as far as Badaun, Tabarhindh, Sanam,

Samana, and the Siwalik Hills, accordingly sent to Ulugh Khan, inviting him to return. Arslan Khan led an army out of Tabarhindh, Ban Khan came forth from Sanam and Mansurpur, and Ulugh Khan collected his forces in Nagor and the Siwalik Hills. Malik Jalal-ad-din Mas'ud Shah ibn Sultan joined them from Lahore, and they marched upon the capital.

Imad-ad-din Rihan advised his Majesty to go forth and repress the malcontents, and accordingly he led his army toward Sanam. Ulugh Khan was in the neighbourhood of Tabarhindh with several other chiefs. On the twenty-seventh of Ramazan, 652 A. H. (Nov. 10, 1254 A. D.), the opposing armies drew near to each other, the outposts met, and great disquietude arose. The festival of the end of the fast of Ramazan was passed at Sanam, and on Saturday, the eighth of Shawwal (Nov. 21), the royal army fell back to Hansi. Malik Jalal-ad-din, Ulugh Khan, and the nobles with them proceeded to Kaithal, whereupon the chiefs and nobles on both sides deemed it desirable to hold a parley. Karra Jamak, a personal attendant of Ulugh Khan and well known for his integrity, acted on the part of the insurgents; and the noble of the black banner, Hisam-ad-din Katlagh, a man of conciliatory character and great probity, was deputed to meet him.

The discontented nobles represented to his Majesty that they were all willing to obey his commands, but that they had no security against the machinations and outrageous conduct of Imad-ad-din Rihan. If he were banished from the court, they would all submit and would willingly obey the orders of the Sultan. The royal army marched from Hansi to Jind, and on Saturday, the twenty-second of Shawwal, 652 A. H. (Dec. 5, 1254 A. D.), Imad-ad-din was dismissed from his office of minister (thanks be to God for it!) and was given, instead, the privileges attaching to the government of Badaun.

Izz-ad-din Balban, deputy of the lord chamberlain, repaired to the camp of Ulugh Khan, and on Tuesday, the third of Zu-l-ka'da, Ban Khan Aybek Khitai came to the royal camp to make the final arrangements regarding the terms of peace. An extraordinary plot was now formed, since Imad-ad-din Khan, aided by a number of Turks of low degree, who were inimical to Ulugh Khan, resolved to murder Ban Khan Aybek Khitai at the entrance of the royal tent, in order that Ulugh Khan, on hearing of the assassination, might slay Izz-ad-din Balban in retaliation. Peace would thus be prevented, Imad-ad-din would retain his position in safety, and Ulugh Khan would be unable to come to court. Kutb-ad-din Hasan heard of the conspiracy and sent one of the chief attendants of the chamberlain to Ban Khan, advising him not to go to the royal tent in the morning, but to remain at his own lodging. Ban Khan acted on this advice, and the plot failed. The facts became known, and Imad-ad-din was sent off to Badaun at the command of the Sultan.

On Tuesday, the seventeenth of Zu-l-ka'da, his Majesty, in his desire of making peace, directed Minhaj-as-Siraj, the author of this history, to offer terms of agreement to all. On the next day, Ulugh Khan came to court with the other nobles and had the honour of kissing hands. The Sultan then turned homewards, accompanied by Ulugh Khan, and reached the capital on Wednesday, the ninth of Zu-l-hijja. The kindness of the Almighty now became manifest. For a long time there had been no rain, but upon the approach of Ulugh Khan the Almighty displayed His mercy, and the rain, which is the life of herbs and plants, and of men and animals, descended upon the earth. No wonder, then, that men regarded the return of Ulugh Khan as a happy omen, that his compeers rejoiced over it, and that all were grateful to the Almighty for His bounty.

The year 653 A. H. (1255 A. D.) opened. Something happened in the royal harem of which no one had accurate knowledge, but Katlagh Khan, the stepfather of the Sultan, was directed to take charge of the government of Oudh, and thither he proceeded. At the same time the government of Bahraich was given to Imad-ad-din Rihan. The success of Ulugh Khan shone forth with brilliant radiance, the garden of the world began to put forth leaf, and the key of divine mercy opened the doors of the hearts of men who had been driven into seclusion.

After Katlagh Khan had been in Oudh some time, the course of events rendered him disaffected. Repeated and imperative orders were sent to him from court, but he paid no heed to them. Imad-ad-din Rihan busied himself in stirring up strife, and endeavoured by intrigue and deceit to cast the dust of his selfish plots on the prosperity of Ulugh Khan and to cloud the glory of that dignitary with the emanations of his malice. But "Divine mercy is for ever sufficient," and it prevented the success of these schemes. Malik Taj-ad-din Sanjar had been confined in prison by Katlagh Khan. By a bold device the captive escaped from Oudh and crossing the river Saru (Gogra) in a boat, he proceeded with a few horsemen to Bahraich. By the decree of fate, the fortune of the Turks now triumphed, and the power of the Hindus was levelled to the dust. Imad-ad-din was defeated and taken prisoner, and was put to death in Bahraich in the month of Rajab, 653 A. H. (Aug., 1255 A. D.). With him Katlagh Khan's fortunes declined.

When these disturbances arose in Hindustan, several of the chief nobles of the court were drawn away from their allegiance, and it became necessary to put down the insurrection and to punish the disaffected nobles. The army accordingly left Delhi, on the new moon of Shawwal, 653 A. H. (Dec., 1255 A. D.), and marched toward Hindustan. Delay had occurred in assembling the forces of the Siwalik Hills, which were included in the government of Ulugh Khan, so he hastened to Hansi. He arrived there on the seventeenth of Zu-l-ka'da, and so exerted himself that in fourteen days the soldiers of the Siwalik Hills, Hansi, Sarsuti, Jind, Barwala, and the neighbouring regions were collected, and marched in great force to Delhi, where they arrived on the third of Zu-l-hijja. Ulugh Khan remained in

Delhi eighteen days, recruiting and refitting the army of Mewat and the hills.

On the nineteenth of the month he marched with a brave and well equipped army to the royal camp, and reached Oudh in the month of Muharram, 654 A. H.

A MOHAMMEDAN TOMB AT DELHI.

(Feb., 1256 A. D.). Katlagh Khan and the nobles who were in league with him were all subjects of the Sultan, but adverse circumstances led them to revolt. From Oudh they retreated over the river Saru, and by royal command Ulugh Khan pursued them with a strong force. They had got a good start, however, the jungles were dense, the roads difficult, and the trees numerous, so that he could not come up with them. Nevertheless, he advanced as far as Bishanpur, on the confines of Tirhut, and returned with great spoil to the royal camp. When Ulugh Khan crossed the Saru from Oudh on his return from the pursuit, his Majesty marched toward the capital, and Ulugh Khan joined the royal army at Kasmandi. On Tuesday, the sixth of Rabi'-al-awwal, 654 A. H. (May, 1256 A. D.), they arrived at Delhi.

Katlagh Khan had found no place in Hindustan where he could make a stand, so in the midst of the campaign he proceeded toward Santur and strengthened himself in the hills of that country. The chiefs paid him every respect, for he was a noble of high rank, a grandee of the court, and one of the principal Turks. He had strong claims, therefore, upon his compeers, and wherever he went he was treated with great consideration.

He made himself secure in the hills of Santur, where he was joined by the Raja Debal Hindi, who held a prominent rank among the Hindus. When the news of this alliance reached the royal camp, the army marched toward Santur, at the beginning of Rabi'-al-awwal, 655 A. H. (Mar., 1257 A. D.). With great difficulty and after much fighting, Ulugh Khan, with the royal army and some officers of the court, made his way into the hills and seized upon the passes and defiles. He penetrated as far as Salmur, a fort and district belonging to the raja, who fled before Ulugh Khan, while the city and markets of Salmur fell into the hands of the army of Islam. By the favour of

God the soldiers of Ulugh Khan thus subdued a place which the Mohammedan armies had never reached before, and they returned laden with plunder to the capital, where they arrived on the fifth of Rabi'-al-akhir, 655 A. H. (April, 1257 A. D.).

When the royal army had returned to Delhi, Katlagh Khan issued from the mountains of Salmur, and Malik Balban Kishlu Khan came from Sind to the banks of the Biyah, where the two chiefs joined their forces and marched toward Samana and Kahram, taking possession of the country. The Sultan sent Ulugh Khan, Kishli Khan, and several other nobles to quell this revolt. Ulugh Khan left Delhi on Thursday, the fifteenth of Jumada-l-awwal, 655 A. H. (May 31, 1257 A. D.), and hastened with all speed to Kaithal. Katlagh Khan was in the vicinity, and the two armies approached each other. Ulugh Khan deemed it expedient to detach the household troops from the main army, and placed them under the command of his cousin, Sher Khan. The main body, together with the elephants, he put under the command of his own brother, Kishli Khan, the lord chamberlain, thus forming two distinct divisions.

The opposing armies drew near to each other in the vicinity of Samana and Kaithal, and their lines were within view on either side. While they were thus confronting each other, a man came as a spy from the camp of Malik Balban Kishlu Khan, representing that he was sent on behalf of the chiefs and nobles that were with Malik Balban, who were desirous of joining

Ulugh Khan. If a promise of immunity and fair treatment were given them, and a grant made for the support of the bearer of these overtures, he would win over all the chiefs and nobles who were with Balban, and would arrange matters as far as other officers were concerned.

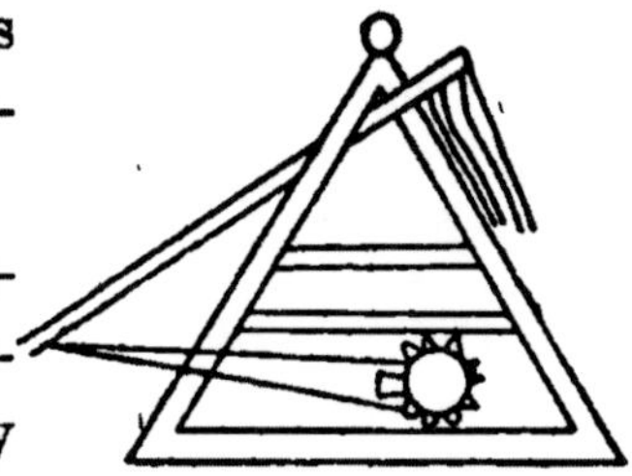

AN ENGINE OF WAR.

Perceiving the fellow's intentions, Ulugh Khan gave orders that the whole of the army should be shown to him; and all the troops, munitions, and implements of war, as well as the elephants and horses, were accordingly displayed before his eyes. The Khan then dictated a letter to the chiefs and nobles in the following terms: "Your letter has reached me, and its import has been understood. I have no doubt that, if you submit, grants will be made to you all, and your maintenance will be most amply provided for; but if you take a different course, then, on this very day, the world shall learn how your pretensions will be settled by the wounds of the trenchant sword and the flaming spear, and how you will be carried fettered with the bonds of fate to the foot of the royal standard." This letter was delivered to the spy, and he returned.

When the letter was delivered to the officers of Malik Balban, those of them who were wise perceived its drift, and knew that the dissensions between the nobles and generals would be settled elsewhere. Fresh letters now arrived from Delhi, and Malik Balban and

Katlagh Khan set forth in that direction and showed no intention of returning. Two days later, Ulugh Khan became aware of their design, and his mind was troubled as to what might happen to the throne and capital. After this extraordinary incident, letters reached him from Delhi, and he turned thither, reaching the city in safety.

After Ulugh Khan had remained quietly in the capital for seven months, news came that the army of the infidel Moghuls, under the command of Salin Nawin, had made a descent upon Sind. When these tidings reached the capital, Ulugh Khan advised his Majesty to set the royal army in motion, and it marched forth accordingly on the second of Muharram, 656 A. H. (January 9, 1258 A. D.), encamping within sight of the city. Orders were sent to all parts of the kingdom, directing the nobles and officers to collect what forces they could and to join the army.

With a numerous and well-appointed army, Ulugh Khan marched in company with his Majesty and all the nobles, attended by their followers. When the infidel Moghul heard of this host on the frontier which he had assailed, he advanced no farther and showed no spirit. It seemed expedient, therefore, for the royal army to remain within sight of the city of Delhi for four months or more, making various forays. At length word came that the accursed foe had retreated, and all disquietude on his account was at an end.

Ulugh Khan was now informed that Arslan Khan Sanjar and Kalij Khan Mas'ud Khani had taken alarm at the orders which they had received to join the royal camp, and were meditating revolt. Ulugh Khan advised his Majesty to nip this project in the bud and to smother their intentions before they had time to form and gather strength. The advice was approved and followed, although it was the hot season and the army was depleted by the inroad of the Moghuls. On Tuesday, the sixth of Jumada-l-akhir, the royal forces marched toward Hindustan and reached the neighbourhood of Karra and Manikpur, where Ulugh Khan exerted himself most strenuously in punishing the rebellious Hindus.

Upon the arrival of Ulugh Khan, the two confederates, Arslan Khan and Kalij Khan, parted, and were obliged to send their families and dependents among the Mawas. They also deputed some trusty persons to wait on Ulugh Khan and prevail upon him to inform the Sultan that they had been obliged to disperse their followers, and that they were ready to promise to come to the capital and do homage as soon as the royal army was withdrawn. Upon this representation the forces were recalled and reached the capital on Monday, the second of Ramazan, 656 A. H. (Sept. 2, 1258 A. D.). Arslan Khan and Kalij Khan repaired to court, where Ulugh Khan exerted himself so generously and strenuously in their behalf that their rebellion was forgiven, and in the course of two months Kalij Khan was appointed to govern Lakhnauti, while Arslan Khan was sent to rule over Karra.

On the thirteenth of Muharram, at the beginning

of the year 657 A. H. (Jan., 1259 A. D.), the royal forces again marched from Delhi. Ulugh Khan now very properly used his influence in favour of his nephew, Sher Khan, and on Sunday, the twenty-first of Safar (Feb. 17, 1259 A. D.), all the territories of Bayana, Kol, Jalesar, and Gwalior were assigned to him. There was nothing to require the action of the army during the rest of the year. On Wednesday, the fourth of Jumada-l-akhir (May 29, 1259 A. D.), treasure, wealth, and many valuables, together with two elephants, were brought to court from Lakhnauti, as presents from Izz-ad-din Balban Uzbeg, who was grantee of Lakhnauti; and by the influence of Ulugh Khan the grant was confirmed, and honours were bestowed upon him.

At the beginning of 658 A. H. (Dec., 1259 A. D.), Ulugh Khan resolved upon a campaign in the hills near Delhi. These hills were inhabited by a turbulent people, who committed depredations on the roads, plundered the goods of Mussulmans, drove away the cultivators, and ravaged the villages in the districts of Harriana, the Siwalik Hills, and Bayana. Three years before, they had carried off from Hansi a drove of camels and a number of the people of Ulugh Khan. Their chief was a Hindu named Malka, a fierce and desperate fellow, who had carried off the camels and fomented disturbances among the Hindus from the hills to Rantambhor. He did these things, however, at a moment when the army was otherwise engaged and the soldiers and followers of Ulugh Khan had not the means to transport their baggage and implements. Ulugh Khan and

THE TOMB OF MOHAMMAD GHAUS AT GWALIOR.

all the princes and nobles were sorely vexed, but it was then impossible to do anything, as the army was fully employed in repelling the Moghul forces which had attacked the frontiers of Islam in Sind, at Lahore, and in the vicinity of the river Biyah. At this time, ambassadors to the Sultan came to Khorasan from Irak, on behalf of Hulaku Mughal, son of Toli, son of Chingiz Khan, and orders were given that the embassy was to halt at Maruta.

Ulugh Khan and other nobles, with the royal troops and their own followers, suddenly resolved upon a campaign in the hills, and started on Monday, the fourth of Safar, 658 A. H. (Jan., 1260 A. D.). In their first forced march they accomplished nearly fifty leagues and fell unexpectedly upon the rebels, who retreated to the tops of the mountains and to defiles, deep gorges, and narrow valleys, only to be taken and put to the sword. For twenty days the troops traversed the hills in all directions. The villages and habitations of the mountaineers were on the summits of the loftiest hills and rocks and were of great strength, but they were all stormed and ravaged by order of Ulugh Khan, and the inhabitants were slain. A piece of silver was offered for every head, and two pieces for every man brought in alive. Eager for these rewards, the soldiers, especially the Afghans, climbed the highest hills and penetrated the deepest gorges, bringing in heads and captives. Fortune now favoured Ulugh Khan so that he was able to penetrate to a fastness which no Mussulman army had ever reached, and thus the Hindu rebel,

Malka, who had carried off the camels, was taken prisoner with his children and dependents, while 250 of the chiefs of the rebels were captured.

In the course of twenty days this great work was accomplished, and the army returned to Delhi on the twenty-fourth of Rabi'-al-awwal, 658 A. H. (Mar. 9, 1260 A. D.). His Majesty, with a great retinue of chiefs and

A GROUP OF AFGHANS.

(Copyright by Underwood & Underwood, New York.)

nobles, went forth to the plain of Hauz-rani, to meet the conqueror, and a grand durbar was held, in which many honours and rewards were bestowed. After a stay of two days in the capital, the court again went forth to Hauz-rani on a mission of revenge. The elephants were prepared, and the Turks made ready their trenchant swords. By royal command many of the rebels were cast under the feet of elephants, and the fierce Turks cut the bodies of the Hindus in two. About a hundred met their death at the hands of the flayers, being skinned from head to foot, after which their skins were all stuffed with straw, and some of them were hung over each gate of the city. The plain of Hauz-rani and the gates of Delhi remembered no punishment like this, nor had any one ever heard such a tale of horror.

Ulugh Khan now represented to the Sultan that the Moghul ambassadors in Khorasan should be brought to court and granted an interview. On Wednesday, the seventh of Rabi'-al-akhir, the court accordingly proceeded to the Green Palace, and Ulugh Khan gave orders for armed men to be collected from all quarters round Delhi to the number of two hundred thousand foot and fifty thousand horse, with banners and accoutrements. Great numbers of armed men of all ranks went forth from the capital and assembled at the royal residence in the new city of Kilu-ghari, where they were drawn up shoulder to shoulder in twenty lines. When the ambassadors entered the city, they were received with the utmost honour and were conducted before the throne with the highest possible ceremony. The palace was decked out in the most splendid array, all the princes, nobles, and officers attended in gorgeous dresses, and a poem written by the author of this work was recited before the throne. After the reception the ambassadors were conducted in great state to the place appointed for their abode.

When Ulugh Khan carried war into the hills and punished the rebels in the way we have related, a number of them escaped by flight. These survivors again took to plundering on the highways and murdering Mussulmans to such an extent that the roads became dangerous. When this matter was reported to Ulugh Khan, he sent emissaries and spies to find out the places where the rebels had taken refuge, and to make a full report of their state and condition. On Monday, the twenty-fourth of Rajab, 658 A. H. (July, 1260 A. D.), he marched from Delhi with his own troops, the main army, and the forces of several chiefs. He hastened toward the hills, and, accomplishing more than fifty leagues in one day's journey, he fell upon the insurgents unawares and captured them all, to the number of twelve thousand—men, women, and children—whom he put to the sword. All their valleys and strongholds were overrun and cleared, and great booty was captured. Thanks be to God for this victory of Islam!'

This concludes the principal events of Ulugh Khan's career until the death of his royal master, Nasir-ad-din, six years later, in 1266 A. D., when Ulugh, the great statesman and general, became king himself under the title of Balban, as already described by Professor Lane-Poole in the third volume of this series.

A SILVER COIN OF ALA-AD-DIN.

CHAPTER VII

ALA-AD-DIN'S CONQUESTS IN THE DECCAN

1310 A. D.

AFTER Balban, the supremacy of the Slave Kings gave place to the Khalji Rulers, so called from their place of origin, the village of Khalj in Afghanistan. The greatest of these sovereigns was Ala-ad-din, who sat upon the throne of Delhi for twenty years (1296-1316 A. D.) and stretched his conquering arm even over the Deccan and the south of India.

The main events of Ala-ad-din's reign have been previously given in this history, but an excerpt from the annals of the Mohammedan writer Amir Khusru, narrating the story of the campaign in Ma'bar (710 A. H., 1310 A. D.), may be appropriate as a record contemporaneous with the events described. Ma'bar appears to have been situated on the lower western coast of India (Malabar?), although some have claimed that it was located on the eastern shore. The style of Amir Khusru's narrative possesses a special interest as an example of a certain kind of Oriental writing, and the stanch Mohammedan orthodoxy of the author is manifest from the exultant note which marks the opening paragraph of his description of the conquest of Ma'bar, an event which he regards as a memorable victory of Islam over the Hindu religion. His account follows.

'The tongue of the sword of the caliphate of the time, which is the tongue of the flame of Islam, has imparted light to the entire darkness of Hindustan by the illumination of its guidance. On the one side an iron wall of royal swords has been raised before the infidel Magog-like Tartars, so that all of that God-forsaken tribe drew their feet within their skirts among the hills of Ghazni, and even their advance-arrows had not strength enough to reach into Sind. On the other side so much dust arose from the battered temple of Somnath that even the sea was not able to lay it, and the army has conquered right and left from sea to sea, and several capitals of the gods of the Hindus, in which Satanism has prevailed since the time of the Jinns, have been demolished. All these impurities of unbelief have been cleansed by the Sultan Ala-ad-din's destruction of idol-temples, beginning with his first holy expedition against Deogir, and now the flames of the light of the law illumine all these unholy countries, and places are exalted on high for the criers to prayer, and prayers are read in mosques. God be praised!

Now, the country of Ma'bar is so far distant from the city of Delhi that a man travelling with all speed could reach it only in a journey of twelve months, nor had the arrow of any holy warrior as yet reached there, but this world-conquering king, Ala-ad-din, determined to carry his army to that distant country and to spread the light of the Mohammedan religion there.

Malik Naib Barbak was accordingly appointed to

THE SO-CALLED GATES OF SOMNATH.

command the army for this expedition, and a royal canopy was sent with him. The Malik represented that on the coast of Ma'bar there were five hundred elephants, larger than those which had been presented to the Sultan from Arangal, and that when he was engaged in the conquest of that place he had thought of possessing himself of them, so that now, since the wise determination of the king had combined the extirpation of idolaters with this object, he was more than ever rejoiced to enter on this grand enterprise.

The army left Delhi on the twenty-fourth of Jumada-l-akhir, 710 A. H. (Oct. 31, 1309 A. D.), and after marching by the banks of the Jumna, halted at Tankal for fourteen days, where a muster of the army was taken. "After that the royal soldiers, like swift greyhounds, made lengthened marches for twenty-one days until they arrived at Kanhun, and in the course of seventeen days more, they arrived at Gurganw. During these seventeen days the Ghats were passed and great heights and depths were seen among the hills, where even the elephants became nearly invisible. Three large rivers, moreover, had to be crossed, and the passage of them caused the greatest fear. Two of them were equal to each other, but neither of them equalled the Narbada."

After crossing those rivers, hills, and many depths, the raja of Telingana sent twenty-three powerful elephants for the royal service. For the space of twenty days the victorious army remained at Telingana, for the purpose of sending on the elephants, and they took a muster of the men present and absent, until the whole number was counted. And, according to the command of the king, they suspended swords from the standard poles, in order that the inhabitants of Ma'bar might be aware that the day of resurrection had arrived among them, and that the accursed Hindus would all be despatched by the sword to their brothers in hell, so that fire, the improper object of their worship, might mete out proper punishment to them.

The tempestuous army moved swiftly, like a hurricane, to Gurganw. Everywhere the accursed tree that produced no religion was found and torn up by the roots, and the people who were destroyed were like trunks carried along in the torrent of the Jihun, or like straw tossed up and down in a whirlwind and carried forward. When the army reached the Tawi (Tapti), they saw a river like the sea. The soldiers crossed it by a ford quicker than the hurricane which they resembled, and afterwards employed themselves in cutting down jungles and destroying gardens.

On Thursday, the 13th of Ramazan, 709 A. H. (Feb. 14, 1310 A. D.), the royal canopy cast its shadow on Deogir, which had been protected by the angels, and there the army determined to make all preparations for extirpating Billal Deo and other Deos (demons). The Maharaja, Ram Deo, who had heard safety proclaimed by the dreadful Mohammedan timbals, considered himself secure under the protection assured to him, and, true to his allegiance, forwarded with all his heart the preparations necessary for the equipment of the army sent by the court, so as to render it available for the extermination of rebels and the destruction of the Bir and Dhur Samundar. The city was adorned in honour of the occasion, and food and clothes were supplied in abundance to the Mussulmans.

Dalvi, a Hindu, who had been sent on to hold the

gates of access to the Bir and Dhur Samundar, was directed by the Maharaja to attend on the Mussulman camp, and he was anxious to see the conquest of the

A GROUP OF INDIAN MUSSULMANS.

whole of Dhur Samundar by the fortunate devotees of the Ka'ba of religion. The Mohammedan army remained for three days and departed on the seventeenth of Ramazan from the Imanabad Deogir to the

Kharababad of Paras Deo Dalvi, advancing for five stages, in which three large rivers, the Sini, Godavari, and Binhur, were crossed and also some other frightful streams. On the fifth day they arrived at Bandri, in the country (*ikta'*) of Paras Deo Dalvi, who was obedient to his exalted Majesty, and who desired that, by the force of the arms of the victorious Mohammedan soldiers, Bir Dhul and Bir Pandya might be reduced into one cup,[1] together with the seas which encircle them.

Here Ala-ad-din halted to inquire about the countries in advance, and was informed that the two rajas of Ma'bar, the elder named Bir Pandya, the younger Sundar Pandya, who had continued on friendly terms up to that time, had advanced against each other with hostile intentions, and that Billal Deo, the raja of Dhur Samundar, on learning this fact, had marched for the purpose of sacking their two empty cities and of plundering the merchants; but that, on hearing of the advance of the Mohammedan army, he had returned to his own country.

On Sunday, the twenty-third of Ramazan, 709 A. H. (Feb. 24, 1310 A. D.), after holding a council of his chief officers, Ala-ad-din took a select body of cavalry with him and pressed on against Billal Deo, reaching the fort of Dhur Samundar on the fifth of Shawwal (March 8) after a difficult march of twelve days over the hills and valleys, and through thorny forests.

[1] There is much punning here about wells (*bir*) and buckets (*dalvi*), which it is impossible to render into English so as to make it comprehensible.

The fire-worshipping raja, when he learnt that his idol temple was likely to be converted into a mosque, despatched Kisu Mal to ascertain the strength and condition of the Mussulmans, but the latter returned with such alarming accounts that the raja despatched Balak Deo Naik the next day to the royal canopy, to say to the Sultan: "Your slave Billal Deo is ready to swear allegiance to the mighty emperor, like Laddar Deo and Ram Deo, and whatever the Solomon of the age may order, I am ready to obey. If you desire horses like demons, and elephants like fiends, and valuables like those of Deogir, they are all present. If you wish to destroy the four walls of this fort, they are no obstacle to your advance. The fort is the fort of the king; take it." The commander replied that he was sent with the object either of converting him to Islam or of slaying him, if the terms were not assented to. When the raja received this reply, he said he was ready to give up all he possessed, except his sacred thread.

On Friday, the sixth of Shawwal, the raja sent Balak Deo Naik, Narain Deo, and Jit Mal, with some others, to bow before the royal tent, and these envoys were accompanied by six elephants. Next day some horses followed and on Sunday, the sun-worshipper, Billal Deo, seeing the splendour of the sword of Islam above his head, bowed beneath it, descended from his fortress, and came before the shadow of the shadow of God, in whose presence, trembling and abject, he prostrated himself upon the earth and rubbed the forehead of subjection on the ground. He then returned to fetch his treasures and was engaged all night in bringing them out, and next day he conveyed them before the royal tent and made them over to the king's treasurer.

The commander remained twelve days in that city, which is four months' distance from Delhi, and sent the captured elephants and horses to that capital.

On Wednesday, the eighteenth of Shawwal (March 21), Ala-ad-din's general, Malik Kafur, beat his drums, loaded his camels for his expedition to Ma'bar, and after five days arrived at the mountains which divide Ma'bar from Dhur Samundar. In this range there are two passes—one Sarmali, the other Tabar. After traversing the passes, they arrived at night on the banks of the river Kanobari and bivouacked on the sands. Thence they departed for Birdhul, massacring and devastating all around it. The Raja Bir intended at first to flee for refuge to his islands in the ocean, but as he was not able to carry out this plan, his attendants counselled him to flee by land. With a small amount of treasure and property he deserted the city and fled to Kandur, yet even there he dared not remain, but fled again to the jungles.

Thither the Malik pursued "the yellow-faced Bir," and at Kandur was joined by some Mussulmans who had been subjects of the Hindus, now no longer able to offer them protection. They were half-Hindus and not strict in their religious observances, but as they could repeat the profession of faith, the Sultan of Islam spared their lives. Though they were worthy of death, yet, as they were Mussulmans, they were pardoned.

After returning to Birdhul, Malik Kafur again pursued the raja to Kandur and took 108 elephants, one of which was laden with jewels. The raja again es-

A RICHLY CAPARISONED ELEPHANT.

caped him, and then Malik Kafur ordered a general massacre at Kandur. It was thereupon ascertained that the raja had fled to Jalkota, "an old city of the ancestors of Bir." Malik Kafur, the general of Ala-ad-din, closely pursued him thither, but he had again escaped to the jungles, which the general found himself unable to penetrate, and he therefore returned to Kandur, where he searched for more elephants.

Here he heard that in Brahmastpuri there was a golden idol, round which many elephants were stabled. The Malik started on a night expedition against this place and in the morning seized no less than 250 elephants. He then determined to raze the magnificent temple to the ground. The beauty of this shrine was such that you might say that it was the Paradise of Shaddad, which those hellites had found after it was lost, or that it was the golden Lanka of Rama. The roof was covered with rubies and emeralds, and, in short, it was a holy place of the Hindus. Nevertheless Malik Kafur dug it up absolutely from its foundations, and the heads of the Brahmans and the idolaters danced from their necks and fell to the ground at their feet, and blood flowed in torrents.

These stone idols, called Ling Mahadeo, had long been established at that place, but up to this time the kick of the horse of Islam had not attempted to break them, and now the Mussulmans destroyed all these images, and Deo Narain fell down, and the other gods, who had fixed their seats there, jumped so high that the idols themselves would have fled had they had any legs to stand on. Much gold and valuable jewels fell into the hands of the Mussulmans, who returned to the royal tent, after executing their holy project, on the thirteenth of Zu-l-ka'da, 710 A. H. (April, 1311 A. D.).

After five days, the royal tent was moved from

Birdhul on Thursday, the seventeenth of Zu-l-ka'da, and set up at Kham, and five days later the army arrived at the city of Mathra (Madura, in Southern India), the dwelling-place of the brother of the Raja Sundar Pandya. They found the city empty, for the raja had fled with his queens, but he had left two or

THE TEMPLE AT MADURA.

three elephants in the temple of Jagannath. The elephants were captured and the temple was burned.

When Malik Kafur came to take a muster of his captured elephants, they extended over a length of three parasangs and amounted to 512, besides five thousand Arabian and Syrian horses, and five hundred *mans* of jewels of every description—diamonds, pearls, emeralds, and rubies.

On Sunday, the fourth of Zu-l-hijja, 710 A. H. (Apr. 24, 1311 A. D), Malik Kafur, accompanied by his army, returned toward Delhi with all the plunder, and arrived in safety on Monday, the fourth of Jumada-s-sani, 711 A. H. Sultan Ala-ad-din held a public durbar in front of the Golden Palace, and all the nobles and chiefs stood on the right and on the left, according to their rank. Malik Kafur, with the officers who had accompanied him, were presented to the Sultan, before whom the rich booty was exhibited. The Sultan was much gratified, loaded the warriors with honour, and then dissolved the durbar.'

GOLD COIN OF FIROZ, STRUCK AT AHSANABAD, 807 A. H. (1404-1405 A. D.).

CHAPTER VIII

SOME MEASURES OF MOHAMMAD TAGHLAK AND OF FIROZ SHAH

MOHAMMAD TAGHLAK SHAH (1325 - 1351 A. D.) was a man of ideas, but his innovations and reforms were a failure, and the schemes which he sought to carry out resulted only in making him unpopular. His reign was one of the most unsuccessful in the entire history of India, and reasons for this fact may be gathered from a half-dozen of his measures which are described by the historian Barani, who lived under Taghlak's rule and under that of Firoz Shah, his successor. The illustrations are significant enough to show the view of a contemporary, and that, too, of one who was close to the throne during the emperor's entire reign. He writes as follows regarding some of the monarch's ill-considered plans.

'Sultan Mohammad Taghlak planned in his own heart three or four projects by which the whole of the habitable world was to be brought under the rule of his servants, but he never talked over these projects with any of his counsellors and friends. Whatever he conceived he considered to be good, but in promulgating and enforcing his schemes he lost his hold upon the territories he possessed, disgusted his people, and emptied his treasury. Embarrassment followed embarrassment, and confusion became worse confounded.

The ill feeling among his subjects gave rise to outbreaks and revolts, and the rules for enforcing the royal schemes became daily more oppressive to them. More and more the people became disaffected, and more and more the mind of the king was set against them, so that the number of those brought to punishment was constantly on the increase. The tribute of most of the distant countries and districts was lost, many of the soldiers and servants were scattered and left in distant lands, and deficiencies appeared in the treasury. The mind of the Sultan lost its true equilibrium, and in the extreme weakness and harshness of his temper he gave himself up to severity. Gujarat and Deogir (Devagiri) were the only distant possessions that remained, while in the old territories dependent upon Delhi, the capital, there sprang up disaffection and rebellion.

By the will of fate many different projects occurred to the mind of the Sultan, which appeared to him moderate and suitable and were enforced for several years, but the people could not endure them. These schemes effected the ruin of the Sultan's empire and the decay of the people. Every one of them that was enforced wrought some wrong and mischief, and the minds of all men, high and low, were alienated from their ruler, and territories and districts which had been securely settled were lost.

When the Sultan found that his projects did not work so well as he desired, he became still more embittered against his people. He punished them and cut them down like weeds. So many hired wretches were ready to slaughter true and orthodox Mussulmans as had never before been created from the day of Adam. If the twenty prophets of Islam had been given into the hands of these minions, I verily believe that they would not have allowed them to live one night.

The first project which the Sultan formed, and which operated to the ruin of the country and the distress of the people, was based on the idea that he ought to get five or ten per cent. more tribute from the lands in the Doab than heretofore. To accomplish this he invented some oppressive taxes, and made stoppages from the land-revenues until the backs of the peasants were broken. The taxes were collected so rigorously that the peasants were impoverished and reduced to beggary. Those who were rich and had property became rebels, the lands were ruined, and cultivation was entirely arrested.

When the peasants in distant countries heard of the distress and ruin of the farmers in the Doab, through fear of the same evil befalling them, they threw off their allegiance and betook themselves to the jungles. The decline of cultivation and the distress of the peasants in the Doab, combined with the failure of convoys of corn from Hindustan, produced a fatal famine in Delhi and its environs as well as throughout the Doab. Grain became dear. There was a deficiency of rain, so the famine became general. It continued for some years, and thousands upon thousands of people perished of want. Communities were reduced to misery, and families were broken up. From this time the glory of the state and the power of the government of Sultan Mohammad withered and decayed.

A PEASANT WOMAN GRINDING CORN.

The second project of Sultan Mohammad Taghlak, which was ruinous to the capital of the empire and distressing to the chief men of the country, was that of making Deogir his capital, under the name of Daulatabad. This place held a central situation, being about equidistant from Delhi, Gujarat, Lakhnauti, Satganw, Sunarganw, Telingana, Ma'bar, Dhur Samundar, and Kampila. Without any consultation and without carefully looking into the advantages and disadvantages on every side, he brought ruin upon Delhi, which had grown in prosperity for 170 or 180 years and now rivalled Baghdad and Cairo. The city, which, with its buildings and its suburbs and villages, spread over four or five leagues, was utterly destroyed. So complete was the ruin, that not a cat or a dog was left among the buildings of the city, in its palaces, or in its suburbs. Troops of the natives, with their families and dependents, wives and children, men-servants and maid-servants, were forced to remove. The people, who for many years and for generations had been natives and inhabitants of the land, were broken-hearted. Many, from the toils of the long journey, perished on the road, and those who arrived at Deogir (Devagiri) could not endure the pain of exile. In despondency they pined to death. All around Deogir, which is an infidel land, there sprung up graveyards of Mussulmans.

The Sultan was bounteous in his liberality and favours to the emigrants, both on their journey and after their arrival; but they were tender and could not endure the exile and suffering. They laid down their heads in that heathen land, and of all the multitudes of emigrants, few only survived to return to their home. Thus this city, the envy of the cities of the inhabited world, was reduced to ruin. The Sultan brought learned men and gentlemen, tradesmen and landholders, into the city from certain towns in his territory and made them reside there; but this importation of strangers did not populate the city; many of them died there, and more returned to their native homes. These changes and alterations were a cause of great injury to the country.

The third project also did great harm to the country. It increased the daring and arrogance of the disaffected in Hindustan and augmented the pride and prosperity of all the Hindus. This was the issue of copper money. Mohammad Taghlak, in his lofty ambition, had conceived it to be his task to subdue the whole habitable world and bring it under his rule. To accomplish this impossible design, an army of countless numbers was necessary, and this could not be obtained without vast sums of money. The Sultan's bounty and munificence had caused a great deficiency in the treasury, so he introduced his copper money and gave orders that it should be used in buying and selling, and should pass current, just as the gold and silver coins had passed.

The promulgation of this edict turned the house of every Hindu into a mint, and the Hindus of the various provinces coined crores and lacs of copper coins. With these they paid their tribute, and with these they purchased horses, arms, and fine things of all kinds. The governors, the village headmen, and the landowners grew rich and strong upon these copper coins, but the state was impoverished. No long time passed before distant countries would take the copper *tanka* only as copper. In those places where fear of the Sultan's edict prevailed, the gold *tanka* rose to be worth a hundred of the copper *tankas*. Every goldsmith struck copper coins in his workshop, and the treasury was filled with these copper coins. So low did they fall that they were not valued more than pebbles or potsherds. The old coin, from its great scarcity, rose fourfold and fivefold in value.

When trade was interrupted on every side, and when the copper *tankas* had become more worthless than clods, and of no use, the Sultan repealed his edict and in great wrath proclaimed that whoever possessed copper coins should bring them to the treasury and receive the old gold coins in exchange. Thousands of men from various quarters, who possessed thousands of these copper coins, and caring nothing for them, had flung them into corners along with their copper pots, now brought them to the treasury and received in exchange gold *tankas* and silver *tankas*, and other

A GOLDSMITH AT LUCKNOW.

coins, which they carried to their homes. So many of these copper *tankas* were brought to the treasury, that heaps of them rose up in Taghlakabad like mountains. Great sums went out of the treasury in exchange for the copper, and a great deficit was thus caused. When the Sultan found that his project had failed and that great loss had been entailed upon the treasury through his copper coins, he turned against his subjects more than ever.

The fourth project which diminished his treasure and so brought distress upon the country, was his design of conquering Khorasan and Irak. In pursuance of this object, vast sums were lavished upon the officials and leading men of those countries. These great men came to him with insinuating proposals and deceitful representations, and as far as they knew how, or were able, they robbed the throne of its wealth. The coveted countries, however, were not acquired, and those which he already possessed were lost, while his treasure, which is the true source of political power, was spent.

The fifth project was the raising of an immense army for the campaign against Khorasan. Three hundred and seventy thousand horse were enrolled in the muster-master's office and were supported and paid for a whole year; but as they were not employed in war and conquest or enabled to maintain themselves on plunder, there was not sufficient in the treasury or in the feudal estates to support them when the next year came round. The army broke up; each man took his own course and engaged in his own occupations. But hundreds and thousands of rupees had been thus expended from the treasury.

The sixth project, which inflicted a heavy loss upon the army, was the design which Mohammad Taghlak formed of capturing the mountain of Kara-jal. His plan was that, as he had undertaken the conquest of Khorasan, he would first bring under the dominion of Islam this mountain, which lies between the territories of Hind and those of China, so that the passage for horses and soldiers and the march of the army might be rendered easy. To effect this object a large force, under distinguished commanders and generals, was sent to the mountain of Kara-jal, with orders to take it. In obedience to imperial command, the army marched into the hills and encamped in various places, but the Hindus closed the passes and cut off its retreat. The whole force was thus destroyed at one stroke, and out of all this chosen body of men only ten horsemen returned to Delhi to spread the news of the disaster.'

From these ill-advised measures, as described by Barani, we may easily understand how the sixteen years of Mohammad Taghlak's reign were a succession of uprisings, insurrections, and rebellions down to the time of his death, in 1351, near Thatta on the banks of the Indus. His successor was Firoz III, or Firoz Shah, sometimes called Firoz the Builder.

Firoz Shah, unlike his predecessor, enjoyed a long and prosperous reign of nearly forty years (1351-1388 A. D.). Abounding in good works, loved by his people, and rejoicing in his own piety, he advanced his kingdom in every way that he could. His munificent rule was described by contemporary Mohammedan writers, but, in addition to these records, we have a brief outline of the more important "Triumphs" of his reign, written by Firoz Shah himself.

This interesting little memoir, covering about thirty pages, has been translated into English by Professor

Dowson and incorporated in Sir Henry Elliot's history. A selection from it — autobiographic in charac-

A MOHAMMEDAN TOMB AT THATTA.

ter — is here given to show the character of Firoz Shah, his aims and his ideals. They may be best summarized in his own words descriptive of his reasons for writing, which were as follows: "My desire is that I should, to the best of my power, recount and pay my thanks for the many blessings which God has bestowed upon me, so that I may be numbered among His grateful servants."

The royal author then proceeds to show in a dozen different ways the clemency and justice of his rule. One of his first reforms was to abolish the barbarous methods of punishment which had prevailed under his predecessors. His sense of justice was next shown by a re-arrangement of taxes upon grounds of greater equity, and his Moslem orthodoxy was manifested by his strengthening the hold of his subjects upon the Religion of the Prophet and repressing idolatry, while his common sense was indicated by his introducing at court a simpler manner of living and by exemplifying it himself. But most striking of all, perhaps, was his enthusiasm for building and for restoring structures that had fallen into decay. His own words justify his title to be called Firoz the Builder, and, judging from what follows, we might add, Firoz the Wise.

'Among the gifts which God bestowed upon me, His humble servant, was a desire to erect public buildings. So I built many mosques and colleges and monasteries, that the learned and the elders, the devout and the holy, might worship God in these edifices and aid the kind builder with their prayers. The digging of canals, the planting of trees, and the endowing with lands are in accordance with the directions of the Law of Islam. The learned doctors of the Law of Islam have many troubles; of this there is no doubt. I settled allowances upon them in proportion to their necessary expenses, so that they might regularly receive the income.

Again, by the guidance of God, I was led to repair and rebuild the edifices and structures of former kings and ancient nobles, which had fallen into decay from lapse of time, and I gave the restoration of these buildings the priority over my own works. The Masjid-i Jami' of old Delhi, which was built by Sultan Mu'izz-ad-din Sam, had fallen into decay from age, and needed repair and restoration. I so repaired it that it was quite renovated.

The western wall of the tomb of the same Sultan, and the planks of the sepulchre's door, had become old and rotten. I restored this, and, in place of the balcony, I furnished it with doors, arches, and ornaments of sandalwood.

The minar of Sultan Mu'izz-ad-din Sam had been struck by lightning. I repaired it and raised it higher than it was before.

The Hauz-i Shamsi, or tank of Altamish, had been deprived of water by some graceless men, who stopped up the channels of supply. I punished these incorrigible men severely and opened again the closed up channels.

The Hauz-i Alai, or tank of Ala-ad-din, had no water in it and was filled up. People carried on cultivation in it, and had dug wells and sold the water from them. After a generation had passed I cleaned the reservoir out, so that this great tank might again be filled from year to year.

The Madrasa (college) of Sultan Shams-ad-din Altamish had been destroyed. I rebuilt it and furnished it with sandalwood doors. The columns of the tomb, which had fallen down, I restored better than they had been before. When the tomb was built, its court had not been made curved, but I now made it so. I enlarged the hewn-stone staircase of the dome, and I re-erected the fallen piers of the four towers.

A MINAR AT AHMADABAD

The tomb of Sultan Mu'izz-ad-din, son of Sultan Shams-ad-din, which is situated in Malikpur, had fallen into such ruin that the sepulchres were undistinguishable. I restored the dome, the terrace, and the enclosing wall.

The tomb of Sultan Rukn-ad-din, son of Shams-ad-din, in Malikpur, needed restoration. I repaired the enclosing wall, built a new dome, and erected a monastery.

The tomb of Sultan Jalal-ad-din I repaired, and I supplied it with new doors.

The tomb of Sultan Ala-ad-din I repaired and furnished it with sandalwood doors. I repaired the wall of the *ābdārkhānah*, or reservoir house, and the west wall of the mosque, which is within the college, and I also restored the tesselated pavement.

I likewise repaired and renovated the tomb of Sultan Kutb-ad-din and the other sons of Sultan Ala-ad-din, namely, Khizr Khan, Shadi Khan, Farid Khan, Sultan Shihab-ad-din, Sikandar Khan, Mohammad Khan, Osman Khan, and his grandsons, and the sons of his grandsons.

I furthermore repaired the doors of the dome and the latticework of the tomb of Shaikh-al-Islam Nizam-al-hakk-wa-ad-din, which were made of sandalwood. I suspended the golden chandeliers by chains of gold in the four recesses of the dome, and I built an assembly room, for there was none there previously.

Among other buildings which I restored was the tomb of Malik Taj-al-Mulk Kafuri, the great vizir of Sultan Ala-ad-din and master of fifty-two thousand horsemen. He was a most wise and intelligent minister, and acquired many countries on which the horses of former sovereigns had never placed their hoofs, and he caused the public prayer to be repeated there in the name of Sultan Ala-ad-din. His grave had been levelled with the ground, and his tomb laid low. I caused the sepulchre to be entirely renewed, for he was a devoted and faithful subject.

The Dar-al-aman, or House of Rest, is the bed and resting-place of great men. I had new sandalwood doors made for it, and over the tombs of these distinguished men I caused curtains and hangings to be suspended.

The expense of repairing and renewing these tombs and colleges was provided from their ancient endowments. In those cases where no income had been settled on these foundations in former times for purchasing carpets, lights, and furniture for the use of travellers and pilgrims in the least of these places, I had villages assigned to them, the revenues of which would suffice in perpetuity for the expenditure necessary for their maintenance.

The Jahan-panah, a foundation of the late Sultan Mohammad Shah, my kind patron, by whose bounty I was reared and educated, I restored.

A MOHAMMEDAN TOMB.

All the fortifications which had been built by former sovereigns at Delhi I repaired.

Furthermore, for the benefit of travellers and pilgrims that resort to the tombs of illustrious kings and celebrated saints, and for providing the things necessary in these holy places, I confirmed and gave effect to the grants of villages, lands, and other endowments which had been conferred upon them in olden times. In those cases where no endowment had been settled, I made provision that these establishments might for ever be secure of an income, to afford comfort to travellers and wayfarers, to holy men and learned men. May they remember those ancient benefactors and me in their prayers!

I was enabled by God's help to build a Dar-ash-shifa, or hospital, for the benefit of every one of high or low degree who was suddenly attacked by illness and overcome by suffering. Physicians attend there to diagnose the disease, to look after the cure, to regulate the diet, and to give medicine. The cost of the medicines and the food is defrayed from my endowments. All sick persons, residents and travellers, gentle and simple, bond and free, resort thither; their maladies are treated, and, under God's blessing, they are cured.

Under the guidance of the Almighty I arranged that the heirs of those persons who had been put to death in the reign of my late lord and patron Sultan Mohammad Taghlak Shah, and those who themselves had been deprived of a limb, nose, eye, hand, or foot, should be reconciled to the late Sultan and be appeased with gifts, so that they executed deeds declaring their satisfaction, duly attested by witnesses. These deeds were put into a chest, which was placed in the Dar-al-aman at the head of the tomb of the late Sultan, in the hope that God, in his great clemency, would show mercy to my late friend and patron and make those persons feel reconciled to him.

Another instance of divine guidance was this. Villages, lands, and ancient patrimonies of every kind had been wrested from the hands of their owners in former reigns and had been brought under the exchequer. I directed that every one who had a claim to property should bring it forward in the law-court, and that upon establishing his title, the village, the land, or whatever other property it was, should be restored to him. By God's grace I was impelled to this good action, and men obtained their just rights.

I encouraged my infidel subjects to embrace the religion of the Prophet, and I proclaimed that every one who repeated the creed and became a Mussulman should be exempt from the *jizya*, or poll-tax imposed on non-believers. When this information came to the ears of the people at large, great numbers of Hindus presented themselves and were admitted to the honour of Islam. Thus they came forward day by day from every quarter, and, adopting the faith, were exonerated from the jizya and were favoured with presents and distinctions.

Through God's mercy the lands and property of His servants have been safe and secure, protected and guarded during my reign, and I have not allowed the smallest particle of any man's property to be wrested from him. Men often spoke to me officiously, saying that such and such a merchant had made so many lacs, and that such and such a revenue collector had so many lacs. By reproofs and punishments I made these informers hold their tongues, so that the people might be safe from the malignity of such meddlesome persons, and through this kindness men became my friends and supporters.

"Labour to earn for generous deeds a name,
Nor seek for riches to extend thy fame;
Better one word of praise than stores of gold,
Better one grateful prayer than wealth untold."

Under God's favour my heart was occupied with an earnest desire to succour the poor and needy and to comfort their hearts. Wherever I heard of a holy devotee, or religious recluse, I went to visit him and ministered to his necessities, so that I might attain the blessing promised to those who befriend the poor.

Whenever a person had completed the natural term of life and become full of years, I first provided for his support, and then I advised and admonished him to direct his thoughts to making preparation for the life to come, to repent of all things which he had done contrary to the Law and Religion of Islam in his youth, and to wean his affections from this world and fix them on the world to come.

I desired to act upon the principle of these lines:

"The practice of the great should be
To succour honest men;
And when a good man dies, to see
His children find a friend."

When any government servant filling an important and responsible position was carried off under the decrees of God to the happy future life, I gave his place and employment to his son, so that he might occupy the same position and rank as his father and suffer no injury.

"Kings should make their rule of life
To love the great and wise;
And when death ends this mortal strife,
To dry their loved ones' eyes."

The greatest and best of honours that I obtained through God's mercy was, that by my obedience and

TEACHING ISLAM TO THE YOUTH.

piety, and friendliness and submission to the caliph, the representative of the holy Prophet, my authority was confirmed; for it is by his sanction that the power of kings is assured, and no king is secure until he has submitted himself to the caliph and has received a confirmation from the sacred throne. A diploma was sent to me fully confirming my authority as deputy of the caliphate, and the leader of the faithful was graciously pleased to honour me with the title of *Sayyid-as-Salā-tīn*, "Chief of Sultans." He also bestowed upon me robes, a banner, a sword, a ring, and a footprint as badges of honour and distinction.

My object in writing this book has been, first of all, to express my gratitude to the All-bountiful God for the many and various blessings which He has bestowed upon me. Secondly, that men who desire to be good and prosperous may read it and learn what is the proper course. There is a brief maxim, by observing which a man may obtain God's guidance: "Men will be judged according to their works and rewarded for the good that they have done."'

AN INDIAN DECORATIVE DESIGN.

CHAPTER IX

TIMUR'S ACCOUNT OF HIS INVASION OF INDIA AND SACK OF DELHI

1398 - 1399 A. D.

AFTER his victorious sweep over Persia and Mesopotamia to Asia Minor on the west and his occupation of Afghanistan on the south, Timur Lang, or Tamerlane, the great conqueror, turned his attention to India as the next country in which to wage a holy war and from which to carry away rich spoils sanctified by religion. China also had attracted his eye, so that his mind wavered for a moment as to which country he should invade, but an omen from the Koran settled his decision, and he determined to make the expedition against Hindustan. We have a somewhat detailed account of his campaign recorded in autobiographic memoirs which he caused to be written down, and a translation of these, made from the Turkish language into Persian two centuries after his death, serves as a valuable record of the great conqueror's exploits, which were inspired also by a pious zeal for the renown of having been a Champion of the Faith of Mohammed. Excerpts from the rendering by Chapman and Dowson in Elliot's collection are here given.

'About the year 800 A. H. (1398 A. D.), there arose in my heart the desire to lead an expedition against the infidels and to become a Champion of the Faith, for it had reached my ears that the slayer of infidels is a Champion and that, if he is slain, he becomes a martyr. It was for this reason that I formed my resolution, but I was undetermined in my mind whether I should direct my expedition against the infidels of China or against the infidels and polytheists of India. In this matter I sought an omen from the Koran, and the verse to which I opened was this: "O Prophet, make war upon infidels and unbelievers, and treat them with severity."

My chief officers told me that the inhabitants of Hindustan were infidels and unbelievers. In obedience to the mandate of Almighty God, I determined to make an expedition against them, and I issued orders to the amirs of mature years and to the leaders in war to assemble in my presence, and when they had come together, I questioned the assembly as to whether I should invade Hindustan or China, and said to them: "By the command of God and of His Prophet I needs must make war upon these infidels and polytheists." Throwing themselves upon their knees, they all wished me good fortune. I then asked the warrior chieftains whether I should direct my expedition against the infidels of Hindustan or of China. At first they repeated fables and wise sayings, and then said that in

THE RIVER INDUS AT KHUSHALGARH.

the country of Hindustan there are four defences, and if any one invades this extensive country and breaks down these four defences, he becomes the conqueror of the land.

The first defence consists of five large rivers, which flow from the mountains of Kashmir, after which they unite in their course, pass through the country of Sind, and flow into the Arabian Sea, nor is it possible to cross them without boats and bridges. The second defence consists of woods and forests and trees, which, interweaving stem with stem and branch with branch, render it extremely difficult to penetrate into the country. The third defence is the soldiery, and landholders, and princes, and rajas of that country, who inhabit fastnesses in those forests and dwell there like wild beasts. The fourth defence consists of the elephants, for in the day of battle the rulers of that country equip elephants in mail, put them in the van of their army, and place great confidence in them; and they have trained them to such a degree that with their trunks they lift a horse with his rider, and whirling him in the air, they dash him to the ground.

Some of the nobles replied that Sultan Mahmud Sabuktagin had conquered the country of Hindustan with thirty thousand horse and had established his own servants as rulers of that region, after which he had carried off many thousand loads of gold and silver and jewels from that country, besides subjecting it to a regular tribute. "Is then," they cried, "our lord inferior to Sultan Mahmud? No! thanks to Almighty God! To-day one hundred thousand valiant Tartar horsemen wait at the stirrup of our prince; and, if he determines upon this expedition, God on high will give him victory, and he will become a conqueror and a crusader before God, and we shall be attendants on an amir who is a conqueror; and the army will be contented, and the treasury rich and well filled; and with the gold of Hindustan our prince will become a conqueror of the world and be renowned among the kings of earth."

At that juncture Prince Shah Rukh said: "India is an extensive land; whatever Sultan conquers it becomes supreme over the four quarters of the globe, and thus, if we subdue with our lord as leader, we shall become rulers over the seven climes. I have read in the history of Persia," he continued, "that, in the days of the Persian Sultans, the King of India was called Darai with all honour and glory. On account of his dignity he bore no other name; and the Emperor of Rome was called Cæsar; and the Sultan of Persia was called Kisra; and the Sultan of the Tartars, Khakan; and the Emperor of China, Faghfur; but the King of Iran and Turan bore the title of Shahinshah, or King of Kings, and the orders of the Shahinshah were always paramount over the princes and rajas of Hindustan. Praise be to God that at this time we are Shahinshah of Iran and Turan, for it would be a pity that we should not be supreme over the realm of Hindustan."

I was exceedingly pleased with these words of Prince Shah Rukh, and after that Prince Mohammad Sultan said: "The whole country of India is full of gold and jewels, and in it there are seventeen mines of gold and silver, diamonds and rubies, emeralds and tin, iron and steel, copper and quicksilver, and many metals more; and among the plants which grow there are those fit for making wearing-apparel, and aromatic shrubs, and the sugar-cane; and it is a country which is always green and verdant, and the whole aspect of the land is pleasant and delightful. Now, since the inhabitants are chiefly polytheists and infidels and idolaters and worshippers of the sun, it is meet, according to the mandate of God and of His Prophet, for us to conquer them."

Some of the nobles said: "By the favour of Almighty God we may conquer India, but if we establish ourselves permanently therein, our race will degenerate, and our children will become like the natives of those regions, and in a few generations their strength and valour will diminish." The commanders of regiments were disturbed at these words, but I said to them: "My object in the invasion of Hindustan is to lead an expedition against the infidels that, according to the law of Mohammed (upon whom and his family be the blessing and peace of God!), we may convert the people of that country to the true faith and purify the land itself from infidelity and polytheism, and that we may overthrow their temples and idols and become conquerors and crusaders before God." They gave an unwilling consent, but I placed no reliance upon them.

At this time the wise men of Islam came before me, and a conversation began about the propriety of a war against infidels and polytheists, whereupon they declared that it is the duty of the Sultan of Islam and of all who profess that "there is no god but Allah, and Mohammed is the prophet of Allah," to exert their utmost endeavour for the suppression of the enemies of their faith, for the sake of preserving their religion and strengthening their law. They likewise said that it is the duty of every Moslem and true believer to use his utmost exertions in obedience to his ruler. When the edifying words of the wise men reached the ears of the nobles, all their hearts were set upon a holy war in Hindustan, and throwing themselves on their knees, they repeated the Chapter of Victory which opens the Koran.

When I girded up my loins for the expedition, I wrote to Hazrat Shaikh Zain-ad-din to the effect that I had determined on a religious war in Hindustan. He wrote in the margin of my letter: "Be it known to Abu-l-Ghazi Timur that great prosperity in this world and the next will result to him from this undertaking, and that he will go and return in safety." He also sent me a large sword which I made my sceptre.

In the meanwhile there came a petition from Prince Pir Mohammad Jahangir on the confines of Kabulistan, the government of which, from the boundaries of Kunduz and Bakalan and Kabul and Ghazni and Kandahar, was vested in him. When I looked at this petition it read thus:

"From the very moment that I arrived in this country, according to your order, I have acted toward all people conformably to the exalted mandates and wise counsels of the king.

"When I had satisfied my mind with the conquest

and settlement of this kingdom, I turned my thoughts toward the acquisition of some of the provinces of Hindustan. I inquired concerning the condition of that country and received the following account: that the city of Delhi is the capital of the sovereigns of India, and that after the death of Sultan Firoz Shah, two brothers among his nobility, one of whom was named Mallu and the other Sarang, became very powerful and established their independence; so that, though they gave the nominal sovereignty to one of the sons of Sultan Firoz Shah, Sultan Mahmud by name, they kept the real power in their own hands and virtually governed the empire. Mallu, the elder brother, lives at Delhi, at the court of Sultan Mahmud, while Sarang is established in the city of Multan for the protection of that country.

SHAH TIMUR.
(From an old Persian print.)

"When I became acquainted with these matters, I acted according to the practice of the great king, and wrote a letter which I sent to Sarang by an ambassador, declaring that since the fame of the victories and conquests and of the extensive empire of the great king is spread over all the world, it certainly must have reached him also. The great king has appointed me to the government of those provinces which lie on the borders of Hindustan, and has commanded: 'If the rulers of Hindustan come before me with tribute, I will not interfere with their lives, property, or kingdoms; but if they are negligent in proffering obedience and submission, I will put forth my strength for the conquest of the realms of India. At all events, if they set any value upon their lives, property, and reputation, they will pay me a yearly tribute; and if not, they shall hear of my arrival with my powerful armies. Farewell.'

"When the ambassador reached the presence of Sarang at Multan, he was treated with great respect and consideration; but in reply to his letter, Sarang said: 'It is difficult to take an empire to your bosom, like a bride, without trouble and difficulty and the clashing of swords. The desire of your prince is to take this kingdom with its rich revenue. Well, let him wrest it from us by force of arms if he be able. I have numerous armies and formidable elephants, and am quite prepared for war.' With these words he dismissed the ambassador.

"When this unsatisfactory answer was brought back to me, I issued immediate orders for the armies to assemble from all quarters, together with those nobles who were in my province, such as Amir Saikal Kandahari, and other amirs and soldiers. I made preparations for the invasion of Hindustan, plundering and

devastating the country of the Aghanis who inhabit the mountain Sulaiman, and marching steadily forward until I crossed the river Indus and assaulted the city of Uchh, which I captured through the good fortune of the great king. Leaving a body of men there as a garrison, I proceeded to Multan, which I besieged; but as Sarang had carefully fortified and strengthened this fortress, the siege has been protracted for some days, and, indeed, I am at this moment engaged in the siege, giving an assault twice every day. All the nobles have displayed great valour and intrepidity, especially Timur Khwaja, the son of Amir Akugha, and I am awaiting further instructions."

When I had read this letter, my previous resolution was confirmed and strengthened, and I acted in such a manner that by spring (800 A. H., 1398 A. D.) I had collected the soldiery from all parts of the country under my sway.

In this same year 800 I selected ten battalions from my army, and giving the command to Prince Shah Rukh, I left him in charge of the remaining forces and baggage in Tilak Ghunan and Diktur, while I myself placed my foot in the stirrup to chastise the infidel Kators.[1] Setting spurs to my horse, I marched forward in great haste, accomplishing two days' journey within twenty-four hours. When I arrived at a place called Paryan, I detached Prince Rustam and Burhan Aghlan Jujitar, who were reckoned among my chief nobles, to invade

[1] The description of this entire campaign against the Kators is interesting because of the details it gives regarding Timur's military operations.

the country of the Siyah-poshes, which lay on the left hand. With them I sent some of the nobility and a body of ten thousand cavalry, while I myself pursued my march toward the mountains of Kator.

When I made inquiries concerning the extent and condition of that kingdom from Muzid, who was the chief man of Indarab, he informed me that the length of the kingdom of Kator stretches from the frontier of Kashmir to the mountains of Kabul, and that there are many towns and villages in this country. One of their large cities is called Shokal, and another Jorkal, the latter being the residence of their ruler. The country produces fruit in large quantities, such as grapes, apples, apricots, and various other kinds. Rice and other grains are cultivated. Much wine is made, and all people, great and small, drink of it. The people eat swine's flesh, and cattle and sheep abound in the country. Most of the inhabitants are idolaters; they are men of a powerful frame and fair complexion, and speak a language distinct from Turkish, Persian, Hindi, and Kashmiri. Their weapons are arrows, swords, and slings, and their ruler is called Adalshu.

When I arrived at Khawak, I perceived a dilapidated fort which I resolved to repair. I therefore gave immediate orders to the soldiers to that effect, and they were speedily executed. As most of the route was rocky and precipitous, I ordered most of the nobles and all the soldiers to leave their horses, camels, and superfluous baggage in this fort. In obedience to this order, most of the nobles and all the soldiers accom-

Ruins at Kabul.

panied me on foot, while I, relying on the assistance of Almighty God, pressed steadily forward to the conquest of Kator and began to ascend the mountains. Despite the heat of the wind, there was so much snow on the hills that the feet of both men and cattle sank in it helplessly. I was obliged, therefore, to halt during

AN AFGHAN FORTRESS.

the day; but at night, when the snow congealed, I pursued my way over the frozen surface of the ice till I reached the top of the mountain. At daybreak, when the ice thawed, carpets and horse-rugs were spread upon its surface and the horses were kept upon them. At nightfall we again proceeded as before, and in this manner I crossed several lofty mountains, although the nobles were obliged to send back to the fort several of the horses they had brought with them.

When I reached the top of a lofty mountain, I found that the infidels had taken up their position in caverns which had their entrances blocked with snow so that they were almost inaccessible, nor, in spite of all my exertions, could I find a way to descend the mountain. I was accordingly obliged to give orders to my brave soldiers to get down as best they could. The nobles and soldiery now began the descent. Some, lying down on their sides and sliding over the snow, rolled to the bottom. Others, fastening cords and long tent-ropes to their waists and attaching one end of the ropes to the trees and rocks which were on the top, let themselves gently down. As for myself, I gave orders that they should make me a basket of planks and wicker-work. When they had made the basket, they attached a rope 150 yards in length to each of its four corners. Since I had undertaken this expedition against the infidels and had made up my mind to undergo all manner of trouble and fatigue, I took my seat in the basket. Thereupon a body of men took hold of the ends of these ropes and lowered the basket gently till the rope had all run out, after which some soldiers scrambled down to before where I was, cleared away the snow and ice with spades and mattocks, and made a place for me to stand on. By that time the first body of men had descended to this place, and they again lowered me gently down as far as the ropes would reach. At the fifth repetition of this manœuvre I reached the bottom of the mountain. When all the nobles and soldiers had got down in this fashion, some of my own horses were lowered by attaching ropes to their legs and shoulders; but out of the whole number only two reached the bottom in safety, all the rest being dashed to pieces.

When no more of my people remained above, since my object was the extermination of the infidels, I grasped my sceptre-sword in my hand and marched forward on foot one parasang into that rocky country, together with my nobility and troops. At the earnest petition of the nobles I remounted, but all the chiefs and their soldiers marched steadily on foot at my stirrup. The ruler of Kator had a fort, bounded on one side by a river, beyond which a lofty mountain reached down to the water. As the infidels in this fort had gained intelligence of my approach a day before my arrival, and dread had taken possession of their hearts, they had removed their wealth and property from the fort, and, after crossing the river, had taken refuge in the mountain, which was very lofty and abounded in caves that were very difficult of access. Since I was given to understand that this fort was the most important stronghold of the ruler of Kator in those parts, I resolved to subdue it; but when I advanced into the neighbourhood of the fort, I did not perceive a trace of the infidels, and when I came to the place itself, I saw that they had abandoned it and fled. I obtained a booty of many sheep and some other things here, and ordered my soldiers to set fire to the houses and buildings of the city, in the midst of which the fort was built, and to level it to the ground.

Crossing the river in haste and pursuing the enemy, I reached the skirts of the mountain on whose top the infidels had fortified themselves in defiles and other strong places. I immediately ordered my valiant and experienced troops to ascend, whereupon they raised the war-cry of "God is most great" and rushed to the attack. Before all the rest Shaikh Arslan Aztuman Kabak Khan, who is a lion in the day of battle, mounted the hill on the left hand and commenced the fight. Leading his men against the infidels, he put them to flight, and following up the enemy, he entered the fastnesses of the rock and slew vast numbers of the unbelievers. Tawachi Ali Sultan also made a valiant assault upon the foe, and with his own regiment charged and routed the infidel enemy, killing them in multitudes. Amir Shah Malik likewise displayed great valour, slaughtering hosts of the infidels and driving them completely out of the mountain. Mubashir Bahadur, and Mankali Khwaja, and Sunjak Bahadur, and other valiant nobles used their swords equally well. They all proved their zeal for Islam on the unbelieving foe, and having overpowered the infidels, they put many of them to death and took possession of their fastnesses. Only a few of the enemy succeeded in sheltering themselves in their caverns, wounded and worn out with fatigue. Of my troops only fourteen lost their lives, and that was in effecting the passage of the mountain.

Some of the infidels held out in their defiles for three

days and nights, but sending my valiant troops against them, I so pressed them that they were obliged to surrender and beg for quarter. I sent Ak Sultan to them with the message that if they would submit unconditionally and would all become Mussulmans and repeat the creed, I would grant them quarter, but otherwise I would exterminate them to a man. When Ak Sultan reached the infidels with this message, which he explained to them through the medium of an interpreter conversant both with their language and with Turkish, they all proffered submission, and repeating the necessary formula, embraced the Mohammedan faith. Relying upon this external conversion, I spared their lives and property, and gave orders that no one should interfere with their lives, belongings, or estates. I then clothed some of them in dresses of honour and dismissed them. I halted my army there for the night, whereupon these black-hearted infidels made a nocturnal attack on the regiment of Amir Shah Malik, but as this leader was on his guard, the enemy were foiled in their intentions. Numbers of them were slain, and 150 fell into our hands alive and were afterwards put to death by my enraged soldiery.

As soon as it was day, I ordered my troops to attack on all four sides at once, to force their way into the defiles, and to kill the men, imprison the women and children, and plunder and lay waste their property. In obedience to these orders, my nobles and troops made a valiant assault on all sides at once and put the remnant of the infidels to the sword, after which they made prisoners of their women and children and secured an enormous booty. I directed towers of the skulls of those obstinate unbelievers to be built on the mountain, and I ordered an engraver on stone, who was in my camp, to cut an inscription somewhere on those defiles to the effect that I had reached this country by such and such a route, in the auspicious month of Ramazan, A. H. 800 (May, 1398), so that, if chance should conduct any one to that spot, he might know how I had reached it.

Thus far I had received no intelligence of Prince Rustam and Burhan Aghlan, whom I had detached against the country of the Siyah-poshes, and since this same Burhan Aghlan had displayed great sloth and military incapacity on a former occasion, when I had appointed him commander of a predatory incursion (to retrieve which negligence I had given him the command on the present occasion), doubts entered my mind as to what he might be doing. One night, too, I dreamt that my sword was bent, and interpreted this as a sure sign that Burhan Aghlan had been defeated. I immediately appointed one of my household slaves, named Mohammad Azad, to go and ascertain something respecting him, and I placed under his command Daulat Shah and Shaikh Ali, the son of Airakuli Adighur, and Shaikh Mohammad, and Ali Bahadur, with a body of four hundred men, of whom one hundred were Tartars and the rest Tajiks, and gave them a native of Kator as a guide. Mohammad Azad and his band of heroes immediately commenced the march, and after crossing lofty mountains full of snow and ice and passing through narrow defiles, rolling in many places over precipices and sliding over the icy surface, they finally got out of the mountains and into the open country.

AN AFGHAN PASS.

When Mohammad Azad had extricated himself from the mountains and reached the fortress of the Siyah-poshes, he found it deserted, for they had abandoned it from their dread of the army of Islam and had taken refuge in their mountain defiles.

Now Burhan Aghlan's adventure had been as follows:—When he reached the fort of the Siyah-poshes, he found it empty, whereupon he incautiously pushed on to the defiles, following the footsteps of the enemy. Having left only a few troopers and a few foot-soldiers as a guard below, the infidels, rising from their ambushes, fiercely assailed the true believers. Such was the cowardice and military incapacity of Burhan Aghlan that he threw away his arms and fled without striking a blow. When the troops saw the flight of their leader, they lost heart and were defeated, and the infidels, following them closely, raised full many a true believer to the rank of a martyr. Of the amirs of the regiments, Daulat Shah and Shaikh Husain Suchi and Adina Bahadur displayed great valour, but after slaying many of the infidels, they finally drank the sherbet of martyrdom. Burhan Aghlan, however, escaped, leaving many horses and suits of armour a prey to the infidels.

When Mohammad Azad arrived at the deserted fort of the Siyah-poshes with his four hundred men, he followed the track of the enemy toward the mountain. On arriving at the scene of Burhan Aghlan's defeat and flight, he was attacked by the infidels who had defeated Burhan Aghlan, but he fought so gallantly that he routed them with great slaughter and recovered all the horses and armour which they had captured from the soldiers of Burhan Aghlan, besides taking much booty in the way of wealth and property. Marching homeward, he met Burhan Aghlan on that very day, and restored to each of his soldiers his own horse and arms. On the same day they reached a pass, where Mohammad Azad proposed to Burhan Aghlan that they should halt, but the cowardice and inefficiency of the latter would hear of no delay, so they went through the pass. Certainly, from the days of Chingiz Khan to the present time, no man has shown such a lack of energy and courage.

When I had despatched Mohammad Azad from Kator and satisfied myself with the subjugation of that country, I sent Ali Sistani and Jalal-al-Islam to discover a road and make clear halting-places for me. In obedience to this order, they went forward, clearing the snow and ice from the road in many places. Having made a passage for me, they returned, whereupon I mounted immediately and set forward, while the nobles and soldiery marched along with me on foot; and thus I proceeded in triumph along the track which they had made, till I reached Khawak, where I had left the horses in the fort.

I had been absent eighteen days on this expedition against the infidels, and the nobles and soldiery, who had hitherto fought on foot, now regained their horses. Leaving a body of men to garrison the fort which I had built, I directed my own course toward the heavy baggage, and arrived at Tilak Ghunan and Diktur, where the local princes and amirs came out to meet me with congratulations on my victory. There, too, Burhan Aghlan and Mohammad Azad joined my victorious camp, but I gave orders that they should refuse admittance to Burhan Aghlan and on no account allow him to enter my presence; for it is the decree of God Most High that if twenty true believers engage boldly and steadily in fight with ten times the number of infidels they shall prevail against them, and yet Burhan Aghlan, with ten thousand men under his command, was put to rout and flight by a small number of infidels, exposing Mussulmans to disgrace and death. On the other hand, I loaded honours and benefits on Mohammad Azad, who, with only four hundred men, had fought a valiant action against the greatly superior numbers of the unbelievers. I exalted his rank above his fellows and gave him a regiment, nor did I omit to shower my princely favours on his companions in victory.'

Timur next proceeds to describe, step by step, the conquests made by his invading host as it fought its way toward Delhi. When he reached the historic field of Panipat, he prepared for the decisive battle which should place the capital city in his hands. His own description follows.

'For my intended attack on Delhi in this same year 800 A. H. (1398 A. D.), I arranged my forces so that the army extended over a distance of twenty leagues. Being satisfied with my disposition of the troops, I began my march on Delhi. On the twenty-second of Rabi'-al-awwal (Dec. 2) I arrived and encamped at the fort of the village of Aspandi, where I found, in answer to my inquiries, that Samana was seven leagues distant. The people of Samana and Kaithal and Aspandi are all heretics, idolaters, infidels, and misbelievers. They had now set fire to their houses and had fled with their children and property toward Delhi, so that the whole country was deserted.

On the next day, the twenty-third of the month, I started from the fort of Aspandi, and after marching six leagues, arrived at the village of Taghlak-pur, at which I encamped opposite the fort of that same name. When the people of the fort had heard of the approach of my army, they had abandoned it and scattered throughout the country. From the information supplied me I learned that these people were called *Sanawī* [that is, Fire-worshippers, Zoroastrians, or Ghebers]. Many of this perverse creed believe that there are two gods. One is called Yazdan, and all the good they have they believe proceeds from him. The other god they call Ahriman, and every sin and wickedness of which they are guilty they hold is caused by him. These misbe-

INDIAN CHILDREN.

lievers do not know that whatsoever there is of good or evil comes from God, and that man is the mere instrument of its execution. I ordered the houses of these heretics to be burned and their fort and buildings to be razed to the ground.

On the following day, the twenty-fourth of the month, I marched to Panipat, where I encamped. There I found that, in obedience to orders received from the ruler of Delhi, all the inhabitants had deserted their dwellings and had taken flight. When the soldiers entered the fort, they reported to me that they had found a large store of wheat, which I ordered to be weighed, to ascertain the real weight, and then to be distributed among the soldiers.

On the next day I marched six leagues from Panipat and encamped on the banks of a river which is by the road. I set forth from this place on Friday, the twenty-sixth of the month, and gave orders that the officers and soldiers of my army should put on their armour, and that every man should keep in his proper regiment and place, and be in perfect readiness. We reached a village called Kanhi-gazin, where we encamped, and where I issued my commands that on the morrow, the twenty-eighth of the month, a force of cavalry should proceed on a plundering excursion against the palace of Jahan-numa, a fine building erected by Sultan Firoz Shah on the top of a hill by the banks of the Jumna, which is one of the chief rivers of Hindustan. Their orders were to plunder and destroy, and to kill every one they met. Next day, in obedience to my commands, the division proceeded to the palace of Jahan-numa, which is situated five miles from Delhi. They plundered every village and place they came to, killed the men, and carried off all the valuables and cattle, securing much booty; after which they returned, bringing with them a number of Hindu prisoners, both male and female.

On the twenty-ninth I again set forth and reached the river Jumna. On the other side of the river I descried a fort, and upon making inquiry about it, I was informed that it consisted of a town and fort called Loni, and that it was held by an officer named Maimun on behalf of Sultan Mahmud. I determined to take that fort at once, and as pasture was scant where I was, I crossed the river Jumna on the same day. I sent Amir Jahan Shah and Amir Shah Malik and Amir Allah-dad to besiege the fort of Loni, and I pitched my camp opposite to it. At this time a holy shaikh who dwelt in the town came out very wisely and waited upon me, yet although he was greatly honoured by the people, they would not listen to his advice, but determined to fight rather than surrender to me. These people were Hindus belonging to the faction of Mallu Khan, wherefore they despised the counsels of the venerable father and resolved to resist.

When I was informed of their decision, I ordered all the amirs and soldiers to assemble and invest the fort. They accordingly gathered with alacrity round the fort, and in the course of one watch of the day they carried the place, which was situated between the Jumna and the Halin, the latter being a large canal which had been cut from the river Kalini and brought to Firozabad, and there connected with the Jumna by Sultan Firoz Shah. Many of the Rajputs placed their wives and children in their houses and burned them, after which they rushed into battle and were killed. Others of the garrison fought and were slain, and a vast number were taken prisoners. Next day I gave orders that the Mussulman prisoners should be separated and saved, but that the infidels should all be put to death with the proselyting sword. I also commanded that the homes of the *sayyids* (or lineal descendants of the Prophet), shaikhs, and learned Mussulmans should be preserved, but that all the other houses should be plundered and the fort destroyed. It was done as I directed, and great booty was obtained.

When my heart was satisfied with the conquest of Loni, I rode away from thence on the first of Rabi'-al-akhir (Dec. 11) to examine the fords of the Jumna, and when I came opposite the palace Jahan-numa, I found some places where the river might be crossed. At the time of midday prayer I returned to the camp and gave orders to the princes and amirs, after which I held a council about the attack upon Delhi and the operations against Sultan Mahmud.

After much discussion in the Council of War, where every one had something to say and an opinion to offer, it appeared that the soldiers of my army had heard strange tales about the strength and prowess and appearance of the elephants of Hindustan. They had been told that in the fight one would take up a horseman and his horse with his trunk and hurl them in the air, but these stories, fortunately, had been met by suitable answers from some of the bold troopers. The Council of War at length agreed that a plentiful supply of grain must first be secured and stored in

MUSSULMAN PRIESTS OF INDIA.

the fort of Loni as provision for the army, and that after this was done, we might proceed to attack the fort and city of Delhi. When the council was over, I ordered Amir Jahan Shah, Amir Sulaiman Shah, and others to cross the Jumna and to forage in the environs of Delhi, bringing off all the corn they could find for the use of the army.

It now occurred to me that I would cross the Jumna with a small party of horse to examine the palace of Jahan-numa, and to reconnoitre the ground on which a battle might be fought. I accordingly took an escort of seven hundred horsemen clad in armour and started off, sending Ali Sultan Tawachi and Junaid Bur-uldai forward as an advance-guard. Crossing the Jumna, I reached Jahan-numa and inspected the whole building, and I discovered a plain fit for a battle-field. Meanwhile, Ali Sultan and Junaid, my advance-guard, each brought in a man belonging to the vanguard of the enemy, and when I had interrogated Ali Sultan's captive about the matters of Sultan Mahmud and Mallu Khan, I ordered him to be put to death as an augury of good.

My scouts now brought me information that Mallu Khan with four thousand horsemen in armour, five thousand infantry, and twenty-seven fierce war elephants, fully accoutred, had come out of the gardens of the city and had drawn up in battle array. I left Sayyid Khwaja and Mubashar Bahadur with three hundred Turkish horsemen on gray horses in the Jahan-numa and withdrew toward my camp. Mallu Khan advanced boldly toward Jahan-numa, and Sayyid Khwaja and Mubashar went forth to meet him. A conflict ensued, in which my men fought valiantly; and as soon as I heard of the action, I sent Sunjak Bahadur and Amir Allah-dad with two regiments to their support. At the earliest practicable moment, they assailed the enemy with arrows and then charged them. At the second and third onslaught the enemy was defeated and fled toward Delhi in disorder, while many fell under the swords and arrows of my men. When the men fled, an extraordinary incident occurred, in that one of the great war elephants fell down and died. When I heard of it, I declared it to be a good omen. My victorious troops pursued the enemy to the vicinity of the city and then returned to present themselves at my tent, where I congratulated them on their victory and praised their conduct. On the next day, Friday, the third of the month (Dec. 13), I left the fort of Loni and marched to a position opposite to Jahan-numa, where I encamped.

I now held a court, issuing a summons to the princes, amirs, and minor officers, all of whom came to my tent. Each of my soldiers was a brave veteran, and had used his sword manfully under my own eyes, but there were none that had seen so many conflicts and battles as I had beheld, and no one of the amirs or heroes of the army that could compare with me in the amount of fighting I had gone through and the experience I had gained. I therefore gave them instructions as to the mode of carrying on war; on making and meeting attacks; on arraying their men; on giving support to each other; and on all the precautions to be observed in warring with an enemy. I ordered the amirs of the right wing, the left wing, the van, and the centre to take their proper positions, and cautioned them not to be too forward or too backward, but to act with the utmost prudence and caution in their operations. When I had finished, the amirs and others testified their approbation, and, carefully treasuring up my counsel, they departed, expressing their blessings and thanks.

At this court Amir Jahan Shah, Amir Sulaiman Shah, and other amirs of experience informed me that, from the time of entering Hindustan up to the present we had taken more than one hundred thousand infidels and Hindus prisoners, and that they were all in my camp. On the previous day, when the enemy's forces attacked us, the prisoners made signs of rejoicing, uttered imprecations against us, and were ready, as soon as they heard of the enemy's success, to form themselves into a body, break their bonds, plunder our tents, and then to join the enemy, and so increase his numbers and strength. I asked the amirs for advice about the prisoners, and they said that on the day of battle these one hundred thousand prisoners could not be left with the baggage, and that it would be entirely opposed to the rules of war to set these idolaters and foes of Islam at liberty, so that no course remained but to make them all food for the sword.

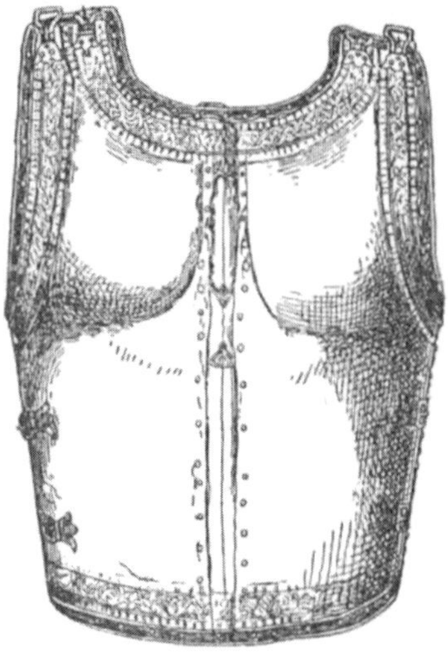

MOHAMMEDAN ARMOUR.

When I heard these words, I found them to be in accordance with the rules of war, and I immediately directed the commanders to proclaim throughout the camp that every man who had infidel prisoners was to put them to death, and that whoever neglected to do so, should himself be executed and his property given to the informer. When this order became known to the champions of Islam, they drew their swords and put their prisoners to death. One hundred thousand infidels, impious idolaters, were slain on that day. Maulana Nasir-ad-din Omar, a counsellor and man of learning, who had never killed a sparrow in all his life, now, in execution of my order, killed fifteen idolatrous Hindus, who were his captives.

AN INDIAN DAGGER.

After all the vile idolaters had been despatched, I gave orders that one man out of every ten should be told off to guard the property, cattle, and horses which had been captured in the invasion, while all the other soldiers were to march with me. At the time of midday prayer the signal was given for the march, and I proceeded to the spot selected for crossing the Jumna, and there encamped. The astrologers who accompanied the army consulted their books and almanacs as to the time propitious for battle, and they represented that the aspects of the stars made a short delay advisable. In all matters, small and great, I placed my reliance on the favour and kindness of God, and I knew that victory and conquest, defeat and flight, are each ordained by Him, so that I gave no credence to the words of the astrologers and star-gazers, but besought the Giver of victory to favour my arms.

I did not wish the war to be of long continuance; so as soon as night was over and morning came, I arose to my devotions. I said the morning prayers in the congregation, and repeated my private prayers, after which I took the Koran, opened it at random, and placed my finger at a venture on a verse in the chapter of the Bee, which I received as a propitious indication, and acted in full reliance on its command and on the favour of God.

On the fifth of Rabi'-al-akhir (Dec. 15) I passed the Jumna by a ford, and pitched my tents on the other side of the river; after which I gave orders to the amirs and other officers to station their men as near my tent as possible; and also directed that the ground around the camp should be parcelled out among them, and that each one should have a deep ditch dug in front of his allotment. All the soldiers, great and small, assembled to dig the ditch, which was constructed around the entire camp in two watches of the day. I then rode out to inspect it, and ordered that the trees in the vicinity should be cut down, and brought within the ditch; that their branches should be formed into a strong *abattis*, and that in some places planks should be set up.

It had been constantly dinned into the ears of my soldiers that the chief reliance of the armies of Hindustan was on their mighty elephants, which, completely encased in armour, marched into battle in front of their forces; that arrows and swords were of no use against them; that in height and bulk they were like small mountains, while their strength was such that at a given signal they could tear up great trees and knock down strongly built walls; and that in the battle-field they could take up the horse and his rider with their trunks and hurl them into the air. Some of the soldiers, with the timidity natural to man, brought some little of what they had heard to my attention; so when I assigned their respective positions to the princes and amirs of the right and left wing and of the centre, I made special inquiry of the holy and learned men who accompanied my army where they would like to be placed in the day of battle. They had been with me in many campaigns, and had witnessed many a great battle, but the stories about the elephants of India had so affected them that they instantly replied that they would like to be placed with the ladies while the battle was in progress. To allay the apprehensions of this class of men, I gave orders that all the buffalos which had been taken and placed with the baggage should be brought up; I then had their heads and necks fastened to their legs, and put them inside the *abattis*.

I gave orders for the camp to be carefully guarded all night to prevent a surprise by the enemy, and the night was passed with the caution and care which are necessary in war. When the morn of victory dawned, I said my prayers in the congregation; and after I had discharged that duty, I gave directions for the drums and other musical instruments to be sounded. The princes and amirs armed themselves completely, and marched with their respective forces in regular order, while I mounted my horse and rode forth to marshal my array. When I had arranged my right and left wings, I placed the right wing under the command of Prince Pir Mohammad Jahangir, Amir Yadgar Birlas, and other high officers; the left wing I put under the command of Prince Sultan Husain, Prince Khalil Sultan, Amir Jahan Shah, and their colleagues; and the advance-guard I placed under such generals as Prince Rustam and Amir Shaikh Nur-ad-din. I took my own place with the centre.

When all the forces were arrayed, I ordered the vanguard to go forward and obtain some knowledge of the enemy. One of the advance-guard captured a man belonging to the enemy's van and brought him in to me. When I asked this prisoner about the position of the enemy, he told me that Sultan Mahmud had drawn up his army with the intention of fighting. His right wing was commanded by Mu'in-ad-din, Malik Hadi, and other officers; his left wing was under Taghi Khan, Mir Ali, and others, and the Sultan had taken up his own position with the centre, and had appointed a body of troops to act as rear-guard. His whole force amounted to ten thousand veteran horse and forty thousand warlike infantry, in addition to 125 elephants covered with armour, most of them carrying howdahs in which were men to hurl grenades, fireworks, and rockets. Thus they came up to battle.

The enemy's forces now made their appearance and I accordingly rode to the top of a little hill which was hard by, where I carefully scrutinized their array and said to myself that, with the favour of God, I would defeat them and gain a victory. I alighted from my horse on the top of that hill and performed my devotions, bowing my head to the ground and beseeching the Almighty for victory. As I did this, I perceived signs that my prayers were heard, so that, when I had finished, I mounted my horse in the full assurance of God's assistance. I returned to the centre and took up my position under the imperial standard, after which I directed Ali Sultan Tawachi, Altun Bakhshi, and other leaders to march with their regiments to strengthen the right wing, also commanding the remaining officers to proceed with their men to the support of the vanguard. It so happened that Amir Yadgar Birlas and Sulaiman Shah, who were with the right wing, and Amir Shaikh Nur-ad-din and Amir Shah Malik, who were with the vanguard, had conceived this very idea at the same instant, and had remarked to each other that they would look upon any reinforcement received from the centre as a presage of victory. It was just then that the Almighty put it into my mind to send them assistance.

The two armies now confronted each other, the drums were beaten on both sides, shouts and cries were raised, the ground trembled, and a great noise was heard. At this instant Sunjak Bahadur, Sayyid Khwaja, Allah-dad, and others separated from the vanguard, and when they perceived that Sultan Mahmud's forces were approaching, they moved off to the right, and getting secretly behind the enemy's advance-guard as it came on unsuspecting, they rushed from their ambush, and falling upon the foe in the rear, sword in hand, they scattered them as hungry lions scatter a flock of sheep, and killed six hundred of them in this single charge. Prince Pir Mohammad Jahangir, who commanded the right wing, moved his own forces forward, and with Amir Sulaiman Shah and his regiments of brave cavalry attacked the left wing of the enemy, which was commanded by Taghi Khan, and poured a shower of arrows upon it, so that my brave soldiers, pressing like furious elephants upon this part of the enemy's host, compelled it to take refuge in flight.

The left wing of my army, under Prince Sultan Husain, Amir Jahan Shah, Amir Ghiyas-ad-din, and other amirs, bravely attacked the enemy's right wing, which was commanded by Malik Mu'in-ad-din and Malik Hadi. They so pressed it with the trenchant sword and piercing arrows that they compelled the enemy to break and fly. Jahan Shah pursued them, and attacked them again and again until they reached the gates of the city of Delhi.

Simultaneously, Sultan Mahmud with Mallu Khan and the army of the centre, with its officers and soldiers more numerous than ants or locusts, and with its strong war elephants, made an attack upon my centre, where Prince Rustam, Amir Shaikh Nur-ad-din, and their colleagues met it with a brave and resolute resistance. While they were thus engaged, Daulat Timur Tawachi, Mangali Khwaja, and other amirs came up with their respective forces and assailed the enemy. I now gave the order to a party of brave fellows who were in attendance upon me, and they cut

GATEWAY OF THE MOSQUE OF ALA-AD-DIN AT DELHI.

their way to the sides of the amirs, who were fighting in the forefront of the battle. They brought the elephant drivers to the ground with their arrows and killed them, after which they attacked and wounded the elephants with their swords. The soldiers of Sultan Mahmud and Mallu Khan showed no lack of courage, and bore themselves manfully in the fight, but they could not withstand the successive onslaughts of my soldiers. Seeing their own plight and that of the soldiers and elephants around them, their courage fell and they took to flight. Sultan Mahmud and Mallu Khan reached the city with a thousand difficulties, and shut themselves up close in the fortifications.

The whole of Sultan Mahmud's army was defeated; part was slain, and part had found refuge in the fort, toward which I marched, exalted with victory. When I reached its gates, I carefully reconnoitred its towers and walls, and then returned to the side of the Hauz-i Khas, a reservoir constructed by Sultan Firoz Shah, and faced all around with stone and cement. Each side of this reservoir is more than a bow-shot long, and buildings are placed around it. It is filled by the rains in the rainy season and supplies the people of the city with water throughout the year. The tomb of Sultan Firoz Shah stands on its bank.

When I had pitched my camp here, the princes and amirs, and all the generals and officers, came to pay their respects and to offer me their congratulations on this great victory. I embraced them all and praised them for the exertions and courage which I myself had seen. When I recounted the favours and mercies I had received from the Almighty, my excellent sons, the brave and renowned amirs who served under me, and the great and glorious victories I had achieved, my heart melted and tears fell from my eyes. I cast myself upon the ground and poured forth my thanksgivings to the All-beneficent. All who were present raised their voices in prayer, and expressed their earnest wishes for the continuance of my prosperity and the prolongation of my reign.

I called up the heavy baggage and formed my camp, issuing orders for my soldiers to be very cautious and

TOMB OF FIROZ SHAH AT DELHI.

watchful. After their defeat, Sultan Mahmud and Mallu Khan, in wretched plight, had taken refuge in the fort. They now repented of the course they had taken, and regretted that they had not made submission to me and thus avoided the evil which had befallen them.

They saw that if they remained in the fort, they would be captured and made prisoners, so in the middle of that night, the seventh of Rabi'-al-akhir (Dec. 17), Sultan Mahmud and Mallu Khan left the fort of Jahan-panah and fled toward the mountains and jungles.

As soon as I heard of this, I immediately sent Amir Sa'id and other officers in pursuit. They followed with all speed, and coming up with the fugitives, they killed many of them and obtained great booty. Malik Sharf-ad-din and Malik Khudai-dad, sons of Rashid Mallu Khan, were taken prisoners, with many others, and brought back to my camp. On the same night that I heard of the flight of the Sultan and his generals from Delhi, I sent Amir Allah-dad and other officers to watch the gate of Hauz-rani, through which Mahmud had escaped, and that of Baraka, by which Mallu Khan had gone out. I also sent men to all the other gates, with orders to prevent the inhabitants from escaping.

I then mounted my horse and rode toward the gate of the public square, alighting at the *'īd-gāh*, or court of celebrations and festivities, a lofty and extensive building, where I directed my throne to be set up. I took my seat upon the throne and held a court, which was attended by Sayyids, the judges, the learned Mussulmans, the shaikhs, and the great men and chiefs. I had them introduced one by one, whereupon they made their obeisances and were admitted to the honour of kissing my throne. I received every one of them with respect and kindness, and directed them to be seated. Fazl-allah Balkhi was viceroy and deputy of

Mallu Khan, and he came out to wait upon me and do homage, accompanied by a party of the officials and clerks of the government of Sultan Mahmud and Mallu Khan. Thereupon all the Sayyids, scholars, shaikhs, and other leading Mussulmans arose, and making the princes their mediators, they begged that quarter might be given to the people of Delhi, and that their lives might be spared. Out of respect to the Sayyids and scholars, whom I had always held in great esteem and honour, I granted quarter to the inhabitants of the city, after which I then ordered my ensign and royal standard to be raised, and the drums to be beaten and music played on the tops of the gates of Delhi. Rejoicings for the victory followed, and some of the clever men and poets that accompanied me worked the date of the victory into a verse, which they presented to me. Of all these memorial verses, however, I have introduced only this one into my memoirs:

> "On Wednesday, the eighth of Rabi' the second (Dec. 17, 1398),
> The Emperor Sahib-Kiran took the city of Delhi."

I rewarded and honourably distinguished the literary men and poets who presented these verses to me.

I sent a party of men into the city to bring out the elephants which Sultan Mahmud had abandoned when he fled. They found 120 enormous elephants and several rhinoceroses, which they brought out to my court. As the elephants passed by me, I was greatly amused to see the tricks which their drivers had taught them. Every animal, at the sign of his driver, bowed his head to the ground, made his obeisance, and uttered a cry. At the direction of their drivers they picked up any object from the ground with their trunks and placed it in their drivers' hands, or put it into their mouths and kept it. When I saw these mighty animals, so well trained and so obedient to weak man, I was greatly astonished, and I ordered that they should be sent to Turan and Iran, to Fars and Azur and Rum (Byzantium), so that the princes and nobles throughout my dominions might behold these animals. Accordingly I sent five to Samarkand, two to Tabriz, one to Shiraz, five to Herat, one to Sharwan, and one to Azarbaijan.

When Friday came, I sent Maulana Nasir-ad-din Omar, together with certain other holy and learned men who accompanied my camp, to the Jami' Masjid, with directions to say the prayers for the Sabbath, and to recite the official prayer of my reign in the metropolis of Delhi. This petition was accordingly repeated in my name in the pulpits of the mosques of the city of Delhi, and I rewarded the preachers with costly robes and presents.

When the preparations for holding a court in Delhi were completed, I gave orders for the princes, amirs, and other officers, as well as the Sayyids, scholars, shaikhs, and all the principal men of the city, to attend my court. When all had arrived, I entered and took my seat upon the throne. The Turkish and Arab musicians and singers began to play and sing, and wine, sherbet, sweetmeats, and all kinds of bread and meat were served. I bestowed rich robes, caps, girdles, swords, daggers, horses, and the like upon the princes and amirs and other leading men of my army, especially upon those heroes who had distinguished themselves by deeds of valour under my own observation. To some I gave regiments and raised their dignity, while to the Sayyids and scholars of the city I presented robes and gifts.

I ordered my secretaries to draw up despatches announcing my victories in Hindustan and to circulate them with all speed throughout my dominions; and I also directed my revenue officers to make provision for collecting the ransom-money assessed upon the entire city, excepting the Sayyids, scholars, and shaikhs. The collectors proceeded about their work, and I remained in my quarters for several days, holding courts, giving feasts, and partaking of pleasure and enjoyment.

On the sixteenth of the month (Dec. 26), certain incidents occurred which led to the sack of the city of Delhi and to the slaughter of many of the infidel inhabitants. One was this. A party of fierce Turkish soldiers had assembled at one of the gates of the city to look about them and enjoy themselves, and some of them had laid riotous hands upon the goods of the inhabitants. When I heard of this violence, I sent some amirs, who were present in Delhi, to restrain the Turks, and a party of soldiers accompanied these officers into the city. Another reason was that some of the ladies of my harem expressed a wish to go into the city and see the Palace of a Thousand Columns which Malik Jauna had built in the fort called Jahan-panah. I granted this request, and I sent a party of soldiers to escort the litters of the ladies. Another reason was that Jalal Islam and other officials had entered Delhi with a party of soldiers to collect the contribution laid upon the city. Another reason was that some thousand troopers with orders for grain, oil, sugar, and flour had gone into the city to collect these supplies. Another reason was that it had come to my knowledge that great numbers of Hindus and infidels had come into the city from all the country round with their wives and children, and goods and valuables, and consequently I had sent some amirs with their regiments into Delhi and directed them to pay no attention to the remonstrances of the inhabitants, but to seize these fugitives and bring them out.

For these various reasons a great number of fierce Turkish troops were in the city. When the soldiers proceeded to apprehend the Hindus and infidels who had fled to Delhi, many of them drew their swords and offered resistance. The flames of strife thus lighted spread through the entire city from Jahan-panah and Siri to Old Delhi, consuming all they reached. The savage Turks fell to killing and plundering, while the Hindus set fire to their houses with their own hands, burned their wives and children in them, and rushed into the fight and were killed. The Hindus and infidels of the city showed much alacrity and boldness in fighting. The amirs who were in charge of the gates prevented any more soldiers from entering Delhi, but the flames of war had risen too high for this precaution to be of any avail in extinguishing them. All day Thursday and throughout the night, nearly fifteen thou-

HINDU WOMEN.

sand Turks were engaged in slaying, plundering, and destroying.

When Friday morning dawned, my entire army, no longer under control, went off to the city and thought of nothing but killing, plundering, and making prisoners. The sack was general during the whole day, and continued throughout the following day, Saturday, the seventeenth (Dec. 27), the spoil being so great that each man secured from fifty to a hundred prisoners, men, women, and children, while no soldier took less than twenty. There was likewise an immense booty in rubies, diamonds, garnets, pearls, and other gems; jewels of gold and silver; gold and silver money of the celebrated Alai coinage; vessels of gold and silver; and brocades and silks of great value. Gold and silver ornaments of the Hindu women were obtained in such quantities as to exceed all account. Excepting the quarter of the Sayyids, the scholars, and the other Mussulmans, the whole city was sacked. The pen of fate had written down this destiny for the people of this city, and although I was desirous of sparing them, I could not succeed, for it was the will of God that this calamity should befall the city.

On the following day, Sunday, it was brought to my knowledge that a great number of infidel Hindus had assembled in the Jami' Masjid of Old Delhi, where they had carried arms and provisions, and had prepared to defend themselves. Some of my people who had gone that way on business were wounded by them, whereupon I immediately ordered Amir Shah Malik and Ali Sultan Tawachi to take a party of men and clear the house of God of infidels and idolaters. They accordingly attacked these infidels and put them to death, after which Old Delhi was plundered.

I ordered that all the artisans and clever mechanics who were masters of their respective crafts should be selected from among the prisoners and set aside, and accordingly some thousands of craftsmen were bidden to await my command. All these I distributed among the princes and amirs who were present, or who were officially engaged in other parts of my dominions. I

THE MAUSOLEUM OF TIMUR AT SAMARKAND.

had determined to build a Jami' Masjid in Samarkand, the seat of my empire, which should be without a rival in any country; and for this reason I ordered that all builders and stone-masons should be set apart for my own especial service.

By the will of God, and by no wish or direction of mine, all the three cities of Delhi, Siri, Jahan-panah, and Old Delhi, had been plundered. The official prayer of my sovereignty, which is an assurance of safety and protection, had been read in the city, and it was, therefore, my earnest wish that no evil might happen to the people of the place. It was ordained by God, however, that the city should be ruined, and he accordingly inspired the infidel inhabitants with a spirit of resistance, so that they brought on themselves that fate which was inevitable.

When my mind was no longer occupied with the destruction of the people of Delhi, I took a ride around the cities. Siri is a round city, with lofty buildings surrounded by strong fortifications built of stone and brick. Old Delhi has a similar strong fort, but it is larger than that of Siri, and from the fort of Siri to that of Old Delhi, which is a considerable distance, there runs a strong wall, built of stone and cement. The district called Jahan-panah is situated in the midst of the inhabited city. The fortifications of the three cities have thirty gates. Jahan-panah has thirteen gates, seven on the south side bearing toward the east, and six on the north side bearing toward the west. Siri has seven gates, four toward the outside and three on the inside toward Jahan-panah. The fortifications of Old Delhi have ten gates, some opening to the exterior and some toward the interior of the city.

When I was tired of examining the city, I went to the chief mosque, where I found a congregation of Sayyids, lawyers, shaikhs, and other principal Mussulmans, together with the inhabitants of their parts of the city, to whom they had been a protection and defence. I called them to my presence, consoled them, treated them with every respect, and bestowed upon them many presents and honours. I also appointed an officer to protect their quarter of the city, and guard them against annoyance, after which I remounted and returned to my quarters.

INTERIOR OF TIMUR'S TOMB AT SAMARKAND.

After spending fifteen days at Delhi, passing my time in pleasure and enjoyment, and in holding royal courts and giving great feasts, I reflected that I had come to Hindustan to war against infidels, and that my enterprise had been so blessed that wherever I had gone I had been victorious. I had triumphed over my adversaries, I had put to death hundreds of thousands of infidels and idolaters, I had dyed my proselyting sword with the blood of the enemies of the Faith, and now that I had gained this crowning victory, I felt that I ought not to indulge in ease, but rather to exert myself still further in warring against the infidels of Hindustan. Having made these reflections, on the twenty-second of Rabi'-al-akhir, 800 A. H. (Jan.

1, 1399 A. D.), I again drew my sword to wage a religious war.'

Timur's memoirs then proceed to describe his taking of Mirat by storm, his frightful slaughter of the inhabitants, his capture of Hardwar, and his devastation of the territory along the Ganges, until he turned his army on the homeward march to Samarkand, fighting his way at every step until he left India.

CHAPTER X

THE MEMOIRS OF THE EMPEROR BABAR

IT is generally agreed that the Memoirs of the Emperor Babar form one of the best and most faithful pieces of autobiography that exist. They are considered to be decidedly superior to those of Timur and Jahangir, and may compare favourably with Xenophon's Anabasis or Cæsar's Commentaries, as they are fully equal to the latter in the matter of simplicity and are much more straightforward.

These autobiographical records were written by Babar in remarkably pure Chagatai Turkish, and are extant in a very few copies, one of which may be found reproduced in facsimile in the Gibb Memorial series of publications. A Persian translation of the famous journal was made in Akbar's time and presented to that monarch. The Memoirs have since been turned into German, Russian, and French, as well as into English by Leyden and Erskine. The extracts from the latter's version as given below, with slight alterations and omissions, give a detailed account of some of Babar's operations in India in 1519 A. D. and the following years.

'When we left Bajaur, on the fourteenth of Safar,

925 A. H. (Feb. 15, 1519 A. D.), we did it with the intention of attacking Bahrah, the country on the Jihlam, or Hydaspes, near the town of that name, but chiefly on the right bank of the river, before we returned to Kabul. We were always full of the idea of invading Hindustan, but this had been prevented by various circumstances. For the three or four months that the army had been detained in Bajaur, it had got no plunder of value. As Bahrah is on the borders of Hindustan and was near at hand, I thought that, if I were now to push on without baggage, the soldiers might light upon some booty. Moving on with this idea, and plundering the Afghans in our progress, I was advised by several of my principal adherents, when I reached Makam, that if we were to enter Hindustan, we should do it on a proper footing and with an adequate force. Though the advice was perfectly judicious, we made the inroad in spite of all these objections.

Early next morning we marched toward the passage over the Sind. I despatched Mir Mohammad Jala-ban in advance, with his brothers and some troops to escort them, for the purpose of examining the banks of the river, both above and below. After sending the army forward toward the river, I myself set off for Sawati, which they likewise call Kark-khanah, to hunt the rhinoceros. We started many rhinoceroses, but as the country abounded in brushwood, we could not get at them.

Next morning, being Thursday, the seventeenth of Safar (Feb. 18), we crossed the ford with our horses, camels, and baggage, while the camp bazaar and the infantry were floated over on rafts. The same day the inhabitants of Nilab (fifteen miles below Attok on the Sind) waited on me, bringing a horse clad in full panoply and three hundred *Shāh-rukhīs* (almost £15) as a present. That same day at noonday prayers, as soon as we had got all our people across, we proceeded on our march, which we continued for one watch of the night, halting at the river of Kachah-kot (the modern Haroh). Marching thence before daybreak, we crossed the river of Kachah-kot, and the same evening we surmounted the pass of Sangdaki, where we halted. Sayyid Kasim, who brought up the rear-guard on the march, captured a few Gujars who followed the camp, cut off the heads of some of them, and brought them in.

Marching at dawn from Sangdaki and crossing the river Sohan (a stream lying between the Sind and the Jihlam), we encamped about the hour of noonday prayers. Our stragglers, however, continued to come in till midnight, for it was an uncommonly long and severe march, and as it was made when our horses were lean and weak, it was peculiarly hard on them, so that many of the animals were worn out and fell down by the way. Seven leagues to the north of Bahrah (possibly Bhira, south of the Swan) there is a hill, which, in the Zafar Namah and some other books, is called the hill of Jud. At first I was ignorant of the origin of its name, but afterward discovered that on it there were two races of men descended from the same father, one tribe being called Jud, and the other Janjuhah.

As I always had the conquest of Hindustan at heart, and as Bahrah, Khushab, Chinab, and Chaniut, where I now was, had long been in the possession of the

MOHAMMEDANS AT NOONDAY PRAYERS.

Turks, I regarded them as my own domains, and was resolved to gain possession of them either by war or by peace. It was, therefore, right and necessary that the people of the hill should be well treated, and I accordingly issued orders that no one should molest or trouble their flocks and herds, or take from them so much as a bit of thread or a broken needle.

Marching thence rather late, about noonday prayers, we reached a place of some size named Kaldah-kahar (the modern Kallar-kahar), where we halted, setting forth again at dawn on the following day. In various places on the very top of the Pass of Hambatu we met men bringing gifts of small value and coming to tender their submission. About luncheon-time we reached the bottom of the pass, where we halted, and having cleared the pass and emerged from the wooded ground, I formed the army in regular array, with right and left wings and centre, and marched toward Bahrah. When we had almost reached that place, Deo Hindu and the son of Saktu, who were servants of Ali Khan, the son of Daulat Khan Yusuf Khail, accompanied by the head men of Bahrah, met us, each bringing a horse and camel as a gift, and tendering his submission and service. Noonday prayers were over when we halted on the banks of the river Behat to the east of Bahrah, on a green field of grass, without having done the people of that town the least injury or damage.

From the time that Timur Beg (Tamerlane) had invaded Hindustan and left it again, these countries of Bahrah, Khushab, Chinab, and Chaniut had remained in the possession of the family of Timur Beg and of their dependents and adherents. Sultan Mas'ud Mirza, the grandson of Shah Rukh Mirza and son of Siurghnamsh Mirza, was, in those days, the ruler and chief of Kabul and Zabul, on which account he got the title of Sultan Mas'ud Kabuli.

Next morning I sent out foraging parties in proper

directions, and afterwards rode round Bahrah. On Wednesday, the 22d (Feb. 23), I sent for the head men and chief craftsmen of Bahrah and agreed with them for the sum of four hundred thousand *Shāh-rukhīs* (nearly £20,000 sterling) as the ransom of their property, whereupon collectors were appointed to receive the amount. Having learned that the troops had exercised some severity toward the inhabitants of Bahrah and were misusing them, I sent out a party, which seized a few of the soldiers who had been guilty of excesses. I then put some of them to death and slit the noses of others, and commanded them to be led about the camp in that condition; for I considered the countries that had belonged to the Turks as my own territories, and therefore allowed no plundering or pillage.

People were always saying that if ambassadors were to be sent in a friendly and peaceable way into the countries that had been occupied by the Turks, it could do no harm. I therefore despatched Mulla Murshid to Sultan Ibrahim, whose father, Sultan Iskandar, had died five or six months before, and who had succeeded his parent in the empire of Hindustan; and giving my envoy the name and style of ambassador, I sent him to demand that the countries which had belonged to the Turks from days of old should be given up to me. Besides these letters for Sultan Ibrahim, I gave Mulla Murshid letters to Daulat Khan, and having also delivered verbal instructions to him, I dismissed him on his mission. The people of Hindustan, and particularly the Afghans, are a strangely foolish and senseless race, possessed of little reflection and less foresight. They can neither persist in a war and manfully support it, nor can they continue in a state of amity and friendship. Mulla Murshid was detained some time in Lahore by Daulat Khan, who would neither see him himself nor suffer him to proceed to Sultan Ibrahim; so that, five months later, he returned to Kabul without receiving any answer.

On Friday, letters of submission came from the people of Khushab. We remained one day in the fort of Bahrah, which they call Jahan-numa, and on the morning of Tuesday set out on our march, encamping on the rising grounds which skirt Bahrah toward the north. Next morning, after the council was dismissed and I had finished my ride, I went on board of a boat and had a drinking party.

In the hill country between Nilab and Bahrah, but apart from the tribes of Jud and Janjuhah and adjoining the hill country of Kashmir, are the Jats, Gujars, and many other men of similar tribes, who build villages and settle on every hillock and in every valley. Their chief was of the Gakkar race, and their government resembled that of the Jud and Janjuhah. At that time the government of these tribes, which skirt the hills, was held by Tatar Gakkar and Hati Gakkar, sons of the same family and cousins. Their strongholds were situated on ravines and steep precipices. The name of Tatar's fortress was Parhalah, and it was considerably lower than the snowy mountains. Hati's country is close to the hills, and he had also won over to his side Baba Khan, who held Kalinjar. Tatar Gakkar had waited on Daulat Khan and was, in a way, subject to him. Hati had never visited him, but remained in an independent turbulent state. At the desire of the amirs of Hindustan, and in conjunction with them, Tatar had taken a position with his army several miles off, and kept Hati in a sort of blockade. At the very time when we were in Bahrah, Hati had

A DISTANT VIEW OF KABUL.

advanced upon Tatar by a stratagem, had surprised and slain him, and had seized his country, his women, and all his property.

Having arranged the affairs of the country in such a way as to give hopes that it would remain quiet, I marched from Bahrah on my return to Kabul on Sunday, the eleventh of Rabi'-al-awwal. Some persons who were acquainted with the country and with the political situation of the neighbouring territories, and particularly with the Janjuhah, who were old enemies of the Gakkars, informed me that Hati Gakkar had been guilty of many acts of violence, had infested the highways by his robberies, and had harassed the inhabitants; so that it was necessary either to effect his expulsion from this quarter, or at least to inflict exemplary punishment on him.

Next morning I accordingly left Khwaja Mir Miran and Miram Nasir in charge of the camp, and set out, about breakfast-time, with a body of light troops, to attack Hati Gakkar, who had killed Tatar a few days before and had seized the country of Parhalah, where he now had taken his stand, as has been mentioned. About afternoon prayers we halted and fed our horses, resuming our march about bedtime prayers. Our guide was a Gujar servant of Malik-hast, named Surpa.

All night long we marched straight on, but halted toward morning and sent Beg Mohammad Mughal toward the enemy's camp. When it was beginning to be light, we mounted again, and about luncheon-time we put on our armour and increased our speed. About a league from the place where we had made this halt, the stronghold of Parhalah began to appear faintly in sight. The skirmishers were now pushed forward and the right wing proceeded to the east of Parhalah, while Kuch Beg, who belonged to that wing, was directed to follow in their rear, as a reserve. The left wing and centre poured in straight toward Parhalah. Dost Beg was appointed to command the party assigned to support the left wing and centre, who made the direct attack on the stronghold.

Parhalah, which stands high in the midst of deep

valleys and ravines, has two roads leading to it. We advanced by the one on the southeast, which runs along the edge of the ravines and has gullies and precipices on either side. Within half a league of Parhalah, the road becomes extremely difficult, and so continues up to the very gates of the city, the ravine road being so narrow and steep in four or five places that only one person can go along it at a time, while for about a bow-shot it is necessary to proceed with the utmost circumspection. The other road is on the northwest, and here also but one man can pass at a time. It advances toward Parhalah through the midst of an open valley. Except these two roads, there is no other on any side. Although the place has no breastwork or battlement, yet it is so situated that it is not assailable, being surrounded by a precipice seven or eight *gaz* (fourteen or sixteen feet) in perpendicular height.

The troops of the left wing passed along the narrows and went pouring on toward the gate. Hati, with thirty or forty horsemen, all, both man and horse, in complete armour, accompanied by a number of foot-soldiers, attacked and drove back the skirmishers. Dost Beg, who commanded the reserve, then came up, and falling on the enemy with great impetuosity, killed a number of them and routed the rest. Hati Gakkar, who distinguished himself by his courage and firmness in the action, could not maintain his ground in spite of all his exertions, and fled. He was unable to hold the narrows, and on reaching the fort, found that it was equally out of his power to defend himself there.

The detachment which followed close on his heels entered the fort along with him, and Hati was accordingly obliged to make his escape, nearly alone, by the northwest entrance. On this occasion Dost Beg again greatly distinguished himself, and I ordered an honorary gift to be given him. At the same time I entered Parhalah and took up my abode at Tatar's palace. During these operations, some men, who had been ordered to remain with me, had joined the skirmishing party, and to punish them for this offence, I gave them the Gujar Surpa for their guide and turned them out disgracefully into the wilds and deserts to find their way back to camp.

On Thursday, the fifteenth of Rabi'-al-awwal, we halted at Andarabah, which lies on the banks of the river Sohan. This fort of Andarabah depended, in ancient times, on the father of Malik-hast, but when Hati Gakkar slew Malik-hast's father, it had been destroyed, and had remained in ruins ever since. Hati, after killing Tatar, had sent to me one Parbat, his relative, with a caparisoned horse and with gifts. He did not meet me, but fell in with that part of the army that had been left behind with the camp; and having arrived along with the division that accompanied the baggage, he now presented his offerings and tribute, and tendered his submission. Langar Khan, who was to be left behind in Bahrah, but who had accompanied the camp to finish some business, also rejoined me; and having brought everything to a conclusion, he took leave of me and returned to Bahrah, accompanied by some *zamīndārs* of that district. After this we continued our march and crossed the river Sohan, encamping on rising ground. I gave a robe of honour to Parbat, Hati Khan's relative; and having written letters to confirm Hati in his good intentions and to remove any misapprehensions he might entertain, I dismissed Parbat in company with a servant of Mohammad Ali Jang-jang.

Marching at the time when the kettle-drum beats (an hour before dawn), we halted about luncheon-time at the foot of the pass of Sangdaki. We renewed our march at noonday, and ascending the pass, we crossed the river and halted on an eminence, where we remained till midnight. In going to examine the ford by which we had crossed on our way to Bahrah, we found a raft loaded with grain, which had stuck fast in the mud and clay, and which the owners had been unable to extricate with all their efforts. We seized this grain, which came very seasonably, and divided it among the men who were with us. Toward evening we halted below the junction of the Sind and Kabul rivers, but above the old Nilab, midway between the two. We brought six boats from Nilab and divided them among the right and left wings and centre, who immediately began to exert themselves in crossing the river. On Monday, being the day on which we arrived, and on Tuesday and the night following, they continued to cross, and a few went over even on Thursday.

Parbat, Hati's relative, who had been sent from the neighbourhood of Andarabah with the servant of Mohammad Ali Jang-jang, returned to us while we were on the banks of the river, bringing from Hati a horse clad in armour, by way of tributary offering. The inhabitants of Nilab likewise brought an armed horse as a gift and tendered their submission. Since Mohammad Ali Jang-jang wished to remain in Bahrah, which had been given to Hindu Beg, I bestowed on him the tract of country between Bahrah and the Sind, together with other estates in the district, such as the Karluk Hazaras, Hati, Ghiyasdal, and Kib.

On Thursday, the twenty-second of Rabi'-al-awwal (March 24, 1519), at sunrise, we moved from the banks of the river, and resumed our march, and six days later I reached Kabul.

On Friday, the first of Safar, in the year 932 A. H. (Nov. 17, 1525 A. D.), when the sun was in Sagittarius, I again set out to invade Hindustan. We made two marches from Bikram (Peshawar); and after the third, on Thursday, the 26th (Dec. 13), we encamped on the banks of the river Sind. On Saturday, the first day of Rabi'-al-awwal, we passed the Sind, and having also crossed the river of Kach-kot, we halted on its banks. The various officials who had been detailed to superintend the embarkation now brought me the return of the troops who were on the service, and reported that, great and small, good and bad, servants and no servants, they amounted to twelve thousand persons.

We then advanced along the skirts of the hills toward Sialkot to secure a proper supply of grain. On coming opposite to the country of the Gakkars we repeatedly found a quantity of standing water in the bed of a brook. These waters were entirely frozen over, and although there was not much of it, the ice was generally a span in thickness. Such ice is uncommon in Hindustan. We met with it here, but in all the years I have been in Hindustan, this is the only time that I met with any trace of ice or snow.

Advancing five marches from the Sind, the sixth brought us close to the hill of Jud, below the hill of Balinat-jogi on the banks of a river at the station of

A GLIMPSE OF LAHORE.

Bakialan, where we encamped. Marching thence, we halted, after fording the river Behat below Jihlam. From this encampment I sent Sayyid Tufan and Sayyid Lachin forward, giving each of them a spare horse, with directions to push on with all speed to Lahore, and to enjoin our troops in that city not to fight, but to form a junction with me at Sialkot or Parsarur; for there was a rumour that Ghazi Khan had collected an army of thirty or forty thousand men; that Daulat Khan, old as he was, had buckled on two swords; and that they would certainly try the fate of a battle. I recollected the proverb which says, "Ten friends are better than nine," and that no advantage might be lost,

I judged it most advisable to form a junction with the detachment of my army that was in Lahore before I offered battle. I therefore sent messengers with instructions to the amirs, and at the second march reached the banks of the river Chinab, where I encamped.

On Friday, the fourteenth of Rabi'-al-awwal, we arrived at Sialkot. Every time that I entered Hindustan, the Jats and Gujars regularly poured down in prodigious numbers from their hills and wilds in order to carry off oxen and buffalos. These were the wretches that really inflicted the chief hardships and were guilty of the severest oppression in the country. These districts had been in a state of revolt in former times and had yielded very little revenue that could be collected. On the present occasion, when I had reduced the whole of the neighbouring districts to subjection, they began to repeat their practices. As my unfortunate people were on their way from Sialkot to the camp, hungry and naked, indigent and in distress, they were attacked along the road with loud shouts and plundered. I sought out the persons guilty of this outrage, discovered them, and ordered two or three of them to be cut in pieces.

A merchant arrived at this same station, bringing the news of the defeat of Ala-ad-din Khan by Sultan Ibrahim. The particulars are as follows: Ala-ad-din Khan, after taking leave of me, had marched forward, despite the scorching heat of the weather, and had reached Lahore, having gone two days' journey every march without any consideration for those who accompanied him. At the very moment that he left me, all the sultans and khans of the Uzbegs had advanced and blockaded Balkh, so that I was obliged to set out for that city as soon as he departed for Hindustan. When Ala-ad-din reached Lahore, he declared to such of my nobles as were in Hindustan that the emperor had ordered them to march to his assistance, and that arrangements had been made for Ghazi Khan to join him and for all to march together upon Delhi and Agra. The nobles answered that, as things were situated, they could not accompany Ghazi Khan with any degree of confidence; but that, if he sent his younger brother Haji Khan to court with his son, or placed them in Lahore as hostages, their instructions would then leave them at liberty to march along with him; that otherwise, they could not; that it was only recently that Ala-ad-din Khan had fought with Ghazi Khan and had been defeated by him, so that mutual confidence between them was impossible; and that altogether it was absolutely inadvisable for Ala-ad-din Khan to allow Ghazi Khan to accompany him in the expedition.

Whatever expostulations they employed to dissuade Ala-ad-din Khan from prosecuting his plan were in vain. He sent his son Sher Khan to confer with Daulat Khan and Ghazi Khan, and the parties themselves met soon afterwards. Dilawar Khan, who had been in confinement very recently, and who had escaped from custody and come to Lahore only two or three months before, was likewise associated with them; and Mahmud Khan Khan-Jahan, to whom the custody of Lahore had been intrusted, was also pressed into their measures. In a word, it was definitively arranged among them at last that Daulat Khan and Ghazi Khan should take command of all the nobles who had been left in Hindustan, and at the same time should assume the government of all the adjacent territories in the Panjab or near Lahore; while Dilawar Khan and Haji Khan were to accompany Ala-ad-din Khan and occupy the whole of the country about Delhi and Agra, and in that neighbourhood. Isma'il Jilwani, and a number of other amirs, waited on Ala-ad-din Khan and acknowledged him, after which he proceeded toward Delhi by forced marches without delay. On reaching Indari, Sulaiman Shaikh-zadah came and joined him, thus raising the numbers of the confederate army to thirty or forty thousand men. They laid siege to Delhi, but were unable either to take the place by storm or to reduce it by famine.

As soon as Sultan Ibrahim heard that they had collected an army and invaded his dominions, he led his troops to oppose them. Having notice of his march as he approached, they raised the siege and advanced to meet him. The confederates agreed that if the battle was fought in the daytime, the Afghans would not flee, out of regard for their reputation with their countrymen; but that if the attack was made by night, when one man could not see another, each chief would shift for himself. Resolving, therefore, to attempt a night surprise, they mounted to proceed against the enemy, who were six leagues distant. Twice they mounted their horses at noon and continued mounted till the second or third watch of the night, without going either backwards or forwards, and without being able to come to any resolution or to agree among themselves. The third time they set out for their surprise when only one watch of the night remained. Their plan was merely for the party to set fire to the tents and pavilions, and to attempt nothing further. They

INDIAN TENTS AND PAVILIONS.

accordingly advanced and set fire to the tents during the last watch of the night, at the same time shouting the war-cry. Jalal Khan Jaghat, and several other amirs, came over and acknowledged Ala-ad-din Khan. Sultan Ibrahim, attended by a body of men composed of his own tribe and family, did not move from the royal pavilion, but continued steady in the same place till morning.

By this time the troops who accompanied Ala-ad-din Khan were dispersed, being busy plundering and pillaging, whereupon Sultan Ibrahim's troops perceived that the enemy were not in great force, and immediately moved forward from the station which they had kept, though very few in number, with only a single elephant. No sooner had the elephant come up, however, than Ala-ad-din Khan's men took to flight without attempting to keep their ground. In the course of his flight Ala-ad-din Khan crossed over to the Doab side of the river, and again recrossed it toward Panipat, where he contrived by a stratagem to get three or four *lacs* (£750 or £1000) from Mian Sulaiman, and went on his way. Isma'il Jilwani, Babin, and Jalal Khan, the eldest son of Ala-ad-din Khan, now left him and betook themselves to the Doab. A small part of the army which Ala-ad-din Khan had collected, such as Saif-ad-din, Darya Khan, Mahmud Khan, Khan-Jahan, Shaikh Jamal Farmuli, and some others deserted before the battle and joined Ibrahim.

After passing Sirhind, Ala-ad-din Khan, Dilawar Khan, and Haji Khan heard of my approach, and that I had taken Milwat; whereupon Dilawar Khan, who had always been attached to my interests and had been detained three or four months in prison on my account, left the others, and coming by way of Sultanpur and Kochi, waited upon me in the neighbourhood of Milwat, three or four days after the reduction of that town. After crossing the Sutlaj, Ala-ad-din Khan and Haji Khan at length reached Kinkuta, a strong castle in the hills between Dun and the plain, where they prepared to defend themselves. One of my detachments, consisting of Afghans and Hazaras, chanced to come up and blockade them, so that only the approach of night prevented them from taking the castle, strong as it was. These noblemen then attempted to escape, but some of their horses fell in the gateway, and they

MODERN TRIBESMEN OF AFGHANISTAN.

could not get out. Some elephants that were along with them were urged forward, and trampled and killed a number of the horses. Although unable to escape on horseback, Ala-ad-din Khan and his followers left the place during a dark night on foot, and after incredible sufferings joined Ghazi Khan, who, in the course of his flight, had directed his course toward the hills, finding that he could not get refuge in Milwat. Ghazi Khan did not give Ala-ad-din Khan a very friendly reception, and this induced him to wait on me below Dun in the neighbourhood of Palhur, where he came and tendered me his allegiance. While I was at Sialkot, some of the troops that I had left in Lahore arrived to inform me that they would all join me by morning.

Next morning I continued my march and halted at Parsarur, where Mohammad Ali Jang-jang, Khwaja Husain, and some others came and waited on me. As the enemy's camp was on the banks of the Ravi toward Lahore, I sent Bujkah with his party to reconnoitre and bring in intelligence. About the end of the third watch of the night, they returned with information that the enemy had fled in consternation as soon as they heard of my detachment's approach, every man shifting for himself.

On the following morning, leaving Shah Mir Husain and some other officers to guard the camp and baggage, I left them and pushed on with all possible speed. About the middle of afternoon prayers we halted at Kalanur, midway between the Ravi and the Bias, where Mohammad Sultan Mirza, Adil Sultan, and the other amirs came and waited on me.

Marching before daybreak from Kalanur, we discovered certain traces on the road that Ghazi Khan and the fugitives were not far off. Mohammadi and Ahmadi, with several of the nobles about my person, whom I had recently promoted at Kabul, were detached to pursue the fugitives without halting. Their orders were to overtake the flying enemy if possible; but if not, to guard every approach and issue of the fort of Milwat with such care that the garrison might not be able to effect their escape. Ghazi Khan was my principal object in these instructions.

After sending this detachment forward, we crossed the river Bias opposite to Kanwahin, and halted there. From thence, after three marches, we encamped in the mouth of the valley in which the fort of Milwat lies. The nobles, who had arrived before us, as well as the amirs of Hindustan, were directed to encamp and lay siege to the fort. Isma'il Khan, who was Daulat Khan's grandson (being the son of Ali Khan, Daulat Khan's eldest son), and who had arrived in our quarters, was sent into the fort to offer terms of capitulation, bearing a message in which we mingled promises and threats. On Friday I made the camp advance and take ground half a league nearer. I myself went out, reconnoitred the fort, and assigned their respective stations to the right and left wings and to the centre, after which I returned to the camp.

Daulat Khan now sent a messenger to inform me that Ghazi Khan had escaped and fled to the hills; but that if I would excuse his own offences, he would come as a slave and deliver up the place. I therefore sent Khwaja Mir Miran to confirm him in his resolution and to bring him back. To expose the rudeness and stupidity of the old man, I directed Mir Miran to take care that Daulat Khan should come out with the same two swords hung round his neck which he had girded at his side to meet me in combat.

Although matters had gone this length, he still contrived frivolous pretexts for delay, but was at length brought out. I ordered the two swords to be taken from his neck. When he came to offer me obeisance, he affected delays in bowing; I directed them to push his leg and make him bow. I then made him sit down before me and desired a man who understood the Hindustani language to explain to him what I said, sentence by sentence, in order to reassure him; and to tell him these words: "I called you Father; I showed you more respect and reverence than you could have desired or expected. The countries held by Tatar Khan, to the amount of three crores (thirty million rupees), I bestowed on you. What evil have I ever done you, that you should come against me thus?" Finally, after further rebukes, it was settled that he and his family should retain their authority in their own tribes, and possession of their villages, but that all the rest of their property should be sequestrated.

Abd-al-Aziz and several other nobles were now directed to enter the fort and to take possession of their treasures and all their property. I examined Ghazi Khan's library, and found in it a number of valuable books, including a number of theological works, but I did not, on the whole, find so many books of value as, from their appearance, I had expected.

I staid in the fort all night, and next morning

returned to the camp. We had been mistaken in imagining that Ghazi Khan was in the fort. The traitorous coward had escaped to the hills with a small number of followers, leaving his father, his elder and younger brothers, his mother, and his elder and younger sisters in Milwat, which I gave to Mohammad Ali Jang-jang, who left his brother Arghun in the place with a body of troops. We then advanced one league from the station at the gorge of Milwat and halted in a valley; and marching thence, and passing the small hills of Ab-kand by Milwat, we reached Dun, which denotes "dale" in the language of Hindustan.

As we were unable to get any certain intelligence of Ghazi Khan, I sent Tardika and Barim Deo Malinhat, with orders to pursue the fugitive wherever he might go, to engage him, and to bring him back a prisoner. In the small hills lying around Dun there are some wonderfully strong castles. To the northeast is a castle called Kutila, which is surrounded by a perpendicular rock seventy or eighty *gaz* (between 140 and 160 feet) in height. At its chief gate, for the space of about seven or eight *gaz* (fourteen or sixteen feet), there is a place, perhaps ten or twelve *gaz* (twenty or twenty-four feet) in width, that permits a drawbridge to be thrown across. The bridge is composed of two long planks, by which their horses and flocks pass out and in. This was one of the forts of the hill country, which Ghazi Khan had put into a state of defence and garrisoned. The detachment that had been sent ahead attacked the place vigorously, and had nearly taken it when night came on. The garrison then abandoned the castle and fled.

After sending a detachment in pursuit of Ghazi Khan, I placed my foot in the stirrup of resolution and my hand on the reins of confidence in God, and proceeded against Sultan Ibrahim, the son of Sultan Iskandar, the son of Sultan Bahlol Lodi Afghan, who then held the throne of Delhi and the dominions of Hindustan with a field-army said to amount to one hundred thousand men, and with nearly one thousand elephants, including those of his amirs.

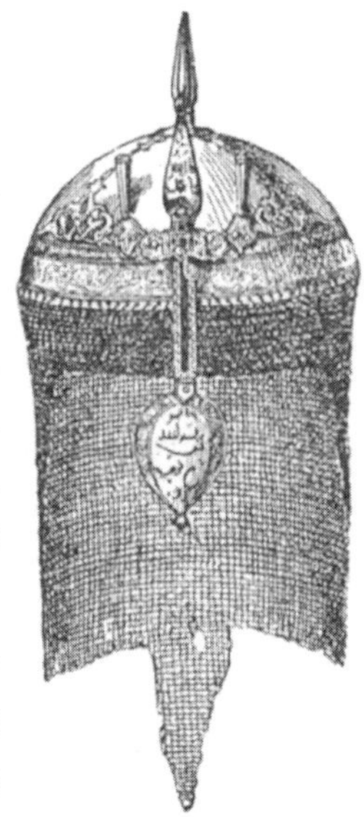

A CHAIN-WORK HELMET.

The detachment which had proceeded to Milwat advanced against Harur, Kahlur, and the forts in that part of the country, among which, from the natural strength of the ground, no enemy had penetrated for a long time. My troops took all these strongholds and returned and joined me, after having plundered the inhabitants of the district. It was at this time that Ala-ad-din Khan, being reduced to great distress, came naked and on foot to meet me. I directed several noblemen of my court to go out to receive him, and also sent him some horses. He waited upon me in this neighbourhood and made his submission.

After marching from Dun we came to Rupur, but

while we stayed there it rained incessantly and was so extremely cold that many of the starving and hungry Hindustanis died. After marching from Rupur, we halted at Karil opposite Sirhind, and there a Hindustani presented himself, assuming the style of an ambassador from Sultan Ibrahim. Though he had no letters or credentials, yet, as he requested that one of my people might accompany him back as my ambassador, I sent a Sawadi Tinkatar along with him. These poor men had no sooner arrived in Ibrahim's camp than he ordered them both to be thrown into prison, but the very day that we defeated Ibrahim, the Sawadi was set at liberty and waited on me.

After two marches more we halted on the banks of the stream of Banur and Sanur, which is a running water, of which there are few in Hindustan, except large rivers. They call it the stream of Kagar, and Chitor stands on its banks. At this station we had information that Sultan Ibrahim, who was on this side of Delhi, was advancing, and that Hamid Khan Khasah-khail, the military collector of revenue for the province of Hisar-Firozah, had also advanced ten or fifteen leagues toward us, with the army of Hisar-Firozah and of the neighbouring districts. I sent Kittah Beg toward Ibrahim's camp to procure intelligence, and despatched Mumin Atkah toward the army of Hisar-Firozah to get information of its movements.

On Sunday, the thirteenth of Jumada-l-awwal, I had marched from Ambala and had halted on the margin of a tank, when Mumin Atkah and Kittah Beg both returned on the same day. I gave the command of the whole right wing to Humayun and other generals, and the next morning, Monday, the fourteenth, he set out with a light force to surprise Hamid Khan, sending as an advance-guard a hundred or a hundred and fifty select men. On coming near the enemy, this detachment went close up to them, hung upon their flanks, and had one or two encounters until the main body of the troops of Humayun appeared in sight. No sooner were these perceived than the enemy took to flight. Our troops brought down one or two hundred men, cut off the heads of half of them, and brought the other half alive into the camp, together with seven or eight elephants. On Monday, the twenty-first, Humayun reached the camp, which was still at the same station, with one hundred prisoners and seven or eight elephants, and waited on me. I ordered Ustad Ali Kuli and the matchlockmen to shoot all the prisoners as an example. This was Humayun's first expedition, and the first service he had seen, so that I accounted his success a very good omen. Some light troops followed the fugitives, took Hisar-Firozah the moment they reached it, and returned after plundering it. Hisar-Firozah, which, with its dependencies and subordinate districts, yielded ten million rupees, I bestowed on Humayun, and also presented him with an equal sum of money.

Marching from that station, we reached Shahabad, where I halted several days and sent envoys toward Sultan Ibrahim's camp to procure intelligence. In this station, on Monday, the twenty-eighth of Jumada-l-awwal, we began to receive repeated information from Ibrahim's camp that he was advancing slowly by a league or two at a time, and halting two or three days at each station. I, for my part, likewise moved to meet him, and after the second march from Shahabad, encamped on the banks of the Jumna, opposite Sirsawah. Haidar Kuli, a servant of Khwaja Kilan, was sent out to procure intelligence, after which I crossed the Jumna by a ford and went to see Sirsawah.

From this station we held down the river for two marches, keeping close along its banks, when Haidar Kuli returned, bringing information that Daud Khan and Haitim Khan had been sent across the river into the Doab with six or seven thousand horse and had encamped three or four leagues in advance of Ibrahim's position on the road toward us. On Sunday, the eighteenth of Jumada-l-akhir, I despatched Chin Timur Sultan against this column, together with the whole of the left wing commanded by Sultan Junaid, as well as part of the centre under Yunas Ali, directing them to advance rapidly and to take the enemy by surprise. Next morning, about the time of early prayers, they came upon the enemy, who put themselves in some kind of order and marched out to meet them; but our troops had no sooner come up than the enemy fled, and were followed in close pursuit and slaughtered all the way to the limits of Ibrahim's camp. The detachment captured Haitim Khan, Daud Khan's eldest brother, and one of the generals, as well as seventy or eighty prisoners and six or eight elephants, all of which they brought in when they waited on me. Several of the

A PROCESSION OF ELEPHANTS.

prisoners were put to death to strike terror into the enemy.

Marching thence, I arranged the whole army in order of battle, with right and left wing and centre, and after reviewing it, performed the *vīm*. The custom of the *vīm* is that after the whole army is mounted, the commander takes a bow or whip in his hand and guesses at the number of the army, declaring that the troops may be so many. The number that I guessed was greater than the army turned out to be.

At this station I directed that, according to the Ottoman custom, the gun-carriages should be joined together with twisted bull-hides, as with chains. Between every two gun-carriages were six or seven breastworks, behind which the matchlockmen stood and discharged their pieces. I halted five or six days in this camp for the purpose of getting this apparatus arranged. After every part of it was in order and ready, I convened all the amirs and men of any experience and knowledge, and held a general council. It was settled that as Panipat was a considerable city, it would cover one of our flanks by its buildings and houses, while we might fortify our front by covered defences and cannon, behind which the matchlockmen and infantry should be placed. With this resolution we broke up camp, and we reached Panipat in two marches on Thursday, the thirtieth of Jumada-l-akhir. On our right were the town and suburbs, and in front I placed the guns and covered defences which I had prepared. On the left, and at various other points, we drew ditches and made ramparts of the boughs of trees, but at the distance of every bow-shot, space was left for a hundred or a hundred and fifty men to make a sortie. Many of the troops were in great tremor and alarm. Now, although trepidation and fear are always unbecoming, since whatsoever Almighty God has decreed from all eternity cannot be reversed, I could not wholly blame them, for they had come two or three months' journey from their own country and were about to battle with strange people, whose very language they did not understand, and who did not understand ours.

The army of the enemy was estimated at one hundred thousand, while the elephants of the emperor and of his officers were said to be nearly one thousand. He possessed the accumulated treasures of his father and grandfather ready for use in current coin. In situations similar to that in which the enemy now were, it is customary in Hindustan to expend sums of money in collecting troops who engage to serve for hire. Had Ibrahim chosen to adopt this plan, he might have engaged one or two hundred thousand more troops, but he had not the heart to satisfy even his own army, and would not part with any of his treasure. Indeed, how was it possible that he should satisfy his troops, when he was himself miserly to the last degree, and avaricious beyond measure in accumulating pelf? He was a young man of no experience; he was negligent in all his movements; he marched without order, retired or halted without plan, and engaged in battle without foresight. While the troops were fortifying their position in Panipat and its vicinity with guns, branches of trees, and ditches, Mohammad Sarban said to me: "You have fortified our ground in such a way that it is impossible that he should ever think of coming here." I answered: "You judge him by the khans and Sultans of the Uzbegs, but you must not estimate our present enemies by those who were then opposed to us, for these opponents have not even the sense to know when to advance and when to retreat." God brought everything to pass favourably, and all happened as I foretold.

During the seven or eight days that we remained in Panipat, a very small party of my men advanced close to the enemy's encampment with its vastly superior force and discharged arrows at them, but, notwithstanding this, they would not move or make any attempt at a sortie. Finally, induced by the persuasion of some Hindustani amirs in my interest, I sent Mahdi Khwaja and other officers with four or five thousand men to make a night attack. They did not assemble properly in the first instance, and as they marched out in confusion, they did not get on well. Even when dawn came on, they continued to linger near the enemy's camp till it was broad daylight, whereupon our opponents beat their kettle-drums, got their elephants ready, and marched out against them. Although our people did not effect anything, yet they returned safe and sound without the loss of a man, despite the multitude of troops that hung upon them in their retreat. Mohammad Ali Jang-jang was wounded with an arrow, and though the wound was not mortal, it prevented him from taking his place in the day of battle.

On learning what had occurred, I immediately sent Humayun and his division a league or so in advance to cover their retreat, while I myself, remaining with the army, drew it out and made ready for action. The party which had marched to surprise the enemy fell in with Humayun and returned with him, after which, as none of the enemy came near us, I drew off the army and led it back to the camp. In the course of the night we had a false alarm, and the call to arms and the uproar continued for almost an hour. Such of the troops as had never before witnessed an alarm of the kind were in great confusion and dismay, but in a short time the disorder subsided.

By the time of early morning prayers, when the light was such that you could distinguish one object from another, notice was brought from the outposts that the enemy were advancing, drawn up in order of battle. We too immediately put on our helmets and armour, and mounted. The right division was led by Humayun and the left by Mohammad Sultan Mirza; the right of the centre was commanded by Chin Timur Sultan and the left of the centre by Khalifa; the vanguard was led by Khusru Gokultash; and Abd-al-Aziz, the master of horse, had command of the reserves. On the flank of the right division I stationed Wali Kizil and others with their Moghuls, to act as a flanking party, and on the extreme left I placed Kara Kuzi and his troops to form the flankers, with instructions that as soon as the enemy approached sufficiently near, they should make a circuit and come round upon their rear.

When the enemy first came in sight, they seemed to direct their chief attack against the right wing, and I therefore detached Abd-al-Aziz, who was stationed with the reserves, to reinforce that division. From the time Sultan Ibrahim's army appeared in sight, it did not halt, but advanced upon us at a quick pace. When the enemy came closer and found my troops drawn up in the order and with the defences already mentioned, they stopped and stood for awhile as if considering, "Shall we halt or not? shall we advance or not?" They could not halt, and yet were unable to advance with the same speed as before. I sent orders to the troops stationed as flankers on the extremes of the right and left divisions to wheel round the enemy's flank with all possible speed and instantly to attack them in the rear, while the right and left divisions were ordered to charge. The flankers accordingly wheeled on the rear of the enemy and began to discharge arrows at them.

Mahdi Khwaja came up before the rest of the left wing, and a body of men with one elephant advanced to meet him. My troops gave them some sharp discharges of arrows, and the enemy's division was at last driven back. I despatched Ahmadi Parwanchi from the main body to the assistance of the left division, but the battle was likewise obstinate on the right, and I accordingly ordered Mohammadi Gokultash to advance in front of the centre and engage. Ustad Ali Kuli also discharged his foreign guns many times in front of the line to good purpose, while Mustafa, the cannoneer, on the left of the centre, managed his artillery with excellent effect.

The right and left divisions, as well as the centre and flankers, having surrounded the enemy and taken them in the rear, were now engaged in hot conflict and were pouring discharges of arrows on them. The

THE GREAT HOWITZER CALLED MALIK-I MAIDAN.

enemy made one or two very poor attacks on our right and left divisions, but my troops, making use of their bows, plied them with arrows and drove them in upon their centre. The troops on the right and left of their centre, being huddled together in one place, threw Ibrahim's army into such confusion that it had no way to flee and was equally unable to advance. The sun had mounted spear-high when the battle began, and the combat lasted till mid-day, when the enemy were completely broken and routed, and my friends victorious and exulting. By the grace and mercy of Almighty God this arduous undertaking was rendered easy for me, and this mighty army was laid in the dust in the space of half a day.

Five or six thousand men were discovered lying slain in one spot near Ibrahim. We reckoned that the number killed in different parts of the field of battle amounted to fifteen or sixteen thousand men. On reaching Agra, we found from the accounts of the natives of Hindustan that forty or fifty thousand men had fallen in this field. After routing the enemy, we continued the pursuit, slaughtering them and taking them prisoners. Those who were ahead began to bring in the amirs and Afghans as captives, and also brought in a very great number of elephants with their drivers, offering them to me as a gift. Having pursued the enemy to some distance, and supposing that Ibrahim had escaped from the battle, I placed Kismai Mirza at the head of a party of my immediate adherents, and ordered him to follow in close pursuit as far as Agra. Having passed through the middle of Ibrahim's camp and visited his pavilions and accommodations, we encamped on the banks of the Kalini.

It was now afternoon prayers, when Tahir Tabari, the younger brother of Khalifa, found Ibrahim lying dead amid a host of slain, cut off his head, and brought it in.

That very day I directed Humayun Mirza to set out without baggage or encumbrances, and to proceed with all possible expedition to occupy Agra and take possession of the treasuries. At the same time I ordered Mahdi Khwaja and others to leave their baggage, to push on by forced marches, and to enter the fort of Delhi and seize the treasuries.

Next morning we broke up camp, and after proceeding about a league, we halted on the banks of the Jumna to refresh our horses. On Tuesday, after two other marches, I visited the mausoleum of Nizam-ad-din Auliya, four or five miles south of Delhi, and at the end of the third march I encamped on the banks of the Jumna near the city. On that same night I circumambulated the tomb of Khwaja Kutb-ad-din and visited the tombs and palaces of Sultan Ghiyas-ad-din Balban and Sultan Ala-ad-din Khalji, also viewing the minaret of the latter, as well as the Shams tank, the royal tank, and the tombs and gardens of Sultan Bahlol and Sultan Sikandar, after which I returned to the camp and went on board of a boat, where we drank arak. I bestowed the office of military collector of Delhi on Wali Kizil, and also made Dost governor of Delhi, directing that the various treasuries be sealed and given into their charge.

On Thursday we moved thence and halted hard by Taghlakabad, on the banks of the Jumna south of Delhi. On Friday we continued to halt in the same station, and Maulana Mahmud, Shaikh Zain, and some others went into Delhi to Friday prayers. There they read the public prayer in my name and distributed some money among the dervishes and beggars, after which they returned. On Saturday we again set out, and proceeded, march after march, toward Agra.

On Friday, the twenty-second of Rajab, I halted at the palace of Sulaiman Farmuli in the suburbs of Agra. As this position was very far from the fort, I moved next morning and took up my quarters at the palace of Jalal Khan Jaghat. The people of the fort had put off Humayun, who arrived before me, with excuses; and he for his part, considering that they were under no sort of control, had taken a position which commanded every exit from the place, wishing to prevent them from plundering the treasure.

Vikramajit, a Hindu, whose family had governed that country for upwards of one hundred years, was raja of Gwalior. Sikandar had remained several years in Agra, seeking to take Gwalior, and afterward, in the reign of Ibrahim, Azim Humayun Sirwan had invested it for some time, attacking it repeatedly and finally succeeding in gaining it by treaty, Shamsabad being given as an indemnification. In the battle in which Ibrahim was defeated, Vikramajit was killed, but his family, as well as the heads of his clan, were in Agra at this moment. When Humayun arrived, Vikramajit's people attempted to escape, but were taken by the parties which Humayun had placed upon the watch, and put in custody. Humayun did not permit them to be plundered. Of their own free will they offered Humayun a gift of jewels and precious stones, including a famous diamond which had been acquired by Sultan Ala-ad-din, and which is so valuable that a judge of diamonds valued it at half of the daily expense of the whole world. On my arrival Humayun presented it to me as a gift, and I gave it back to him as a present.[1]

A district of the value of seven hundred thousand rupees was bestowed on Ibrahim's mother, and districts were also given to each of her amirs. She was con-

TOMB OF BABAR AT KABUL.

ducted with all her effects to a palace about a league below Agra, which was assigned her as her residence. On Thursday, the twenty-eighth of Rajab, I entered Agra about the hour of afternoon prayers and took up my residence in Sultan Ibrahim's palace.

In 925 A. H. (1519 A. D.) I again collected an army, and having taken the fort of Bajaur by storm in two or three hours, I put all the garrison to the sword. I next advanced into Bahrah, where I prevented all

[1] This diamond is thought to have been, perhaps, the famous Koh-i-nur.

marauding and plunder, imposed a contribution on the inhabitants, and levied upon it four hundred thousand Shah-rukhis (almost £20,000 sterling) in money and goods. I then divided the proceeds among the troops who were in my service, after which I returned to my capital, Kabul.

From that time till the year 932 A. H. (1526 A. D.), I devoted myself particularly to the affairs of Hindustan, and in the space of these seven or eight years entered it five times at the head of an army. The fifth time God Most High, in His grace and mercy, cast down and defeated an enemy so mighty as Sultan Ibrahim, and made me the master and conqueror of the powerful empire of Hindustan.'

Babar then proceeds to give a lengthy account of his several campaigns in India during the course of the following years. His memoirs terminate abruptly, the last event chronicled being the third of Muharram, 936 A. H. (March, 1530 A. D.), and his early death at Agra on December 26, 1530, at the age of forty-eight, may account for the absence of further records.

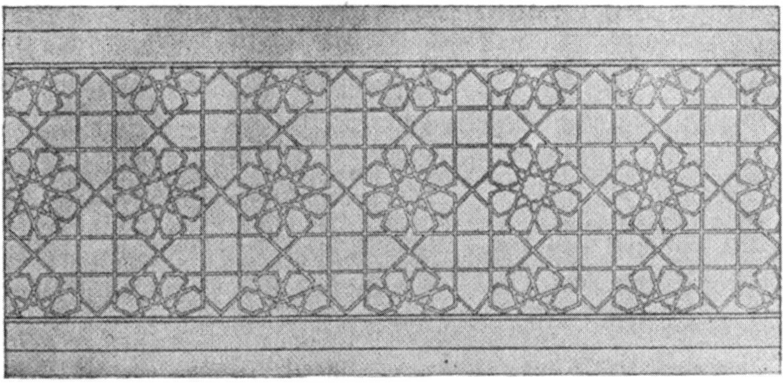

AN INDIAN DECORATIVE DESIGN.

CHAPTER XI

BEGINNING OF THE REIGN OF THE EMPEROR HUMAYUN

1530 - 1556 A. D.

AN interesting account of the opening of Humayun's reign has been preserved from the pen of the historian Khwandamir, who died four years after his sovereign's accession to the throne. The general historical work of this author is well known, and it is worth observing, with Dowson, that in his old age Khwandamir became quite a courtier, abandoning the rôle of the true historian to become a royal panegyrist. A specimen of the Humayun Namah, his last work, will sufficiently illustrate this fact by its somewhat Oriental style. It is chosen here particularly because it gives a picture of court life rather than a description of endless wars and massacres, which are all too common in the history of Mohammedan India.

'When this humble and insignificant slave Ghiyas-ad-din ibn Humam-ad-din, whom men commonly call Khwandamir—may God aid him to surmount all difficulties!—obtained the honour of meeting the great emperor Humayun and the rays of royal kindness shone on the surface of his hopes and circumstances, he conceived the desire and entertained the idea in his mind that he would describe, as a memorial for future days, some of the works and inventions of this monarch; for the histories of kings, by means of the black water of ink, which has the effect of the water of life, are immortalized, and the great names and writings of clever authors, by virtue of their praises of celebrated kings, are stamped on the page of time. For instance, the excellencies of Mahmud were described by Utbi and Unsuri, and the poems of Mu'izzi and Anwari celebrated the character of Sanjar.

> "Who would remember Hakim Anwari,
> Had he not spoken about Sanjar and his works?
> Because Utbi conferred praises on Mahmud,
> Therefore he obtained the object of his desire.
> Sharaf was celebrated in the world
> Because he wrote the eulogy of Timur Gurgan."

Although the compiler of this book withheld his tongue from commencing the history of this renowned monarch's exploits and deeds, since he had but little knowledge and was endowed with no ability, and did not allow the pen which possesses two tongues to describe the character of this most prosperous king, yet he always entertained that desire in his faithful heart and the intention never forsook his mind. On an eve which was full of light, this insignificant creature, the author, having obtained the honour of being present in his Majesty's court at Gwalior, was commanded to sit down, and the fingers of the generosity of that sun of the heaven of glory opened the gates of kindness to him, and the tongue of that king of kings, who was as dignified as Alexander the Great, pronounced these pleasing words: "It seems proper and desirable that the inventions of my auspicious mind and the improvements of my enlightened understanding should be arranged in a series and written down, so that in future ages the light of these happy works may shine among the people of countries far and near." For this cause, the writer, who was wishing for a long time that such a mandate might come to pass, engaged, like his pen, in writing these very interesting subjects; and having commenced to mention the wonderful inventions, he imparted eloquence to the pen which possesses two tongues. He hopes that, through the favour of God on high, these pages, which contain useful matters, may meet the approbation of the most learned personages of the high court, and that they may view these lines of the book of eloquence with the eye of acceptance, and overlook the mistakes which may have been committed therein by the deficient tongue of the pen.

In the beginning of Jumada-l-awwal, 937 A. H. (Dec., 1530 A. D.), when Zahir-ad-din Mohammad Babar, the king who was as dignified as Solomon, whose seat is now in paradise, left the throne of this world for the eternal heaven, the celestial herald of the Supreme Lord raised the pleasing cry, "We have made thee king on earth," to the ears of this rightful prince Humayun, and the hand of the kindness of the Creator of souls and substances put the happy robe of royalty on the person of this able monarch, the Conqueror of the World.

> "The hope which was evoked by prosperity is now realized;
> The desire which the world entertained is satisfied."

On Friday, the ninth of the same month, public prayer was read in the name and title of this noble king in the Jami' Masjid at Agra, and the noise of congratulations which arose from the crowd of the people reached beyond the heavens.

Among other wonderful events which happened to our great prince, one was that in the year in which the late Emperor Babar marched from Kabul toward Kandahar, he left Humayun, this sun of the heaven of royalty and power, in charge of the duties of government. One day the latter mounted his horse and went to ride in the forests, hills, gardens, and meadows. On the road he wished to take an omen, and having called Masih-ad-din Ruh-Allah, who was his tutor, he told him it had just entered his mind that he would ask the names of the first three persons he met and take an omen from them. Masih-ad-din said it would be enough if he asked only one man's name, but the king was firm in his resolution.

After they had gone a little distance, they saw a man about forty years of age; and when they asked him his name, he replied, "Murad Khwaja." After him another man, driving an ass loaded with wood, came

BABAR, HUMAYUN, AKBAR, AND JAHANGIR.

before them; and when they inquired of him his name, he said, "Daulat Khwaja." On this it passed from the secret-telling tongue of the king that if the name of the third person who should happen to meet them should be Sa'adat Khwaja, it might be considered a very curious accident, and the star of success, according to the omen, would rise from the horizon of prosperity. At this moment a boy who was leading cattle to graze came in sight; and when they asked him what was his name, he answered, "Sa'adat Khwaja." This of course excited great wonder and surprise in all who accompanied the king, and they were all sure that this prosperous prince would soon, by divine assistance, attain the highest pitch of fortune and glory, and that the hand of the favour of God would open to him the gates of success in all his sacred and worldly hopes.

When the auspicious throne of royalty was filled by this brave and dignified monarch, all the officers of the state, as well as the inhabitants of the kingdom, were divided into three classes. The brothers and relatives of the king, the nobles and ministers, and the military men were called *Ahl-i Daulat* (officers of the state), since it is evident that no degree of wealth and prosperity can be attained without the assistance of this class of brave subjects; and no one can obtain throne or power without the aid of warriors and heroes.

> "Kings, with the assistance of their armies,
> Place their feet upon the throne of empires.
> He alone can obtain wealth and rank
> Who is assisted by his army."

The divines, the holy men, the Sayyids, the scholars, the officers of the law, the scientists, and the poets, besides other great and respectable men, formed the second class and were denominated *Ahl-i Sa'ādat* (good men), since respect, obedience, and honour paid them, as well as association with them, secure eternal prosperity and enable men to rise to exalted rank and dignity.

> "Virtue is the gift of God;
> It is not in the power of the mighty man to obtain it;
> If thou wouldst obtain fortune,
> Associate thou with virtuous men."

Those who possessed beauty and elegance, those who were young and most lovely, and those who were clever musicians and sweet singers composed the third class, and the appellation of *Ahl-i Murād* (people of pleasure) was conferred upon them, because most people take great delight in the company of such young men of rosy cheeks and sweet voices, and are pleased by hearing their songs and the delightsome sound of musical instruments, such as the harp, the sackbut, and the lute.

> "The hope of the heart of lovers
> Is never realized but when they meet them of rose-hued cheeks;
> He who delighteth in songs and music
> Hath the gates of happiness opened for himself."

The wise king also divided the days of the week according to a similar classification, and appointed one day for each of these three classes. Thus, Saturdays and Thursdays were fixed for pious men, and visits were received on those days from literary and religious folk. On these two days the tree of the hope of this estimable body of the people produced the fruit of prosperity, since they obtained audience in the court, which was like to Paradise. The reason why these two days were appointed for this class was that Saturday is ascribed to Saturn, who is the protector of good and religious men and persons of old families; while Thursday is appropriated to Jupiter, who is the preserver of Sayyids, scholars, and strict followers of the Mohammedan law.

Sundays and Tuesdays were fixed for the state officers, and on these days all the government business and duties connected with the management of the country were discharged. On these days also the king, the destroyer of enemies, sat in the public court, and all the nobles and plebeians were able to obtain the honour of seeing him. The advantage in appointing these two days for opening the court and attending to the state affairs was that Sunday belongs to the Sun, on whom, by the will of God, depends the fate of all rulers and kings; and Tuesday is the day of Mars, who is the patron of warriors and heroes. Hence it is evident that it was most seemly for Humayun to adorn the throne of sovereignty in the public court by his royal sessions and to devote himself to the discharge of government duties on those two days.

Among other customs which were introduced by this just and generous king, one was that when he adorned the throne of royalty, drums were beaten to inform the people, who straightway flocked to see him; and when he left the court, the gunners fired guns to let the people know that they might retire. On those days, moreover, the keeper of the wardrobe used to fetch some suits of fine apparel, while the treasurer brought several purses of money, and they placed them in the court in order that rewards and robes might be given to any one from them, and that no delay should take place. In addition to all this, a number of heroes of most martial bearing donned coats of mail and took blood-drinking swords in their hands, standing before the throne to seize and punish those who might be proved guilty.

Mondays and Wednesdays were allotted for pleasure parties, and on these days some of the emperor's boon companions and chosen friends were convened and a band of musicians and singers was called. The cause of appointing these days for this purpose was that Monday is the day of the Moon and Wednesday of Mercury; and it was, therefore, suitable that on these days he should keep company with young men beautiful as the moon and hear sweet songs and delightful music. On Fridays, as the Arabic name of the day, *jum'a*, or "assembly," implies, he called together all the assemblies and sat with them as long as he could find leisure from his other duties.

Another invention of this king was that he made three arrows of gold and called each after the name of one of the three classes mentioned above. Each of these arrows was given to one of the leading men of the respective classes and he was commissioned to manage all the affairs of the class to which he belonged.

As long as he conducted his duties with such care as to ensure the pleasure of God and the satisfaction of the king, he was maintained in his trust. But when he was intoxicated by the wine of arrogance and pride, or when his foresight was obscured by the dimness of negligence and he did not look after his business, but

THE TOMB OF HUMAYUN AT OLD DELHI.

unfortunately thought only of collecting riches, then the arrow of his wishes failed to hit the target of success, and the pen of destiny removed him from office for his insolent deeds.

Among the customs introduced by this king, one was that of the distribution of arrows which marked the distinction of ranks and stations among the servants of the throne. According to the different standards of gold, the ranks of all the people composing the three classes were divided into twelve orders or arrows, and every one received a grade and rank suitable to himself. The twelfth arrow, which was made of the purest gold, was put in the auspicious quiver of this powerful king and no one dared to touch it; the eleventh arrow belonged to his Majesty's kinsmen and brethren and to all who were in the government employ; the tenth, to the great divines, Sayyids, scholars, and holy men; the ninth, to the great nobles; the eighth, to the courtiers and some of the king's personal attendants; the seventh, to the attendants in general; the sixth, to the harems and to the female attendants; the fifth, to young maid-servants; the fourth, to the treasurers and stewards; the third, to the soldiers; the second, to the menial servants; and the first, to the palace guards, camel-drivers, and the like. Each of these arrows or orders had three grades: the highest, the middle, and the lowest.

Another of the arrangements of this king was that he divided all the affairs of government into four departments according to the number of the four elements, naming them respectively *Ātashī* ("fiery"), *Hawāī* ("airy"), *Ābī* ("watery"), and *Khākī* ("earthy"); and appointed four ministers to conduct the business of these departments. The department which comprised artillery and the making of arms, weapons of war, various sorts of engines, and other such things as require the assistance of fire, was called *Ātashī*; and the superintendence of this department was placed under Khwaja Amid-al-Mulk, the fire of whose solicitude inflamed the ovens of the hearts of those who were employed on these works.

The duties connected with the wardrobe, kitchen, stable, and other great and important offices belonged to the *Hawāī* department, and the care of them was entrusted to Khwaja Lutf-Allah. The digging of canals and all the works which related to water and rivers were comprised in the *Ābī* department, of which Khwaja Hasam was superintendent. Agriculture, building, the administration of government lands, and some household affairs formed a department which was called *Khākī*, and this was placed under the management of Khwaja Jalal-ad-din Mirza Beg. Formerly, one of the nobles was ordered to look after each department. Amir Nasir Kuli, for instance, supervised the fire department and he always used to put on red clothes. After his death, Mir Nihal, that cypress of the garden of dignity and grandeur, was appointed to the same duty; but in the days when these pages were written, the supervision of all four departments was entrusted to that most learned man, Amir Wais Mohammad.

Another great work of this just and generous king was the city of Dinpanah, a haven of rest for holy men. In the month of Sha'ban, 939 A. H. (1533 A. D.), when the fort of Gwalior became an object of envy to the high revolving heavens because of the royal presence, the great king one night ascended the imperial throne, and having ordered all his great courtiers and learned companions to sit down, poured forth from his tongue the secrets of the pearls of these words, that it had long since been his intention to found near the capital of Delhi a great city, whose lofty ramparts should open the tongue of reproach and scorn at Khawarnak and Sawir, the palaces of Bahram Gor, and the keeper of whose bastions might claim equality with Saturn. In this same city, furthermore, a magnificent palace of seven stories should be erected, surrounded by delightful gardens and orchards; and its elegance and beauty should be such that its fame would draw mankind from the remotest corners of the world for its inspection. This city should be the abode of wise and intelligent persons and should be called Dinpanah.

Those who were present in that assembly, which resembled paradise, opened their mouths in approbation and applause of such a scheme. At the same time, the most witty and clever Shihab-ad-din Ahmad Mu'ammai discovered that the numerical value of the words *Shahr-i pādshāh Dīnpanāh* ("the royal city Dinpanah") was 940, and he said that if the city were built in that year it would be a very remarkable fact. These words were immediately brought to the notice of the king, who was greatly struck with them, as were all the officers of the high court. Everybody present began thereupon to sing the following stanza before his Majesty, who understood the excellencies of poetry so well:

"The picture which thy imagination draweth on thy mind
Hath no opposition from the hand of destiny;
What thy understanding doth write upon a leaf
Agreeth with the book of God's own Will."

The king accordingly fixed the resolution in his enlightened mind; and after he had returned from Gwalior to Agra, under the protection of the Almighty God, he turned the reins of his world-travelling horse toward the city of Delhi in the beginning of the month of Zu-l-hijja, 939 A. H. When he had reached the city, which was as beautiful as heaven, and had taken omens and religious advice, a rising ground adjacent to the banks of the stream of Jumna, about three leagues from the city, was selected for the foundation of Dinpanah.

In the middle of the month of Muharram, 940 A. H., at an hour which was prescribed by the most clever astrologers and the greatest astronomers, all the divines, Sayyids, scholars, and elders of the city of Delhi accompanied the king, who was as generous as the ocean, to the new site, where they prayed that God on high might vouchsafe to finish the happy foundation of that city and to strengthen the basis of the king's wealth. His Majesty with his holy hand first laid a brick upon the ground, after which each person from that concourse of great men placed a stone on the earth, and they all made such a crowd there that the army, the people, and the artists, masons, and labourers found neither space nor time to carry stones and mud to the spot. On the same date work was commenced in the king's own palace, and by this time, that is to say, the latter part of the month of Shawwal of the same year, the walls, bastions, ramparts, and gates of the city of Dinpanah are nearly finished.'

THE PACHISI COURT OF AKBAR AT FATHPUR-SIKRI.

CHAPTER XII

AKBAR'S RELIGIOUS VIEWS, AS DESCRIBED BY BADAUNI

Sixteenth Century A. D.

AKBAR the Great was a reformer and innovator, as has been fully shown in the preceding volume. Among the detailed accounts of his reign is a record by Abd-al-Kadir Badauni, who lived and wrote at the great emperor's court and died in 1615 A. D., ten years after his royal patron's death.

The selection here chosen from Badauni's work illustrates the well-known latitudinarianism of Akbar in religious matters and shows how little favour they met with in orthodox Mohammedan eyes like those of Badauni.

'In the year 983 A. H. (1575 A. D.), the buildings of the *Ibādat-Khānah*, or "Hall of Worship," were completed. The cause of their erection was as follows. In the course of the last few years the emperor had gained many great and remarkable victories, and his dominion had grown in extent from day to day, so that not an enemy was left in the world. He had taken a liking for the society of ascetics and the disciples of the celebrated Mu'iniyyah, and spent much time in discussing the Word of God and the sayings of the Prophet, likewise devoting his attention to problems of Sufism, science, philosophy, law, and similar matters. He passed whole nights in meditation upon God and upon the modes of addressing Him, and reverence for the great Giver filled his heart. In order to show his gratitude for his blessings, he would sit many a morning alone in prayer and mortification upon the stone bench of an old cell in a lonely spot near the palace. Thus engaged in meditation, he gathered the bliss of the early hours of dawn.

Having completed the construction of the "Hall of Worship," he made a large chamber in each of its four divisions and also finished the construction of the tank called *anūptalāo*. After prayers on Fridays he would go from the monastery of the Shaikh-al-Islam and hold a meeting in this new building. Shaikhs, learned and pious men, and a few of his own companions and attendants were the only people who were invited, and discussions were carried on upon all kinds of instructive and useful topics. Every Sabbath evening he invited Sayyids, shaikhs, theologians, and nobles, but ill feeling arose in the company about the order of precedence, so that his Majesty commanded that the nobles should sit on the east side, the Sayyids on the west, the theologians on the south, and the shaikhs on the north. His Majesty would go to these various parties from time to time and converse with them to ascertain their

GOLD COINS OF AKBAR.

thoughts. Quantities of perfume were used and large sums of money were distributed as rewards of merit and ability among the worthy people who obtained an entry through the favour of the emperor's attendants. Many fine books which had belonged to Itmad Khan Gujarati and had been acquired in the conquest of

Gujarat were placed in the royal library, but were subsequently brought out and distributed by the emperor among learned and pious men. One night the vein of the neck of the chief theologian of the age swelled up in anger and a great outcry and tumult arose. This annoyed his Majesty, and he said to the humble writer of these lines: " In future, report any one of the assembly whom you find speaking improperly, and I will have him turned out." Thereupon I said quietly to Asaf Khan: " According to this, a good many would be expelled." His Majesty asked what I had said, and when I told him, he was much amused, and repeated my saying to those who were near him.

In the year 983 A. H. (1575 - 1576 A. D.), Hakim Abu-l-Fath Gilani, Hakim Humayun (who subsequently changed his name to Humayun Kuli and finally to Hakim Humam), and Nur-ad-din, who is known as a poet under the name of Karari, arrived at the imperial court. These three were brothers and came from Gilan near the Caspian. The eldest of them obtained an extraordinary ascendency over the emperor by his subserviency, flattering him openly and adapting himself to every change in the religious ideas of his Majesty, so that, by thus pushing forward, he soon became one of Akbar's most intimate friends. Shortly afterward, Mulla Mohammad of Yazd came to court, whom they nicknamed Yazidi [" devil-worshipper "]. He attached himself to the emperor and concocted the most extravagant censures against the Companions of the Prophet (the peace of God be upon them!). He told extraordinary stories about them and tried hard to make the emperor a heretic. This man was far distanced by Birbal, Shaikh Abu-l-Fazl, and Hakim Abu-l-Fath, who turned the emperor from the Faith of the Prophet and made him a perfect sceptic of inspiration, the prophetic office, the miracles, and the law. They carried matters to such an extent that I, the author, could no longer bear them company.

About the same time, his Majesty ordered Kazi Jalal-ad-din and several other learned men to write a commentary upon the Koran, but they fell to squabbling about it. As history was read from day to day, his Majesty's faith in the Companions of the Prophet began to be shaken and the breach grew broader, so that daily prayers, fasts, and prophecies were all pronounced to be delusions opposed to sense. Reason, not revelation, was declared to be the basis of religion. Europeans also paid visits to him and he adopted some of their rationalistic tenets.

His Majesty used frequently to go to the "Hall of Worship" and converse with the theologians and shaikhs, especially on Sabbath evenings, and would sometimes pass the whole night there. The discussions always turned upon the principles and divergencies of religion, and the disputants used to exercise the sword of their tongues upon each other with such sharpness and animosity that the various sects at length took to calling each other infidels and renegades. Innovators and schismatics artfully started their doubts and sophistries, making right appear to be wrong and wrong to be right, and thus his Majesty, who had an excellent understanding and sought after the truth, but was surrounded by low irreligious persons to whom he gave his confidence, was plunged into scepticism. Doubt accumulated upon doubt and the object of his search was lost. The ramparts of the law and of the true faith were broken down, and in the course of five or six years not a single trace of Islam was left in him.

There were many reasons for this, but I shall mention only a few. Learned men of various kinds and from every country, as well as adherents of many different religions and creeds, assembled at his court and were admitted to converse with him. Night and day people did nothing but inquire and investigate. Profound points of science, the subtleties of revelation, the curiosities of history, and the wonders of nature were the continual themes of discussion. His Majesty collected the opinions of every one, especially of those who were not Mohammedans, retaining whatever he approved and rejecting everything which was against his disposition and ran counter to his wishes. From his earliest childhood to his manhood, and from his manhood to old age, his Majesty passed through the most diverse phases and through all sorts of religious practices and sectarian beliefs, and collected everything which people can find in books, with a talent of selection peculiar to him and a spirit of inquiry opposed to every Islamitic principle.

Thus a faith, based on some elementary principles, traced itself on the mirror of his heart, and as the result of all the influences which were brought to bear upon him, there grew (as gradually as the outline on a stone) the conviction in his heart that there were sensible men in all religions, and abstemious thinkers and men endowed with miraculous powers among all na-

AKBAR'S TOMB AT SIKANDRA.

tions. If some true knowledge was thus to be found everywhere, why should truth be confined to one religion or to a creed like Islam, which was comparatively new and scarcely a thousand years old? Why should one sect assert what another denies, and why should one claim a preference without having superiority conferred on itself?

Moreover, Hindu ascetics and Brahmans managed to get frequent private interviews with his Majesty.

As they surpass all other learned men in their treatises on morals and on physical and religious sciences, and since they attain a high degree of knowledge of the future and of spiritual power and human perfection, they brought proofs based on reason and testimony for the truth of their own religion and the falsity of other faiths, and inculcated their doctrines so firmly, and so skilfully represented things as quite self-evident which require consideration, that no man, by expressing his doubts, could now raise a doubt in his Majesty, even though the mountains should crumble to dust or the heavens be torn asunder.

Hence his Majesty cast aside the Islamitic revelations regarding the resurrection, the Day of Judgment, and the details connected with it, together with all ordinances based on the tradition of our Prophet. He listened to every insult which the courtiers heaped on our pure and glorious faith, which can so easily be followed; and eagerly seizing such opportunities, his words and gestures showed his satisfaction at the treatment which his original religion received at the hands of these apostates.

In 986 A. H. (1578 A. D.), the missionaries of Europe, who are termed Padris, and whose chief pontiff, called Papa (Pope), promulgates his interpretations for the use of the people and issues mandates that even kings dare not disobey, brought their Gospel to the king's notice, advanced proofs of the Trinity, affirmed the truth of the Christian faith, and spread abroad the knowledge of the religion of Jesus. The king ordered

HOUSE OF AKBAR'S HINDU MINISTER, BIRBAL, AT FATHPUR-SIKRI.

Prince Murad to learn a few lessons from the Gospel and to treat it with all due respect, while Shaikh Abu-l-Fazl was directed to translate it.

On the other hand, Birbal the Hindu tried to persuade the king that since the sun gives light to all, and ripens all grain, fruits, and products of the earth, and supports the life of mankind, that luminary should be the object of worship and veneration; that the face should be turned toward the rising, not toward the setting, sun; that man should venerate fire, water, stones, trees, and all natural objects, even down to cows and their dung; and that he should adopt the frontal mark and the Brahmanical cord. Several wise men at court confirmed what he said by representing that the sun was the chief light of the world and the benefactor of its inhabitants, that it was a friend to kings and that monarchs established periods and eras in conformity with its motions. This was the cause of the worship paid to the sun on the New Year of the Persian emperor Jalal-ad-din, and the reason why he had been induced to adopt that festival for the celebration of his accession to the throne. Every day, therefore, Akbar used to put on clothes of the particular colour which accorded with that of the regent planet of the day. He began also, at midnight and at early dawn, to mutter the spells which the Hindus taught him for the purpose of subduing the sun to his wishes. He prohibited the slaughter of cows and the eating of their flesh, because the Hindus devoutly worship them and esteem their dung as pure. He likewise declared that physicians had represented the flesh of kine to be productive of sundry kinds of sickness and to be difficult to digest.

Fire-worshippers also came from Nausari in Gujarat, proclaiming the religion of Zardusht [Zoroaster] as the true one and asserting that reverence to fire is superior to every other kind of worship. They attracted the king's regard and taught him the peculiar terms, ordinances, rites, and ceremonies of the ancient Persians; so that at last he directed that the sacred fire should be made over to the charge of Abu-l-Fazl, and that, according to the fashion of the Kings of Iran, in whose temples blazed perpetual fires, he should take care that it was never extinguished either by night or day—for that it is one of the emblems of God and one light from among the many lights of His creation.

From his earliest youth, in compliment to his wives, the daughters of the Rajas of Hind, Akbar had, within the female apartments, continued to burn the *hom*, which is a ceremony derived from fire-worship; but on the New Year festival of the twenty-fifth year after his accession (987 A. H., 1579 A. D.) he prostrated himself both before the sun and before the fire in public, and in the evening the whole court were required to rise up respectfully when the lamps and candles were lighted.

On the festival of the eighth day after the sun's entrance into Virgo in this year, Akbar came forth to the public audience-chamber with his forehead marked like a Hindu and with jewelled strings tied on his wrist by Brahmans as a blessing. The chiefs and nobles adopted the same practice in imitation of him and on that day presented pearls and precious stones suitable to their respective wealth and station. It also became the current custom to wear on the wrist the *rākhī*, an amulet formed of twisted linen rags. In defiance and contempt of the true faith, he treated as manifest and decisive every precept which was enjoined by the doctors of other religions. The teachings of Islam, on the contrary, were esteemed follies, innovations, and inventions of indigent beggars, rebels, and highway robbers; and those who professed that religion were set down as contemptible idiots. These sentiments had long been growing up in his Majesty's mind, and gradually ripened into a firm conviction of their truth.

THE EMPEROR AKBAR.

In this same year, a declaration was issued over the signatures and seals of Makhdum-al-Mulk, Shaikh Abd-an-Nabi, the chief judge, Jalal-ad-din Multani, the chief justice, Sadr-i Jahan, the chief expounder of the law, Shaikh Mubarak, the most learned man of the age, and Ghazi Khan Badakhshi, who had no rival in the science of metaphysics. The object of this document was to establish the complete superiority of the just leader over the chief lawyer and to make the judgment and choice of the latter so preponderating an authority on divers questions that no one could possibly reject his commands, either in religious or political matters.

This declaration ran, in part, as follows: "We have determined and do decree that the rank of a just ruler is higher in the eyes of God than the rank of a chief lawyer. Further, we declare that the Sultan of Islam, the refuge of mankind, the leader of the faithful, and the shadow of God on earth—Abu-l-Fath Jalal-ad-din Mohammad Akbar Padshah-i Ghazi (whose kingdom may God perpetuate!)—is a most just, wise, and God-fearing king. If, therefore, there should be a variance of opinion among the chief lawyers upon questions of religion, and if his Majesty, in his penetrating understanding and unerring judgment, should incline to one opinion and give his decree for the benefit of mankind and for the due regulation of the world, we do hereby agree that such a decree is binding on us and on the whole nation. Furthermore, we declare that should his Majesty, in his unerring judgment, issue an order which is not in opposition to the Koran and which is for the benefit of the nation, it shall be binding and imperative on every man. Opposition to it shall involve damnation in the world to come and loss of religion and property in this life. This document has been written with honest intentions for the glory of God and the propagation of Islam, and is signed by us, the principal divines and lawyers, in the month of Rajab, 987 A. H. (1579 A. D.)."

The draft of this document was in the handwriting of Shaikh Mubarak. The others had signed it against their will, but the Shaikh of his own accord added at the bottom that he had most willingly signed his name, for it was a matter to which he had been anxiously looking forward for several years.

After his Majesty had obtained this legal opinion, the road of deciding religious questions was opened, the superiority of the judgment of the *Imām* was established, and opposition was rendered impossible. The legal distinction between lawful and unlawful was set aside, the judgment of the *Imām* became paramount over the dogmas of the law, and Islam was called a counterfeit. His Majesty had now determined publicly to use the formula: "There is no god but God, and Akbar is the representative of God;" but as he found that the extravagance of this phrase led to commotions, he restricted its use to a few people in the harem.

In 990 A. H. (1582 A. D.), his Majesty was firmly convinced that a period of one thousand years from the mission of the Prophet was the extent of the duration of the religion of Islam, and that this period was now accomplished. There was no longer any obstacle to promulgating the designs which he secretly held, for now he was free from the respect and reverence due to the shaikhs and divines and from the deference owing to their authority. To his entire satisfaction, he was able to carry out his project of overturning the dogmas and principles of Islam, to set up his novel, absurd, and dangerous regulations, and to give currency to his own vicious beliefs.

In 991 A. H. (1583 A. D.) the King erected two buildings outside the city where he might feed holy men, both Mussulman and Hindu. Some of Abu-l-Fazl's

AKBAR'S TOMBSTONE AT SIKANDRA.

people were in charge and used to spend the king's money in procuring food. As Hindu ascetics also used to flock there in great numbers, a separate house was built for them and called *Jogīpūra.* Nightly sessions were held in private with some of these men, and they used to employ themselves in various follies and extravagancies, in contemplations, gestures, addresses, abstractions, and reveries, and in alchemy, incantation, and magic. The king himself studied alchemy and used to exhibit the gold which he made. One night in the year, called *Shīv-rāt* ("the night of Siva"), was appointed for a grand assembly of ascetics from all parts of the country, and on this occasion his Majesty would eat and drink with the best of them, being especially gratified by their assurances that he was destined to live three or four times longer than the natural life of man.'

CHAPTER XIII

FROM THE MEMOIRS OF THE EMPEROR JAHANGIR

1605-1628 A. D.

THE Memoirs of the Emperor Jahangir are written in the form of annals, which give the main events of each year in chronological order. They are preserved in two forms: one set of copies, a first edition, comprises twelve years of the emperor's reign; the other, which is extremely rare, carries the records through the eighteenth year. Having the nature both of a journal and an autobiography, these Memoirs are very valuable and are certainly interesting when taken as a whole, even if some of the detailed items and more special matters are, to some extent, lacking in attractiveness.

The character of the Memoirs in general proves Jahangir to have been a man of more than ordinary ability, and in spite of weaknesses and faults, which he acknowledges and puts on record with unusual candour, they leave on the mind a favourable impression of the emperor's nature and his talents. The first extracts, as given below, relate to the beginning of Jahangir's reign and to the Twelve Institutes which he ordained as regulations throughout his realm.

'On Thursday, the eighth of Jumada-s-sani, 1014 A. H. (Oct. 12, 1605 A. D.), I ascended the throne at Agra, in the thirty-eighth year of my age. The first order which I issued was for the setting up of a Chain of Justice, so that if the officers of the courts of justice should fail in the investigation of the complaints of the oppressed and in granting them redress, the injured persons might come to this chain and shake it, and thus give notice of their wrongs. I ordered that the chain should be made of pure gold and be thirty *gaz* long (about sixty feet), with sixty bells upon it. One end was firmly attached to a battlement of the fort of Agra, the other to a stone column on the bank of the river.

I established twelve ordinances, which were observed as the common rule of practice throughout my dominions.

1. *Prohibition of cesses.*—I forbad the levy of duties under the names of *tamghā* (stamp-taxes) and *mīr-bahrī* (port-dues), together with all forms of taxes which the fief-holders of every province and division had been in the habit of exacting for their own benefit.

2. *Regulation concerning highway robbery and theft.*—In those roads which were the scenes of robbery and theft, and in those portions of road which were far from habitations, the fief-holders of the neighbourhood were required to build a shelter for travellers or a mosque, and were also commanded to sink a well to promote cultivation and to induce people to settle

there. If these places were near lands belonging to the exchequer, the government officials were to carry out these provisions.

3. *Rights of merchants and of inheritance of property.* — First, no one was to open the packages of merchants on the roads without their consent. Secondly, when any infidel or Mussulman died in any part of my dominions, his property and effects were to be allowed to descend by inheritance without interference from any one. When there was no heir, officers were to be appointed to take charge of the property and to expend it according to the law of Islam in building mosques and shelters for travellers, as well as in repairing broken bridges and also in digging tanks and sinking wells.

4. *Of wine and all kinds of intoxicating liquors.*— Wine and all sorts of intoxicating liquor were forbidden and might neither be made nor sold; although I myself have been accustomed to drink wine and from my eighteenth year to the present, which is the thirty-eighth year of my age, have regularly partaken of it. In early days, when I craved for drink, I sometimes took as many as twenty cups of double-distilled liquor. In course of time it seriously affected me and I set about reducing the quantity. In the period of seven years I brought it down to five or six cups. My times of drinking varied; sometimes I began when two or three hours of the day remained; and sometimes I took it at night and a little in the day. I kept this up until my thirtieth year, when I resolved to drink only at night,

The Jami' Masjid at Lahore

The Great Mosque at Lahore was built by Jahangir's son, Aurangzib, and contains several precious relics of the Prophet Mohammed and his family. The edifice is constructed out of red sandstone, to which the three white marble domes and the white flower traceries upon the façade form a pleasing contrast. The grand archway and its ten smaller arches, fronting upon the main court, are effectively balanced by the minaret columns that flank the corners of the building, although these have lost their crowning towers as the result of an earthquake.

and at present I drink wine solely to promote the digestion of my food.

5. *Prohibition of seizing houses and of cutting off the noses and ears of criminals.*—No one was permitted to take up his abode in the dwelling of another. I likewise issued an order prohibiting every one from cutting off the noses or ears of criminals for any offence, and I made a vow to heaven that I would never inflict this punishment on any one.

6. *Prohibition of taking the property of another without his consent.*—Fief-holders and officers of lands belonging to the exchequer were forbidden to take the property of the peasants by force or to cultivate them on their own account; nor were these officials allowed to intermarry with the people in their districts without special permission.

7. *Building of hospitals and appointment of physicians to attend the sick.*—Hospitals were to be built in large cities and doctors were to be appointed to attend the sick. The expenses were to be paid from the royal treasury.

8. *Prohibition of the slaughter of animals on certain days.*—In imitation of my honoured father, the Emperor Akbar, I directed that every year from the eighteenth of Rabi'-al-awwal, my birthday, no animals should be slaughtered for a number of days corresponding to the years of my age. In every week, moreover, two days were to be exempted from slaughter: Thursday, the day of my accession, and Sunday, the birthday of my father.

9. *Respect paid to Sunday.*—My father used to hold Sunday blessed and to pay it great respect, because it

ZODIACAL GOLD MOHRS OF JAHANGIR.

is dedicated to the Great Luminary and because it is the day on which the Creation was begun. Throughout my dominions this was one of the days on which it was forbidden to kill animals.

10. *General confirmation of commands and fiefs.*— I issued a general order that the commands and fiefs of my father's servants should be confirmed, and afterwards I increased the old commands according to the merit of each individual. He who held ten was not advanced to less than twelve, and the augmentation was sometimes as much as from ten to thirty or forty. The allowance of all the guardsmen was advanced from ten to fifteen, and the monthly pay of all the domestics was from ten to twelve, or ten to twenty. The attendants upon the female apartments of my father were advanced according to their position and kinsfolk from ten to twelve, or ten to twenty.

11. *Confirmation of grants.* — All those lands throughout my dominions which were devoted to the purposes of prayer and praise, I confirmed according to the terms of the grant in the hands of each grantee. Miran, who is of the purest race of Sayyids in Hindustan and who held the office of justice in the days of my father, was directed to look after the poor every day.

12. *Amnesty for all prisoners in forts and in prisons of every kind.*—All prisoners who had long been confined in forts or shut up in prisons I ordered to be set free.'

In the second year of his reign Jahangir undertook a journey from Lahore to Kabul, the record of which is especially interesting. The narrative not only shows the inherited Moghul relations between Hindustan and the old capital of Afghanistan, but it brings out into a clearer light certain characteristics of Jahangir. In the words of Dowson, " he was a mighty hunter and took pleasure in the sport even in the later years of his life. He was a lover of nature, both animate and inanimate, and viewed it with a shrewd and observant eye. He mentions the peculiarities of many animals and birds, and shows that he watched their habits with diligence and perseverance. Trees and fruits and flowers also come under his observation, and he gives his opinion upon architecture and gardening like one who had bestowed time and thought upon them." The extracts that follow serve to illustrate this.

' The second new year of my auspicious reign began on the twenty-second of Zu-l-ka'da, 1015 A. H. (March 10, 1606 A. D.), and on the seventh of Zu-l-hijja, 1015 A. H. (April, 1606 A. D.), I left the fort of Lahore at a prosperous hour, and crossing the Ravi, I alighted at the garden of Dilamez, where I stopped four days. On Sunday, which happened to be the day of the sun's entry into Aries, some of my servants were favoured with promotion and ten thousand rupees in cash were given to Husain Beg, the ambassador of the ruler of Iran.

On Monday, I marched from the garden to a village called Haripur, three and a half leagues from the city, and on Tuesday, my flags waved in Jahangirpur, which was one of my hunting-grounds. Near this village a minaret was raised by my orders over an antelope of

THE
MOGHUL EMPIRE
AT THE DEATH OF AKBAR
A.D. 1605
English Miles
Longitude East 80 of Greenwich
CEYLON (Port.)
C. Comorin
Laccadive Islands
Maldive Islands
Coromandel Coast
KHANDAISH
Bombay
Mangalore
Madras
Jaffnapatam
Colombo

mine called "Raj," which was not only the best fighter in my possession, but was the best decoy for wild deer. Mulla Mohammad Husain of Kashmir, who excelled all persons of his profession in calligraphy, had engraved the following words on a piece of stone: "In this delightful spot an antelope was caught by the Emperor Nur-ad-din Mohammad Jahangir, which in the space of a month became entirely tame and was considered the best of all the royal antelopes." Out of regard for this animal, I ordered that no one should hunt antelopes in that forest and that their flesh should be considered as unlawful as that of a cow to the infidel Hindus or as that of swine to the Mussulmans, and I caused the stone on the antelope tomb to be carved in the shape of a deer.

On Thursday, the fourteenth, we encamped in the sub-district of Chandwala, and, after one intervening stage, arrived at Hafizabad on Saturday. In two marches more I reached the banks of the Chinab, and on Thursday, the twenty-first of Zu-l-hijja, I crossed the river by a bridge of boats and pitched my tents in the sub-district of Gujarat. When the Emperor Akbar was proceeding to Kashmir, he built a fort on the other side of this river, where he settled the Gujars, who had hitherto been devoted to plunder. The place was consequently named Gujarat and formed into a separate sub-district. The Gujars live chiefly upon milk and curds, and seldom cultivate land.

On Friday, we arrived at Khawaspur, five leagues from Gujarat, and after two further marches we reached the banks of the Behat, where we pitched our tents. In the night a very strong wind blew, dark clouds obscured the sky, and it rained so heavily that even the oldest persons said they had never seen such floods. The storm ended with showers of hailstones, which were as large as hens' eggs, and the torrent of water, combined with the wind, broke the bridge. I crossed the river in a boat with the ladies of my harem, and as there were but very few boats for the other men, I ordered them to wait till the bridge was repaired. This was accomplished in a week, after which the whole camp crossed the river without trouble.

The source of the river Behat is a fountain in Kashmir called Virnag, a word which in the Hindi language signifies a snake, since it appears that at one time a very large serpent haunted the spot. I visited this source twice during the lifetime of my father. It is about twenty leagues from the city of Kashmir and rises in an octagonal basin about twenty yards in length by twenty in breadth. The neighbourhood contains many vestiges of the abodes of devotees, consisting of numerous caves and chambers made of stone. The water of this spring is so clear that, although its depth is said to be beyond estimation, if a poppy-seed be thrown in, it will be visible till it reaches the bottom. There are very fine fish in it. As I was told that the fountain was unfathomably deep, I ordered a stone to be tied to the end of a rope and thrown into it, and thus it was found that its depth did not exceed the height of a man and a half. After my accession to the

throne, I ordered its sides to be paved with stones, a garden to be made round it, and the stream which flowed from it to be similarly decorated on both sides. Such elegant chambers and edifices were raised on each side of the basin that there is scarcely anything to equal it throughout the inhabited world. The river expands much as it approaches the village of Pampur, which lies ten leagues from the city of Kashmir.

All the saffron of Kashmir is the product of this village, and perhaps there is no other place in the world where saffron is produced so abundantly. I visited this place once with my father in the season in which the plant blossoms. In all other trees we see, they first get the branches, then the leaves, and last of all the flower. But it is quite otherwise with this plant, for it blossoms when it is only about two inches above the ground. Its flower is of a bluish colour, having four leaves and four threads of orange colour, like those of safflower, equal in length to one joint of the finger. The fields of saffron are sometimes half a league or a league in length and they look very beautiful at a distance. In the season when it is collected, the saffron has such a strong smell that people get headache from it, and even though I had taken a glass of wine, yet I myself was affected by it. I asked the Kashmirians who were employed in collecting it whether it had any effect upon them, and was surprised by their reply that "they did not even know what headache was."

The stream that flows from the fountain of Virnag is called Behat in Kashmir, and becomes a large river after being joined by many other smaller ones on both sides. It runs through the city, and in some places its breadth does not exceed a bow-shot. Nobody drinks its water, since it is very dirty and unwholesome, but all quench their thirst from a tank called Dal, which is near the city. After falling into this tank, the Behat takes its course through Barah-Mulah, Pakali, and Damtaur and then enters the Panjab. There are many rivulets and fountains in Kashmir, but Darahlar, which joins the Behat at the village of Shihab-ad-dinpur, is the best of all the streams.

This latter village is one of the most famous places in Kashmir, and in a piece of verdant land in it there are nearly a hundred handsome plane-trees, whose branches interlace and afford a deep and extensive shade. The surface of the land is so covered with green that it requires no carpet to be spread on it. The village was founded by Sultan Zain-al-Abidin, who ruled firmly over Kashmir for fifty-two years. He was there called Baroshah, or the Great King, and is said to have performed many miracles. The remains of many of his buildings are still to be seen there, and among them there is a building called Barin Lanka, which he built with great difficulty in the middle of the lake called Ulur (Wulur), which is three or four leagues in circumference and is exceedingly deep.

To form the foundation of this building, boat-loads of stone were thrown into the lake, but as this proved of no avail, some thousands of boats laden with stones were sunk, and thus with great labour a foundation a hundred yards square was raised above the water and smoothed. On one side of it were erected a palace and a place for the worship of God, than which no finer buildings can anywhere be found. Zain-al-Abidin used

INDIAN GIRLS FROM KASHMIR.

to come to this place in a boat and devote his time to the worship of Almighty God, so that it is said that he passed many periods of forty days there.

Kashmir is a delightful country in the seasons of autumn and spring. I visited it in the former season and found it even more charming than I had anticipated. I was never there in spring, but I hope sometime or other to be there during that season.

On Saturday, the first of Muharram, I marched from the bank of the Behat to Rohtas, with one stage intervening. The fort of Rohtas is one of the buildings of Sher Khan Afghan and is constructed among the ravines, where it seems scarcely conceivable that so strong a position could have been obtained. As this tract is near the country of the Gakkars, a troublesome and turbulent race, he commenced to build this fort for the purpose of overawing and controlling them. Sher Khan died when only a portion of the work was done, but it was completed by his son Salim Khan.

On Tuesday, the fourteenth, I marched four leagues and three-quarters to Tillah, which means "a hill" in the Gakkar language. From that place I proceeded to the village of Bhakra, which in the language of the same people is the name of a shrub with odourless white flowers. From Tillah to Bhakra I marched the whole way through the bed of the Kahan, in which water was then flowing, while the oleander bushes were in full bloom and of exquisite colour, like peach blossoms. These shrubs grew in special abundance at the sides of this stream, so I ordered my personal attendants, both horse and foot, to bind bunches of the flowers in their turbans and directed that the turbans of those who would not decorate themselves in this fashion should be taken off their heads. I thus got up a beautiful garden.

On Thursday, the sixth, the camping-ground was

Hatya, so called from its founder, a Gakkar named Hati. On this march a great many dhak-trees were found in blossom. This shrub has no fragrance in its flowers, which are of a fiery orange colour and the size of a red rose, or even bigger. It was such a sight that it was impossible to take one's eyes off it. As the air was very charming, and as there was a slight shower in consequence of a veil of clouds which obscured the light of the sun, I indulged myself in drinking wine. In short, I enjoyed myself amazingly on this march. The country from Margalla to Hatya is called Pothuwar, and within this tract there are but few crows to be found. Between Rohtas and Hatya is the country of the Bugyals, who are connected with the Gakkars and are of the same stock.

On Friday I marched four leagues and three-quarters to Pakka, so called because it has a caravansarai built of baked bricks, *pakka* in the Hindi language meaning "baked." There was nothing but dust on the road and I found it a very troublesome march in consequence of the annoyances which I experienced. In this place also most of the sorrel brought from Kabul got injured.

On Saturday, the eighth, I marched four and a half leagues through a country very bare of trees to a place called Khar, which in the Gakkar language means "broken ground." This country is very bare of trees. On Sunday, I pitched my camp on the other side of Rawal Pindi, so called because it was founded by a Hindu named Rawal, and in that language Pindi means "a village." Near this place there is a stream of water in a ravine which empties into a tank about a bow-shot in breadth. As the place was not destitute of charms, I remained there for a short time. I asked the Gakkars what the depth of the water was. They gave no specific answer, but said: "We have heard from our fathers that there are alligators in this water which wound and kill every animal that goes into it, so that no one dares to enter it." I ordered a sheep to be thrown into the water, which swam around the whole tank and came out safe. After that I ordered a swimmer to go in and he also emerged unharmed, thus proving that there was no foundation for what the Gakkars asserted.

On Monday I encamped at Kharbuza, which receives its name of "melon" from the shape of a domed structure erected here in ancient days by the Gakkars for the collection of toll from travellers. The following day, the camp moved to Kala-pani, which means in Hindi "black water." On this march the road passes a hill called Margalla. *Mār*, in Hindi, signifies "to rob on the highway," while *galla* denotes "a caravan," so that the entire name implies a place where caravans are plundered. This hill forms the boundary of the country of the Gakkars, who are strange fellows, always squabbling and fighting with one another. I did all I could to effect a reconciliation, but without effect.

On Wednesday, our camp was at Baba Hasan Abdal. About a league to the east of this place there is a cascade, over which the water flows with great rapidity.

On the whole road to Kabul there is no stream like this, but on the road from that city to Kashmir there are two or three of the same kind. Raja Man Singh raised a small edifice in the middle of the basin whence the water flows. There are several fish in it, half or a quarter of a yard long. I stayed three days at this charming spot, drank wine with my intimate companions, and also had some sport in the way of fishing. Up to this time I had never thrown the *safra* net, which in Hindi they call *bhanwar jāl.* This net is one of the commonest kind, but to throw it is a matter of some difficulty. I tried it with my own hand and succeeded in getting twelve fish. I strung pearls in their noses and let them go again in the water.

On the fifteenth of Muharram I encamped at Amardi, a most extraordinary green plain, in which you cannot see a mound or hillock of any kind. At this place and in the neighbourhood there are seven or eight thousand houses of Khaturs and Dilazaks, who practise every kind of turbulence, oppression, and highway robbery. I gave orders that the division of Attok, as well as this tract of country, should be made over to Zafar Khan, the son of Zain Khan Koka, and I gave him directions that before the return of the royal camp from Kabul he should march all the Dilazaks off toward Lahore and should seize the chiefs of the Khaturs and keep them fettered in prison.

On Monday, the seventeenth, I encamped near the fort of Attok on the banks of the river Nilab (the Abbasin or Attals), where I promoted Mahabat Khan to the rank of 2500. This fort, which is very strong, was constructed under the direction and superintendence of Khwaja Shams-ad-din Khwafi by order of my father. In those days the Nilab was very full, insomuch that the bridge consisted of eighteen boats, over which people passed with great ease and security. The chief amir was so weak and sick that I left him at Attok, and as the country around Kabul was not able to support so large a camp as accompanied me, I ordered the paymasters to allow no one to cross the river except my own friends and household, the main camp being ordered to wait at Attok till my return.

On Wednesday, the nineteenth, I embarked with the prince and a few attendants on a raft, and passing over the Nilab in safety, I landed on the bank of the Kama (Kabul), the river which flows under Jalalabad. These rafts are composed of bamboos and grass placed on inflated skins, and in rivers where there are many stones they are safer than boats. I gave twelve thousand rupees to Mir Sharif Amali and the officers who were left on duty at Lahore to be distributed to the poor; and orders were given to Abd-ar-Razak Ma'muri and Bihari Das, paymaster of the guardsmen, to make arrangements for supplying every necessity to the detachment left behind with Zafar Khan.

On the second day following, I reached my camp near Sarai Bara. On the opposite side of the river Kama there is a fort built by Zain Khan Koka when he was appointed to exterminate the Yusufzai Afghans. It is called Naushahra, and nearly fifty thousand ru-

A SCENE NEAR ATTOK.

pees were expended in its construction. Men say that his Majesty Humayun hunted wolves in these parts and I have heard my father declare that he had himself attended his father two or three times on these excursions.

On Tuesday, the twenty-fifth of Muharram, I moved to Sarai Daulatabad, where Ahmad Beg Kabuli, who held the fief of Peshawar, brought the Yusufzai and Ghorya-khail chiefs with him to pay their respects. As I was not pleased with his services, I removed him from the government of that country and bestowed it upon Sher Khan Afghan.

On Wednesday, the twenty-sixth, I arrived at the garden of Sardar Khan, near Peshawar. Ghorkhatri, a famous place of worship among the Hindu ascetics, is in this neighbourhood, and I went to see it in the possible chance of meeting some holy man from whose society I might derive advantage; but such a man is as rare as the Philosopher's Stone or the Roc, and all that I saw was a small fraternity without any knowledge of God, the sight of whom filled my heart with nothing but regret. On Thursday, Jamrud was our encamping ground, and on Friday we went through the Khaibar Pass and encamped at Ali Masjid, thus being fairly within the confines of Afghanistan.'

A final extract relating to Jahangir is presented to complete this chapter; it is a description of Nur Jahan, the beloved wife of the emperor. This famous queen was originally a princess of Persian blood and the wife of an Afghan captain who served under the emperor, although she was born in India, or rather in Kandahar. She was the second daughter of Ghiyas Beg, who gave her in marriage to Sher Afghan, who was in the Moghul army. Some time after her husband's death she chanced to be seen by Jahangir, who took her into his harem in the sixth year of his reign and became so infatuated with her that he exalted her to the position of chief queen and she ultimately became the real head of the kingdom. An account of Nur Jahan is found in the history of Mu'tamad Khan, from which the following extract is taken.

'Among the great events that occurred during the sixth year of the reign of the Emperor Jahangir was his demanding Nur Jahan Begam in marriage. This subject might be expanded into volumes, but we are necessarily confined to a limited space in describing the strange decrees of Fate.

Mirza Ghiyas Beg, the son of Khwaja Mohammad Sharif, was a native of Teheran. Khwaja Mohammad was, first of all, the vizir of Mohammad Khan Taklu, governor of Khorasan, but after the death of Mohammad Khan, he entered the service of the renowned King Tahmasp Safawi and was entrusted with the vizirate of Yazd. The Khwaja had two sons, Aka Tahir and Mirza Ghiyas Beg. For his second son the Khwaja sought in marriage the daughter of Mirza Ala-ad-din, the father of Aka Mulla. After the death of his father, Mirza Ghiyas Beg travelled to Hindustan with two sons and a daughter, but as he was passing through Kandahar, another daughter was born to him by the blessing of God. In the city of Fathpur, he had the good fortune to be presented to the Emperor Akbar, and in a short time, owing to his devotion to the king's service and his intelligence, he was raised to the office of superintendent of the household. He was considered exceedingly clever and skilful, both in writing and in transacting business. He had studied the old poets and had a nice appreciation of the meaning of words, and he wrote *shikastah* (the Persian hand of Arabic script) in a bold and elegant style. His leisure moments were devoted to the study of poetry and style, and his generosity to the poor was such that no one ever turned from his door disappointed. In taking bribes, however, he was very bold and daring.

When his Highness the Emperor Akbar was staying at Lahore, Ali Kuli Beg Istajlu, who had been brought up under Shah Isma'il II, came from the kingdom of Irak and was included among the number of the royal servants. There, as Fate would have it, he married that daughter of Mirza Ghiyas Beg who had been born in Kandahar. Afterwards, in the reign of Jahangir, a suitable post and the title of Sher Afghan were conferred on him, and he later received a fief in the province of Bengal and departed thither to take possession.

After the death of Kutb-ad-din at the hands of this same Ali Kuli Beg, the officials of Bengal, in obedience to the royal command, sent to court the daughter of Ghiyas Beg, and the king, who was greatly distressed at the murder of Kutb-ad-din, entrusted her to the keeping of his own royal mother. There she remained some time without notice. Since, however, Fate had decreed that she should be the Queen of the World and the Princess of the Time, it happened that on the celebration of New Year's Day in the sixth year of the emperor's reign her appearance caught the king's far-seeing eye and so captivated him that he included her among the inmates of his select harem. Day by day her influence and dignity increased. First of all she received the title of *Nūr Mahal*, "Light of the Harem," but was afterwards distinguished by that of *Nūr Jahān Begam*, "Light of the World." All her relatives and kinsfolk were raised to honour and wealth, nor was any grant of lands conferred upon any woman except under her seal.

In addition to giving her the titles that other kings bestow, the emperor granted Nur Jahan the rights of sovereignty and government. Sometimes she would sit in the balcony of her palace, while the nobles would present themselves and listen to her dictates. Coin was struck in her name with this superscription: "By order of the King Jahangir, gold has a hundred splendours added to it by receiving the impression of the name of Nur Jahan, the Queen," while all firmans which received the imperial signature also bore the name of "Nur Jahan, the Queen" [which was one of the greatest compliments possible to be paid to her]. At last her authority reached such a pass that the king was ruler only in name. Repeatedly he gave out that he had bestowed the sovereignty on Nur Jahan Begam, and

Jahangir's Sarcophagus at Lahore.

would say: "I require nothing beyond a *sīr* of wine and half a *sīr* of meat."

It is impossible to describe the beauty and wisdom of the queen. If a difficulty arose in any matter that was presented to her, she immediately solved it. Whoever threw himself upon her protection, was preserved from tyranny and oppression; and if ever she learned that any orphan girl was destitute and friendless, she would bring about her marriage and give her a wedding portion, so that it is probable that during her reign no less than five hundred orphan girls were thus married and portioned.'

CHAPTER XIV

SOME INCIDENTS OF SHAH JAHAN'S REIGN

1628-1659 A. D.

THERE is extant a voluminous native history of Shah Jahan's reign, entitled *Pādshāh-nāmah*, "Book of the King." It was written by Abd-al-Hamid of Lahore, who died in 1654 A. D., five years before the emperor's decease, leaving behind him a most detailed account of his royal patron. These annals cover twenty-one years of the emperor's reign, and, taken together, they make up two large volumes of nearly seventeen hundred pages, which rehearse the more important transactions of the kingdom during that period.

The excerpts which are included in the present volume are chosen because of their general interest, and they are representative of dozens of others in the Eastern chronicler's account. The passages selected refer to a visitation of the plague in Shah Jahan's reign, to the construction of the famous Peacock Throne, and to an attempted conquest of Tibet.

'For an entire year during the rule of the Emperor

Shah Jahan no rain had fallen in the territories of the Balaghat, and the drought had been especially severe about Daulatabad. Even in the following year there had been a deficiency in the bordering countries and a total absence of rain in the Deccan and Gujarat. The inhabitants of these two countries were reduced to the direst extremity. Life was offered for a loaf, but none would buy; rank was to be sold for a cake, but none cared for it; the once bounteous hand was now stretched out to beg for food, and the feet which had always trodden the way of contentment walked about only in search of sustenance. For a long time dog's flesh was sold for goat's flesh and the pounded bones of the dead were mixed with flour and sold, but when this was discovered, the sellers were brought to justice. Destitution at length reached such a pitch that men began to devour each other and the flesh of a son was preferred to his love. The multitude of those who died blocked the roads, and every man whose dire sufferings did not terminate in death and who retained the power to move wandered off to the towns and villages of other countries. Those lands which had been famous for their fertility and plenty now retained no trace of productiveness.

The emperor, in his gracious kindness and bounty, directed the officials of Burhanpur, Ahmadabad, and the country of Surat to establish soup kitchens or almshouses for the benefit of the poor and destitute. Every day sufficient soup and bread were prepared to satisfy the wants of the hungry. It was further ordered that so long as his Majesty remained at Burhanpur, five thousand rupees should be distributed among the deserving poor every Monday, that day being distinguished above all others as the day of the emperor's

A STREET SCENE IN AHMADABAD.

accession to the throne; and on twenty Mondays one hundred thousand rupees were accordingly given away in charity. Ahmadabad had suffered more severely than any other place, and his Majesty therefore ordered the officials to distribute fifty thousand rupees among the famine-stricken people. Want of rain and scarcity of grain had caused great distress in many other countries. Under the directions of the wise and generous emperor, therefore, taxes amounting to nearly seven million rupees were remitted by the revenue officers, a sum equal to an eleventh part of the whole revenue. When such remissions were made from the exchequer, it may be conceived how great were the reductions made by the nobles who held fiefs and commands.'

This short extract is sufficient to show that famine is no new thing in India. The next selection relates to the world-renowned Peacock Throne of Delhi, which is accounted among the richest treasures ever owned by an Oriental monarch. This throne was constructed at the order of Shah Jahan in the eighth year of his reign, early in the seventeenth century (1044 A. H., 1634 A. D.), but it now reposes in the palace of the Shah of Persia, at Teheran, having been carried away from India by Nadir Shah, after his victorious invasion of Hindustan, about the middle of the eighteenth century. Lord Curzon, nevertheless, maintains that the throne now in Teheran is not the original Peacock Throne of Delhi, but was made for Fath Ali Shah more than half a century after Nadir Shah's time. Be that as it may, the description of the jewelled *Takht-i Tā'ūs*, or "Peacock Throne," by Abd-al-Hamid is none the less interesting.

'In the course of years many valuable gems had come into the imperial jewel-house, each one of which might serve as an ear-drop for Venus or as an adornment for the girdle of the Sun. Upon the accession of the emperor, it occurred to him that, in the opinion of far-seeing men, the acquisition of such rare jewels and the keeping of such wonderful brilliants could

SHAH NASIR-AD-DIN OF PERSIA.
From an old Persian print.

render but one service, that of adorning the throne of empire. They ought, therefore, to be put to such a use that beholders might benefit by their splendour and that majesty might shine with increased brilliancy.

It was accordingly ordered that, in addition to the

jewels in the imperial jewel-house, rubies, garnets, diamonds, rich pearls, and emeralds, to the value of twenty million rupees (over £2,200,000), should be brought for the inspection of the emperor, and that they, together with some exquisite jewels exceeding fifty thousand *miskals* (nearly 634 pounds Troy) in weight and worth 8,600,000 rupees (over £950,000), should be carefully selected and handed over to Be-badal Khan, the superintendent of the goldsmiths' department. He was also to receive one hundred thousand *tolas* of pure gold, equal to 250,000 *miskals* (over 334 pounds Troy) in weight and 1,400,000 rupees (over £155,000) in value.

The throne was to be three *gaz* (six feet) in length, two and a half *gaz* (five feet) in breadth, and five *gaz* (ten feet) in height, and was to be set with the jewels already mentioned. The outside of the canopy was to be of enamel work with occasional gems, the inside was to be thickly set with rubies, garnets, and other jewels, and it was to be supported by twelve emerald columns. On the top of each pillar there were to be two peacocks thickly set with gems, and between each two peacocks was to be a tree studded with rubies, diamonds, emeralds, and pearls. The ascent was to consist of three steps set with jewels of fine water.

This throne was completed in the course of seven years at a cost of ten million rupees (over £1,100,000). Of the eleven jewelled recesses formed around it for cushions, the middle one, intended for the seat of the emperor, cost one million rupees (nearly £100,000). Among the jewels set in this recess was a ruby worth a hundred thousand rupees (about £10,000), which Shah Abbas, the King of Iran, had presented to the late Emperor Jahangir, who sent it to his present Majesty

SHAH JAHAN HOLDING AN AUDIENCE.

when he accomplished the conquest of the Deccan. On it were engraved the names of Sahib-kiran (Timur), Mir Shah Rukh, and Mirza Ulugh Beg. When it came into the possession of Shah Abbas in course of time, his name was added, and when Jahangir obtained it, he added the name of himself and of his father. Now it received the addition of the name of his most gracious Majesty Shah Jahan. At the command of the emperor, a poem by Haji Mohammad Jan, the final verse of which contained the date, was placed upon the inside of the canopy in letters of green enamel. On his return to Agra, the emperor held a court and sat for the first time upon his throne.'

The description given by Abd-al-Hamid of Shah Jahan's invasion of Tibet in 1636 A.D. has a special interest because of the comparatively recent expedition by British forces to Lhasa.

'The late Emperor Jahangir had long entertained the design of conquering Tibet and in the course of his reign Hashim Khan, the son of Kasim Khan Mirbahr, the governor of Kashmir, had invaded the country with a large force of horse and foot and local landholders at the bidding of the emperor. Although he entered the country and did his best, he met with no success and was obliged to retreat with great loss and difficulty. In the tenth year of Shah Jahan's reign, 1046 A.H. (1636 A.D.), the imperial order was given that Zafar Khan, then governor of Kashmir, should assemble the forces under his command and effect the conquest of Tibet.

He accordingly collected nearly eight thousand horse and foot, composed of imperial forces, his own men, and retainers of the lords of the marches in his province. He marched by the difficult route of Karcha-barh and in the course of one month reached the district of

Shkardu, the first place of importance in Tibet and on this side of the Nilab (Indus). Upon the summits of two high mountains Ali Rai, father of Abdal, the present lord of the marches of Tibet, had built two strong forts, the higher called Kaharphucha and the lower Kahchana. Each of them had a road of access like the neck of a reed or the curve of a talon. The road of communication between the two was on the top of the mountain. Abdal shut himself up in the fort of Kaharphucha, but placed his minister and general manager in the fort of Kahchana and sent his family and property to the fort of Shakar, which stands upon a high mountain on the other side of the Nilab.

After examining the height and strength of the fortresses, Zafar Khan was of the opinion that it was inexpedient to invest and attack them; but he saw that the military and the peasantry of Tibet were much distressed by the harsh rule of Abdal and he resolved to win them over by kindness. He then sent a detachment to subdue the fort of Shakar and to make prisoners of the family of Abdal. The whole time which the army could keep the field in this country was not more than two months, for if it remained longer, it would be snowed up.

He accordingly sent Mir Fakhr-ad-din with four thousand men against the fort of Shakar, while he himself watched the fort in which Abdal was. He next sent Hasan, the nephew of Abdal, with some other men of Tibet who had entered the imperial service, and some landholders of Kashmir, who had friendly relations with the people of the country, to endeavour to win over the inhabitants by persuasion and promises. Mir Fakhr-ad-din crossed the river Nilab and laid siege to the fort, which was commanded by Abdal's son, Daulat, who was about fifteen years of age. He sallied out to attack the besiegers, but was driven back with heavy loss. The besiegers then advanced and opened their trenches against the gate on the Shkardu side. The son of Abdal was so frightened by these proceedings that, regardless of his father's family in the fort, he packed up the gold, silver, and all that was portable and escaped in the night by the Kashghar gate. Mir Fakhr-ad-din, learning of his flight, entered the fort. He could not restrain his followers from plundering, although he took charge of Abdal's family. A force was sent in pursuit of the son, but the detachment was not able to overtake the fugitive, although it returned with some gold and silver that he had thrown away on the road as he fled.

On hearing of this victory, Zafar Khan pressed the siege of Kaharphucha and Kahchana, and the governor and garrison of the latter accordingly surrendered. Abdal, in despair at the progress made by the invaders and at the loss of his wives and children, likewise opened negotiations and surrendered the fort of Kaharphucha. Zafar Khan was apprehensive that the snow would fall and close the passes and that he might be attacked from the side of Kashmir at the instigation of Abdal. Without making any settlement of the country, therefore, and without searching for Abdal's property, he set out on his return, leaving Mohammad Murad, Abdal's deputy, in charge of Tibet, and taking with him Abdal, his family, and some of the leading men of the enemy.'

GOLD COIN OF AURANGZIB, STRUCK AT BIJAPUR, 1099 A. H. (1687-1688 A. D.).

CHAPTER XV

AURANGZIB

1659-1707 A. D.

AURANGZIB, the Puritan Emperor of India, whose long life of nearly ninety years, including fifty years of sovereignty, was marked by the gradual downfall of the Moghul Empire, stands as a lonely figure amid scenes of the empire's departing grandeur. "Incomparable courage, long-suffering, and judgment" were the qualities accorded him by the verdict of Mohammedan history after his death, and he was always extolled for "devotion, austerity, and justice." Aurangzib's strictness in all matters appertaining to religion is evident from the *Mir'at-i Ālam*, a work written by Mohammad Baka, an official of high rank at court, a man, moreover, who had the opportunity of knowing his sovereign well. Aurangzib's Moslem orthodoxy and his consecrated idea of the kingly office may be read between the lines of the chronicler's account.

'Be it known to the readers of this work that its author, the humble slave of the Almighty, is going to describe in a correct manner the excellent character, the worthy habits, and the refined morals of that most virtuous monarch, Abu-l-Muzaffar Muhi-ad-din Mohammad Aurangzib Alamgir, according as he has witnessed them with his own eyes.

The emperor, a great worshipper of God by natural propensity, is remarkable for his rigid attachment to religion. Having made his ablutions, he always occupies a great part of his time in adoration of the Deity and says the usual prayers, first in the mosque and then at home, both in the congregation and in private, with the most heartfelt devotion. He keeps the appointed fasts on Fridays and other sacred days and reads the Friday prayers in the Jami‘ Masjid of Delhi with the common people of the Mohammedan faith. He keeps vigils during the whole of the sacred nights, and illumines with the light of the favour of God the lamp of religion and prosperity.

Because of his great piety, he passes whole nights in the mosque which is in his palace and keeps company with men of devotion. In privacy he never sits on a throne. Before his accession he gave away in alms a portion of his allowance of lawful food and clothing, and now devotes to the same purpose the income of a few villages in the district of Delhi, as well as the proceeds of two or three salt-producing tracts which are appropriated to his privy purse. The princes also follow the same example. During the entire month of Ramazan he keeps the fast, says the prayers appointed for that season, and reads the holy Koran in the assembly of religious and learned men, with whom he sits for that purpose during six, and sometimes nine, hours of the night. Throughout the last ten days of the month, he performs worship in the mosque, and although he is unable to proceed on a pilgrimage to Mecca for several reasons, yet the care which he takes to promote facilities for pilgrims to that holy place may be considered equivalent to the pilgrimage.

From the dawn of his understanding he has refrained from all that is forbidden, and on account of his great holiness has adopted nothing but that which is pure and lawful. Though he has collected at the foot of his throne those who inspire ravishment in joyous assemblies of pleasure, in the shape of clever instrumental performers and of singers who possess melodious voices, and in the commencement of his reign used sometimes to hear them sing and play, and though he himself understands music well, yet for several years past, on account of his great restraint, self-denial, and observance of the tenets of religion, he has entirely abstained from such amusements. If any of the singers and musicians becomes ashamed of his calling, he makes an allowance for him or grants him land for his maintenance.

He never puts on the clothes prohibited by religion, nor does he ever use vessels of silver or gold. In his sacred court no improper conversation and no word of backbiting or falsehood is allowed. His courtiers, on whom his light is reflected, are cautioned that if they have to say anything which might injure the character of an absent man, they must express themselves in decorous language and in full detail. He appears two or three times every day in his court of audience with a pleasing countenance and mild look to dispense justice to complainants who come in numbers without any hindrance; and as he listens to them with great attention, they make their representations without any fear or hesitation and obtain redress from his impartiality. If any person talks too much or acts in an improper manner, his Majesty is never displeased and never knits his brows. His courtiers have often sought to prohibit people from showing so much boldness, but he remarks that by hearing their very words and by seeing their gestures he acquires the habits of forbearance and tolerance.

All bad characters are expelled from the city of Delhi and the same is ordered to be done in all places throughout the empire. The duties of preserving order and regularity among the people are executed with great efficiency, and in all the empire, notwithstanding its vast extent, no crime can be committed without incurring the due punishment enjoined by the Mohammedan law. He never issues sentence of death under the dictates of anger and passion. In consideration of their rank and merit, he shows much honour and respect to the Sayyids, saints, and learned men, and through his cordial and liberal exertions, the sublime doctrines of the Imam Abu Hanifa and of our pure religion have obtained such prevalence throughout the wide territories of Hindustan as they never enjoyed in the reign of any former king.

Hindu writers have been entirely excluded from holding public offices and all the great temples of these infamous people have been thrown down and destroyed in a manner which excites astonishment at the successful completion of so difficult a task. His Majesty personally teaches the profession of faith

A MOSQUE AT ALIGARH.

to many infidels with success, and invests them with robes of honour and bestows other favours upon them.

Alms and donations are given by this fountain of generosity in such abundance that the emperors of past ages did not bestow even a hundredth part of the amount. In the sacred month of Ramazan sixty thousand rupees, and in the other months less than that amount, are distributed among the poor. Several eating-houses have been established in the capital and other cities, at which food is served out to the poor and helpless, and in places where there were no caravansarais for the lodging of travellers, they have been built by the emperor. All the mosques in the empire are repaired at the expense of the state, and leaders in public prayer, criers to daily prayers, and readers of the sermons have been appointed at each mosque, so that a large sum of money is laid out in these disbursements. In all the cities and towns of this extensive country, pensions, allowances, and land have been given to learned men and professors, while stipends have been fixed for scholars according to their abilities and qualifications.

As it is a great object with this emperor that all Mohammedans should follow the principles of the religion as expounded by the most competent law officers and the followers of the Hanifi persuasion, and as these principles could not be distinctly and clearly learned in consequence of the different opinions of the judges and theologians which have been delivered without any authority, and as there was no book which embodied them all, and as no man could satisfy his mind concerning any disputed problem until he had collected many books and had obtained sufficient leisure, means, and knowledge of theological subjects, therefore his Majesty, the protector of the Faith, determined that a body of eminently learned and able men of Hindustan should take up the voluminous and trustworthy works which were collected in the royal library, and having made a digest of them, should compose a book which might form a standard canon of the law and afford to all an easy and available means of ascertaining the proper and authoritative interpretation.

The chief conductor of this difficult undertaking was Shaikh Nizam, the most learned man of the time, and all the members of the society were very handsomely and liberally paid, so that up to the present time a sum of about two hundred thousand rupees has been expended on this valuable compilation, which contains more than one hundred thousand lines. Another excellence attending this design is, that with a view to afford facility to all, Chulpi Abd-allah and his pupils have been ordered to translate the work into Persian.

Among the greatest liberalities of this king of the faithful is his remission of the transit duties upon all sorts of grain, cloth, and other goods, as well as on tobacco, the duties on which alone amounted to an immense sum. He exempted the Mohammedans from taxes and released the entire people from certain public demands, the revenue of which exceeded three million rupees every year. He relinquished the government claims against the ancestors of the officers of the state, which used to be paid by deductions from the salaries of their descendants. This money formed a very large annual income paid into the public treasury. He also abolished the confiscation of the estates of deceased persons against whom there was no government claim, a practice which had been very strictly observed by the accountants of his predecessors and which was felt as a very grievous oppression by their sorrowful heirs.

Royal orders were also issued to collect the revenues of each province according to the Mohammedan law.

As a single instance of his Majesty's fortitude we may cite the following event. When the royal army arrived at Balkh, Abd-al-Aziz Khan, with a large force which equalled the swarms of locusts and ants, came and arranged his men in order of battle and surrounded the emperor's camp. While the conflict was being carried on with great fury, the time of reading the evening prayers came on, and his Majesty, though dissuaded by some worldly officers, alighted from his horse and said the prayers in a congregation with the utmost indifference and presence of mind. On hearing of this, Abd-al-Aziz was much astonished at the intrepidity of the emperor, who was assisted by God, and put an end to the battle, saying that to fight with such a man was to destroy oneself.

The emperor is perfectly acquainted with the commentaries, traditions, and law, and one of the greatest excellences of this virtuous monarch is that he has learned the Koran by heart. In his early youth he had committed to memory some chapters of that sacred book, but he learned the whole by heart after he ascended the throne, taking great pains and showing much perseverance in impressing it upon his mind. He writes a very elegant Arabic hand and has acquired perfection in this art. He made two copies of the holy book with his own hand, and having finished and adorned them with ornaments and marginal lines at the expense of seven thousand rupees, he sent them to the holy cities of Mecca and Medina. He also writes an excellent Persian hand, and besides being a very elegant stylist in prose, he has acquired proficiency in versification. In obedience to the words of God, "Poets deal in falsehoods," however, he abstains from writing poetry, nor does he care to hear verses except those which contain a moral.

The emperor has given a very liberal education to his fortunate and noble children, who have attained the zenith of perfection by virtue of his attention and care and have made marvellous progress in rectitude, devotion, and piety, and in learning the manners and customs of princes and great men. Through his instruction they have memorized the Book of God, obtained proficiency in the sciences and in polite literature, acquired the art of writing the various Arabic scripts, and learned the Turkish and Persian languages.

In like manner, the ladies of the household have learned the fundamental and necessary tenets of religion in obedience to his command, and all devote their time to the adoration and worship of the Deity, to reading the sacred Koran, and to the performance of virtuous and pious acts. The excellence of character and the purity of morals of this holy monarch are beyond all expression. As long as nature nourishes the tree of existence and keeps the garden of the world fresh, so long may the plant of the prosperity of this preserver of the garden of dignity and honour continue fruitful and abundant!'

The austere side of Aurangzib's character is illustrated by some of his enactments in the eleventh year of his reign. Their effect is thus described in Khafi Khan's *Tārīkh*, or history.

'In the eleventh year of his reign, 1078 A. H. (1668 A. D.), after his Majesty Aurangzib had sat for ten years upon his throne, authors were forbidden to write the events of this just and righteous emperor's reign. Nevertheless, some competent persons disobeyed this mandate, particularly Musta'idd Khan, who secretly wrote an abridged account of the campaign in the Deccan, simply detailing the conquests of the countries and forts without alluding to the misfortunes of the campaign; and Bindraban prepared a brief narrative of the events of some years of the second and third decades. I myself, however, have neither seen nor obtained any history that contains a full and detailed account of the forty remaining years of the reign of Aurangzib. Consequently, from the eleventh to the twenty-first year of the emperor's reign, I have not been able to relate the events in the order in which they occurred, giving the month and year; but after this year, with very great labour and pains, I have managed to collect information from the papers in the public offices and from truthful persons, confidential servants of the emperor, and aged eunuchs. This, together with all that I myself observed for thirty or forty years, after attaining years of discretion, I laid up in the strongbox of my memory, and that I have written. And since I heard that Bindraban Das Bahadur Shahi, who was long an accountant of Shah Alam

CROWDS AT A HINDU FESTIVAL.

during the time he was a prince, had compiled a history and had included in it an account of upwards of thirty years, I made great search for it, being exceedingly anxious to see it. Subsequently, when I obtained a copy after great trouble and examined it carefully from beginning to end in the hope that I might gather the rich fruits of his labours, I discovered that his work did not contain one-half of what I had collected and included in my own history.

The king of happy disposition strove earnestly from day to day to put in force the rules of the Law and to maintain the divine commands and prohibitions. Orders were also issued prohibiting the collection of the tolls, the ground cesses, and other imposts which brought in hundreds of thousands of rupees to the state. Prohibitions were promulgated against intoxicating drinks, against taverns and brothels, and against the meetings called *jātras* or fairs, at which on certain dates countless numbers of Hindus, men and women of every tribe, assemble at their idol-temples, where hundreds of thousands of rupees change hands in buying and selling, while large sums accrue to the provincial treasuries.

The minstrels and singers of reputation that were in the service of the court were made ashamed of their occupation and were advanced to the dignities of commands of horse. Public proclamations were made prohibiting singing and dancing. It is said that one day a number of singers and minstrels gathered together with loud outcries, and having fitted up a bier with great display, round which were grouped the public wailers, they passed under the emperor's interview-window. When he inquired what was intended by the bier and the show, the minstrels said that Music was dead and that they were carrying his corpse for burial. Aurangzib then directed them to place it deep in the ground, that no sound or cry might ever again arise from it.

In the reigns of former kings, and up to this year, the custom of appearing publicly at the palace window had been a regular institution. Even though the king might be suffering from bodily indisposition, he would go to the window once or twice a day at stated times and put his head out of the window to show that he was safe. At Agra and at Delhi this window was constructed on the side looking toward the Jumna. Besides the nobles in attendance at the court, hundreds of thousands of men and women of all classes used to collect under it and offer their blessings and praises. Many Hindus were known by the name of *darsanī*, or "lookers," for until they had seen the person of the king at the window, they put not a morsel of food into their mouths. His religious Majesty looked upon this as one of the forbidden and unlawful practices, so he left off sitting in the window and forbade any assembly of the crowd beneath it.'

The selection chosen to conclude this chapter is an account of the death of Aurangzib in his eighty-ninth year and the fifty-first of his reign, on February 21, 1707. The notice is by Saki Musta'idd Khan, who secretly composed the annals of the emperor's reign, despite the well-known prohibition. The picture of the last period of Aurangzib's life, broken by warfare, old age, and sorrow, has been given in the preceding volume of this series. The final scene of the melancholy drama, depicting practically the end of Moghul power in Aurangzib's decease, is thus portrayed by Musta'idd.

'After the conclusion of the holy wars which rescued the countries of the Deccan from the dominion of the pagans, the army encamped at Ahmadnagar on the sixteenth of Shawwal in the fiftieth year of the reign of Aurangzib (1117 A. H.; 1706 A. D.). A year after this, at the end of Shawwal in the fifty-first year of his reign, the king fell ill and consternation spread among people of all ranks; but by the blessing of Providence his Majesty recovered his health in a short time and resumed once more the administration of affairs.

About this time, the noble Shah Alam was appointed governor of the province of Malwa and Prince Kam Bakhsh was made ruler of Bijapur. Only four or five days had elapsed after the departure of their royal highnesses, when the king was seized with a burning fever which continued unabated for three days. Nevertheless, his Majesty did not relax his devotions and every ordinance of religion was strictly kept. On the evening of Thursday, his Majesty perused a petition from Hamid-ad-din Khan, who stated that he had devoted the sum of four thousand rupees, the price of an elephant, as a propitiatory sacrifice and begged to be permitted to make over this amount to the Kazi Mulla

Haidar for distribution. The king granted the request, and although he was weak and his suffering was great, he nevertheless wrote with his own hand on the petition that it was his earnest wish that this sacrifice should lead to a speedy dissolution of his mortal frame.

On the morning of Friday, the twenty-eighth of

AURANGZIB'S BURIAL-PLACE.

Zu-l-ka'da, 1118 A. H. (February 21, 1707 A. D.), his Majesty performed the consecrated prayers and returned at their conclusion to the sleeping apartments, where he remained absorbed in contemplation of the Deity. Faintness came on and the soul of the aged monarch hovered on the verge of eternity. Even in this dread hour the force of habit prevailed, and the fingers of the dying king continued mechanically to tell the beads of the rosary they held. A quarter of the day later the king breathed his last and thus was fulfilled his wish to die on a Friday.

Great was the grief among all classes of people for the king's death. The shafts of adversity had demolished the edifice of their hopes, and the night of sorrow darkened the joyful noonday. Holy men prepared to perform the funeral rites and kept the corpse in the sleeping apartment pending the arrival of Prince Mohammad A'zam, who was twenty-five leagues distant from the camp. The prince arrived the following day and it is impossible to describe the grief that was depicted on his countenance; never had anything like it been beheld. On Monday he assisted in carrying the corpse through the hall of justice, whence the procession went on without him. May none ever experience the anguish that he felt. People sympathized with the prince's sorrow and shed torrents of tears. Such and so deeply felt were the lamentations for a monarch whose genius only equalled his piety, whose equal the world did not contain, but whose luminous countenance was now hidden from his loving people!

According to the will of the deceased king, his mortal remains were deposited in the tomb constructed during his lifetime near the shrine of the holy Shaikh Zain-ad-din (the mercy of God be upon him!). This place of sepulture, known by the name of Khuldabad, is eight leagues distant from Khujista-bunyad (Aurangabad) and three leagues from Daulatabad. A red stone three yards in length, two in width, and a few inches in depth, is placed above the tomb. In this stone a cavity in the shape of an amulet was hollowed out to receive earth and seeds, and sweet-scented herbs diffuse their fragrance round about the grave of Aurangzib.'

DECORATIVE DESIGN ON A MOHAMMEDAN TOMB.

INDEX

INDEX

A

C

D

K

L

M

T

U

V

W

Y

Published by

Facsimile Publisher
Ashok Vihar, Delhi-110052 (India)
Website: www.facsimilepublisher.com

Distributed by

Gyan Books Pvt. Ltd.
5, Ansari Road, Daryaganj, New Delhi-110002 (India)
E-mail: books@gyanbooks.com, Website: www.gyanbooks.com

8 888000 714569